FOUNDATION FUNDAMENTALS

FOUNDATION FUNDAMENTALS

A Guide for Grantseekers
Sixth Edition

Pattie J. Johnson, Editor
Margaret Morth, Assistant Editor

Contributors

Sarah Collins   Phyllis Edelson   Sara L. Engelhardt
Jeffrey Falkenstein   Margaret Mary Feczko   Joyce Infante
Karen Kingsbury   Ruth Kovacs   Judith B. Margolin
Lorna Mehta   Loren Renz   Rick Schoff
Alyson Tufts

Library of Congress Cataloging–in–Publication Data

Foundation fundamentals : a guide for grantseekers / Pattie J. Johnson, editor,
Margaret Morth, assistant editor.—6th ed.
    p. cm.
  Rev. ed. of: Foundation fundamentals / edited by Mitchell F. Nauffts. 5th ed. 1994.
  Includes index.
  ISBN 0-87954-869-X
  1. Endowments—United States—Information services. 2. Research
grants—United States—Information services. I. Johnson, Pattie J., 1947-
II. Morth, Margaret.

HV41.9.U5 N37 1999
361.7'632—dc21

                                                          99-045399

Contents

List of Figures

Foreword

When the Foundation Center was established in 1956, it was to endeavor, first and foremost, to be a useful resource for anyone seeking information about grant-making foundations. Today, forty-three years later, that remains our primary goal.

Our charter suggested that this goal might best be achieved if the Center were to "collect, organize and make available to the public reports and information about foundations . . . ." Thus, from the beginning, the Center has collected existing information about individual foundations and the foundation field. Now, however, we provide free public access to this information not only at the library at our New York headquarters, but also at four other Center libraries in Washington, Cleveland, San Francisco, and Atlanta, and we assist more than 200 public and academic libraries, community foundations, and other nonprofit organizations that make up the Center's network of Cooperating Collections in making foundation information widely available.

In almost an afterthought, the Center's charter stipulated that "to the extent deemed advisable by its board of trustees," the Center might "compile and publish periodically a general directory of foundations." Beginning in 1960 with the first edition of *The Foundation Directory*, the Center has developed a line of directories and grant guides that covers the full universe of grantmaking foundations. The 1990s brought the possibility of convenient electronic formats, and the Center has developed both a CD-ROM version of its information database on foundations and a World Wide Web site on the Internet that truly is "Your gateway to philanthropy on the World Wide Web." Thus, while our mission remains unchanged, the manner in which we accomplish it has evolved significantly.

Just as our methods of accomplishing our mission have changed, so the foundation field itself has changed. There are many more foundations. And considerably more foundations now recognize the value of making accurate and up-to-date information available to the grantseeking and the wider public. Since the Foundation Center first opened its doors in New York City in the mid-fifties, patterns of foundation type, size, geographic location, and giving priorities have shifted markedly.

Staying abreast of the changes and burgeoning information can be overwhelming, and so the Center has added educational programs in recent years. Now, not only do we collect information about the field of philanthropy and make it available in traditional and cutting-edge ways, we also help grantseekers navigate a course through the sea of information and information technology. An orientation to the funding research process and its tools is offered regularly at all five Center libraries and on the Center's World Wide Web site (www.fdncenter.org). We also publish *The Foundation Center's User-Friendly Guide: A Grantseeker's Guide to Resources* in print and electronically at our Web site to help the first-time grantseeker get a fast start in foundation research. *Foundation Fundamentals*, in contrast, is intended for those who want a more in-depth, systematic orientation to the field, the funding research process, and the many resources for grantseekers that the Foundation Center offers.

We hope you'll find this guide of value in your work. Please call on all of our resources as you make your way through the challenging and exciting process of seeking foundation support.

Sara L. Engelhardt, President
The Foundation Center
August 1999

Introduction

With the dawn of the new millennium, the nonprofit sector plays an increasingly prominent role in society. The downsizing of government that began in 1994 has placed enormous pressure on voluntary agencies to find new ways of financing services previously supported with federal, state, and local tax dollars. Public officials are counting on private generosity to offset decreases in government spending. In addition, a boom in U.S. investment markets, a surge of confidence in the economy, modest inflation, and strong corporate profits during much of the 1990s have added tremendous value to existing foundation endowments, and spurred the creation of new foundations and the increased assets from which corporations make grants and contributions.

Yet, the demand for philanthropic dollars far exceeds the supply. With all indications pointing to a continuation of this trend, the message for grantseekers is clear: in an increasingly competitive environment, the bulk of foundation and corporate giving will go to nonprofits that combine creativity and resourcefulness with a thorough knowledge and understanding of prospective funding sources.

As first-time grantseekers quickly discover, there is no dearth of information on grantmakers, nor on the ways this information can be accessed. If anything, the problem is one of information overload. Fully revised and updated, the sixth edition of *Foundation Fundamentals* is designed to help grantseekers make sense of the wealth of information available to them. Building on previous editions developed by Carol M. Kurzig, Patricia Read, Judith B. Margolin, and Mitchell F. Nauffts, the first three chapters provide a context for understanding foundation giving, and the remaining chapters and appendices introduce the grantseeker to the resources of the Foundation Center, the oldest and most authoritative source of information on grantmaking and grantseeking, and outline a number of research strategies designed to help grantseekers develop a list of potential funders.

The organization and arrangement of the book, with one or two exceptions, follows that of the earlier editions:

Chapter 1 describes the various types of foundations, the regulations that govern their activities, and a brief history of their development. Chapter 2 looks at support from private foundations in relation to other private philanthropy and to other sources of support for nonprofits, including government grants, earned income, and individual donors. Chapter 3 reviews who gets foundation grants in relation to the issue of nonprofit tax exemption.

Chapter 4 discusses the importance of planning your funding research strategies and includes a number of worksheets designed to facilitate the process.

The resources the Foundation Center makes available to grantseekers are described in detail in Chapter 5. The numerous changes in and additions to the Center's traditional print resources over the past few years are noted, and the Center's new electronic resources, whether on the World Wide Web or on CD-ROM, are reviewed at some length.

Chapters 6, 7, and 8 introduce the reader to three research strategies designed to identify potential funders. The subject, geographic, and types of support approaches reflect the content of the Center's print and electronic directories discussed in Chapter 5 and may be employed sequentially or simultaneously. The simultaneous approach has been greatly facilitated by the availability of the Center's database on CD-ROM.

Chapter 9 is devoted to corporate giving, whether by foundations or direct giving programs. Chapter 10 describes the crucial process of presenting your ideas to a funder.

The bibliography in Appendix A has not only been updated, but significantly expanded to include more books, brief descriptions, and relevant Web sites.

This sixth edition of *Foundation Fundamentals* has been updated to include the latest information technology as it relates to the field of funding research. *FC Search: The Foundation Center's Database on CD-ROM* is covered extensively, as well as the Center's World Wide Web site on the Internet. Other CD-ROMs and Web sites are referenced in the text as well as in the bibliography in the appendix. The illustrations and worksheets have been completely updated to reflect the many changes in the form and content of the Center's resources, in both print and electronic formats. You may use the table of contents to zero in on areas of specific interest, focus on particular chapters, or read *Foundation Fundamentals* from cover to cover.

This revision of *Foundation Fundamentals* was truly a collaborative effort. A list of all the people who contributed to the preparation of this edition would include a significant proportion of the Foundation Center staff. Space restraints prohibit a comprehensive list, but major contributors are listed on the title page. I am very grateful for their help.

I especially want to thank Judith B. Margolin, who, having edited a previous edition of the book, was able to offer advice and guidance throughout the process. She also gets the credit for keeping the whole enterprise firmly on track. I also want to thank Sara L. Engelhardt, president of the Foundation Center, who contributed not only the Foreword, but also a substantial revision to Chapter 1, the essential context for the rest of the book.

Margaret Morth, assistant editor for the sixth edition, was absolutely invaluable to this endeavor. She selected many of the illustrations, updated others, and collected and edited most of the information in the appendices. Sarah Collins, manager of bibliographic services, was a great help in pulling together the greatly expanded and very useful bibliography. Cheryl Loe managed the desktop publishing with her usual aplomb. Rick Schoff, senior vice president for information resources and publishing, was most generous with his time and expertise—helping organize two chapters and sharing information from other works in progress.

Last but not least, I want to recognize and thank two staff members of the Foundation Center's Atlanta field office, Kayron Bearden and Candace Springer, for taking on extra duties and responsibilities to allow me the time to edit this book.

Pattie J. Johnson, Editor

Chapter 1

What Is a Foundation?

Carnegie Corporation of New York, the Chicago Community Trust, the Duke Endowment, the GE Fund—what's in a name? Not much, if you're looking for a grantmaking foundation! These four institutions are among the nation's top grantmaking foundations, but none has the word "foundation" in its name. Conversely, many nonprofit organizations that make no grants do.

The difficulty of identifying grantmaking foundations by name alone creates confusion and produces misunderstanding about the scope and activities of the foundation field. That is where the Foundation Center comes in. The Center enables those looking for grants to identify grantmaking foundations that might be prospects for them, and it analyzes trends in growth and grantmaking patterns for the field as a whole. In this chapter, we will describe the various types of grantmaking foundations, with particular reference to the federal laws and regulations relating to them, and provide a brief history of the major types.

Defining a Foundation

The Foundation Center defines a foundation as an entity that is established as a nonprofit corporation or a charitable trust, with a principal purpose of making grants to

1

unrelated organizations or institutions or to individuals for scientific, educational, cultural, religious, or other charitable purposes. This broad definition encompasses two foundation types: private foundations and public foundations. The most common distinguishing characteristic of a private foundation is that most of its funds come from one source, whether an individual, a family, or a corporation. A public foundation, in contrast, normally receives its assets from multiple sources, which may include private foundations, individuals, government agencies, and fees for service. Moreover, a public foundation must continue to seek money from diverse sources in order to retain its public status. Historically, most of the attention on foundations has focused on the private foundation universe, which is much larger than that of public foundations. Indeed, the term "public foundation" has come into common usage only recently to describe organizations in the subset of the public charity universe that operate grantmaking programs as a primary purpose.

The best way to identify private foundations is to refer to the formal determination made by the Internal Revenue Service. Under the rules first set forth by the Tax Reform Act of 1969, those nonprofits determined by the IRS to be "private foundations" are treated differently from other nonprofits. To understand the differences between private and public foundations, it is helpful to trace the path that leads to an IRS determination letter. A nonprofit that has been legally established in one of the states must obtain recognition as a charitable organization from the IRS in order for contributions to it to be tax deductible. Section 501 of the Internal Revenue Code covers many types of organizations that are exempt from federal income tax. Section 501(c)(3) covers those tax-exempt organizations that are "organized and operated exclusively for religious, charitable, scientific, testing for public safety, literary, or educational purposes. . . ."

An organization that meets the definition of Section 501(c)(3) is measured against Section 509(a) of the Internal Revenue Code, which declares that a 501(c)(3) organization is presumed to be a private foundation *unless* it can demonstrate that it meets at least one of four criteria:

- It is an organization described in 170(b)(1)A: churches; schools, colleges, etc.; hospitals, medical research institutes, etc.; support organizations to public colleges or universities; certain governmental units; publicly supported organizations;

- It is an organization that normally receives more than one-third of its support from gifts, grants, or fees and gross receipts from admissions, sales, etc., *and* normally receives not more than one-third of its support from investment income;

- It is a supporting organization that is not publicly supported but is organized for and controlled by another public charity;

- It is an organization organized and operated exclusively for testing for public safety.

Most grantmaking foundations apply for Section 501(c)(3) status. Those that do not meet the requirements for classification as "not a private foundation" are, by default, private foundations. Thus, the IRS defines a private foundation by exclusion: a private foundation is a nonprofit organization that does *not* meet one of the four criteria for exclusion. The IRS does not have a separate classification for "public foundations," so public charities that are significant grantmakers can be difficult to identify using IRS definitions and resources.

The tax laws for private foundations include, among other things, a minimum distribution requirement, an excise tax on investment income, and a limit as to the proportion of a for-profit enterprise they may own, the "excess business holdings" rule. Private foundations must make "qualifying distributions" of at least 5 percent of the average market value of their investment assets in any given fiscal year by the end of the following year, a rule often referred to as "the payout requirement." The excise tax, normally 2 percent of net investment income or 1 percent in special circumstances, counts as a credit toward the 5 percent minimum.

Although they are complex, the definitions of foundations contained in the Internal Revenue Code guide the Center and others because they determine not only the way a foundation must operate but also the information it must make publicly available. All private foundations must file the Form 990-PF, which is a valuable source of information about their finances, board members, and grants. The Center acquires copies of the 990-PFs from the IRS as they are processed. From these it is able to create a database identifying virtually all private foundations.

Because the IRS has no separate designation for them, public foundations follow the same reporting guidelines as other public charities. Public charities with gross receipts over $25,000 in any year must file an information return with the IRS for that year using Form 990. The 990s for public foundations are indistinguishable from those for non-grantmaking public charities, so they are not a useful means of identifying public foundations.

The U.S. Department of the Treasury, Internal Revenue Service, publishes the *Cumulative List of Organizations Described in Section 170(c) of the Internal Revenue Code of 1986* as a three-volume annual set with quarterly supplements. Pub. 78, or the Blue Book, as it is often called, is useful in determining whether an organization is a private foundation and thus files Form 990-PF. Pub. 78 is available at Foundation Center libraries and at some Cooperating Collections. Alternatively, the Center's Web site (www.fdncenter.org) features Foundation Finder, a look-up tool containing approximately 48,000 grantmakers, which is searchable by foundation name. Each entry indicates the foundation's type. Independent, corporate, or operating foundations all file the 990-PF. Chapter 5 contains information on how to obtain copies of individual 990-PF filings.

PRIVATE FOUNDATIONS

It is useful to differentiate the three types of private foundation— independent, corporate, and operating—because of their distinctive operating styles.

Independent foundations are the most prevalent type of private foundation, comprising 88 percent of those in the Foundation Center's database. Their assets are usually provided by an individual or a family in the form of gifts or bequests held as an endowment. Because of the narrow base of their support, they are subject to private foundation laws, intended to assure that they serve the public good.

The Foundation Center includes so-called family foundations in the independent foundation category because the definition of a family foundation is a subjective one rather than a legal or formal designation. Typically, the characteristic that distinguishes a family foundation from other independent foundations is that family members actively determine the foundation's policies and grants. However, use of this term ranges so widely that it is impossible to report comprehensively on family foundations as distinct from other independent foundations.

Corporate, or company-sponsored, foundations are like independent foundations in most respects, except that the source of their assets is a company rather than an individual or family. Although often closely tied to the parent company, a corporate foundation and the company that established it are separate legal entities. A corporate foundation often maintains a small endowment relative to its grants program, with the parent company funding the bulk of its giving through annual gifts to the foundation, augmenting the endowment in good years and allowing it to make grants from its endowment during years in which profits are down. This permits the foundation to maintain a reasonably steady grants program despite business fluctuations.

Many companies make direct gifts, monetary or in-kind, to charities without using the foundation mechanism. Some companies make contributions both directly and through a foundation. As private foundations, corporate foundations are subject to the same IRS rules and regulations that apply to independent foundations. Corporate direct giving programs are not separately incorporated and have no IRS classification. Thus, they do not fit the foundation definition. However, the Foundation Center collects information about them, when available, for its database because of their significance in the total picture of corporate giving in the United States.

Operating foundations are a third type of private foundation. Like independent foundations, the source of their assets is usually an individual or a small group of donors, and they are subject to most of the same rules and regulations. However, they accomplish their charitable purposes largely by operating their own programs rather than by making grants. The Foundation Center compiles basic financial information on all operating foundations. It collects more extensive information on the roughly one-half of operating foundations that also make grants, which are usually for purposes related to the programs they operate.

PUBLIC FOUNDATIONS

A public foundation is a nongovernmental public charity that operates grants programs benefiting unrelated organizations or individuals as one of its primary purposes. As discussed previously, there is no legal or IRS definition of a public foundation, but such a definition is needed to encompass the growing number of grantmaking institutions that are "not a private foundation." Community foundations are the best established category of public foundations, and over 500 of them are currently operating across the United States. Increasingly, foundations have been established to receive funds and make grants for populations with special needs, for specific subject areas, or around other non-geographic communities of interest. Many of these public foundations got their start as a fund within a community foundation, and they often limit their grants to a particular geographic area, but they do not fit the generally accepted definition of a community foundation.

Community foundations receive funds from a variety of sources, including, in some instances, private foundations. They make grants primarily in support of the broad public needs of the geographic community or region in which they are located. Their investments are normally managed by several investment firms, and their endowments are often composed of a wide assortment of individual funds, which may bear the donor's name. Their grantmaking activities are overseen by the governing body or by a distribution committee representative of various community interests, and grants are normally limited to charitable organizations within a particular city, county, state, or other geographically defined area. While community foundations make up only a small portion of the foundation field, their visibility and impact is growing, as more and more communities establish them and as they become known both to potential donors and to grantseekers as important resources for their communities.

Community foundations usually qualify as public charities under the Internal Revenue Code because of the diverse sources of their funds and, therefore, do not file the 990-PF with the IRS. Nonetheless, information about their programs is relatively easy to locate because at least 90 percent of them issue annual or other reports on their work. As a result, the Foundation Center and other directory publishers have been able to document community foundations systematically for many years. Community foundations appear in *The Foundation Directory* and the Center's other major directories, *FC Search: The Foundation Center's Database on CD-ROM*, and its Web-based Foundation Finder. Further, community foundations are the only public foundations included in the Center's statistical analyses, such as *Foundation Giving: Yearbook of Facts and Figures on Private, Corporate and Community Foundations*, because they represent the only type of public foundation for which enough reliable information has been consistently available over time to permit statistical conclusions to be reached.

Other public foundations encompass a range of grantmaking institutions that raise and dispense funds around a particular community of interest. The women's funds that have been established in communities across the country to raise money and make grants to benefit women and girls are one example of population-oriented public foundations. Other public foundations focus their giving on the arts, health, the environment, social change, or any number of other issues at a local, regional, national, or international level. Still another group of public foundations receive funding primarily from an ethnic or religious community, but their grantmaking programs may extend beyond this particular community of interest.

Historical Background

The concept of private philanthropy dates back to ancient times. Legal provision for the creation, control, and protection of charitable funds (the forerunner of U.S. foundations) was first established in 1601 by England's Statute of Charitable Uses, which granted certain privileges to private citizens or groups of citizens in exchange for support or performance of charitable acts intended to serve the public good. Since then, legal doctrines in the common law countries have generally preserved this status for most types of charitable organizations, including foundations, churches, hospitals, and schools, ensuring their existence in perpetuity as well as their right to tax exemption, so long as they serve a charitable purpose.

Most early foundations were established for the benefit of a particular institution, such as a hospital, or to respond to specific social needs, such as educating the poor. Early in the twentieth century, a new kind of foundation began to emerge in the United States. Exemplified by Carnegie Corporation of New York (established in 1911) and the Rockefeller Foundation (established in 1913), these "general purpose foundations" have large endowments and broad charters, enabling them to address major social problems and seek solutions to them. General purpose foundations usually focus their grantmaking on one or more areas for a period of time, but their governing boards have considerable latitude to change the focus of their grantmaking programs as social conditions change. Modern-day foundations may be limited by their charters to specific issues or geographic areas, but within those limitations they may periodically review and adapt their grantmaking strategies or programs.

American foundations began to attract congressional scrutiny soon after the Carnegie and Rockefeller foundations were created. The U.S. Commission on Industrial Relations of the U.S. Congress (called the Walsh Commission for its chairman) launched the first investigation of private foundations in 1915, looking into charges that wealthy capitalists were using the foundation mechanism to protect their economic power, but no major new legislation or restrictions resulted. Two subsequent World Wars and the Great Depression created a relatively quiet period for foundations, as Congress focused on other issues, but in the early 1950s, during a period of rapid expansion spurred by the creation of new wealth and a tax structure favorable to foundation formation, foundations again became the target of congressional criticism. First the Select Committee to Investigate Foundations and Other Organizations (the Cox Committee) in 1952 and then the Special Committee to Investigate Tax-Exempt Foundations and Comparable Organizations (the Reece Committee) in 1954 looked into allegations that the large foundations were promoting "un-American activities" and Communist subversion of the capitalist system. The Cox Committee's *Final Report* found that, ". . . on balance, the record of foundations is good," and the very negative majority report from the Reece Committee hearings was generally discredited. Again, no major new restrictive legislation was passed.

Starting in 1961, an open-ended investigation of foundations initiated by Congressman Wright Patman, chairman of the Select Committee on Small Business, ultimately led to passage in the Tax Reform Act of 1969 of a whole new legal and regulatory framework for private foundations. At the time, it was assumed that the TRA of 1969 spelled the end of private foundation formation, and this prediction seemed to be borne out by the sharp decline in their birth rate in the 1970s. To the surprise of many, the 1980s brought renewed growth in private foundation establishment rates, a trend that has continued well into the 1990s.

Corporate foundations are a more recent phenomenon than independent foundations. Corporate contributions to nonprofit organizations go back to the 1870s, when railroad companies began supporting the development of Young Men's Christian Associations at their divisional and terminal points to provide accommodations for their workers, and until World War I, the YMCA was the only major recipient of corporate contributions. The war prompted major national fundraising drives among corporations by the American National Red Cross, as well as the YMCA. It also led to the creation of "war chests" in local communities, which evolved into Community Chests following the war, with corporations leading the way in their support. The Revenue Act of 1935 greatly increased the corporate income tax, but it also provided, for the first time, a charitable deduction for corporate contributions.

Although a few corporate foundations existed prior to World War II, the higher corporate tax rates of the 1950s led to a boom decade for the creation of new ones. Only ninety-eight corporate foundations currently in the Foundation Center's database existed at the opening of the decade; 377 were created between 1950 and 1960. Also in the 1950s, regulation was increased to prevent the use of the foundation mechanism for private inurement or business purposes. The Revenue Act of 1950 restricted self-dealing and unreasonable accumulation of income, and foundations generally came under congressional scrutiny during the following two decades, culminating in the Tax Reform Act of 1969, which restructured the legal framework for private foundations.

Formation of corporate foundations slowed considerably in the 1970s due both to the new tax law and to the state of the economy. With federal cutbacks in funding for social services, education, and the arts in the early 1980s, the call went out for private sources, notably business, to pick up the slack. During this time, the tax deduction limit for corporate charitable contributions was increased from 5 to 10 percent of a company's pre-tax earnings in an effort to increase corporate giving levels. There was substantial growth in the number of large corporate foundations from the late 1970s through the 1980s. This growth has continued in the 1990s, but it has been undercut by a steep termination rate caused by mergers and buy-outs. Despite this trend, corporate foundation giving has grown in the 1990s, but at a slower rate than giving by independent foundations. With pressure on corporations to create value, they are again focusing their giving more sharply to achieve "direct benefit" to major corporate constituencies and communities, as they did in the early part of the century.

The community foundation movement dates back to the early part of this century, with the establishment of the Cleveland Foundation in 1914. The idea of centralizing the governance of numerous separate trusts that were dedicated to charitable purposes in the community was welcomed by local trust officers, and community trusts or foundations were set up across the country, mostly at the initiative of banks and trust companies and of chambers of commerce. The movement lost momentum during the Great Depression, but following World War II, it was revived by leaders in the community planning arena as a suitable means of strengthening their cities and regions.

The rate of community foundation formation increased dramatically when the regulations for community foundations under the Tax Reform Act of 1969 were finally issued in 1976. These clarified the significant new advantages that community foundations had over private foundations, including fewer limitations on their grant-making, exemption from the excise tax on private foundations, and greater deductibility for donors as a proportion of their pre-tax income. In 1996, the 411 community funds tracked by the Foundation Center (up from seventy-two in 1975) accounted for just 1 percent of the foundations in the United States but about 7 percent of the grant dollars awarded.

The proliferation of other types of public foundations in addition to community foundations in the 1980s and 1990s is probably also due in part to their preferable tax treatment over private foundations. However, it attests, as well, to the success of the community foundation model. In this model, individuals of even modest wealth can pool their philanthropic dollars based on common philanthropic interests and have both the assets and grant programs managed professionally and strategically. This combination of advantages leads to expectations that the number and size of community foundations and other public foundations will continue to grow for the foreseeable future.

The emergence of the additional types of foundations that fit neither the private nor the public foundation definition is probably directly attributable to the post-1969 private foundation rules. Because of the perceived disadvantages of private foundation status, some foundations that appear to fit the definition of a private foundation may have an IRS ruling as other than a private foundation. The Howard Hughes Medical Institute (HHMI), for example, now a prominent funder of education and research in the biomedical sciences, was established as a medical research organization in 1953. Its grantmaking program began in 1987, as part of the settlement of a long-standing dispute with the IRS, which included an agreement that it would disburse $500 million over ten years for grants for medical research. It met the obligation three years ahead of schedule and has continued its grants program beyond the life of the agreement. Because of the importance of its grantmaking, HHMI is included in many resources about foundations, even though it does not fit into any of the usual categories of grantmaking foundations.

Foundations created since 1969 with very large assets from the onset may have difficulty complying with both the private foundation payout and excess business holdings rules in the initial years of operation. The California HealthCare Foundation, one of two foundations created in 1996 as a result of the conversion of the nonprofit Blue Cross of California to a for-profit corporation, was allowed to retain Blue Cross's 501(c)(4) tax status, thereby avoiding the excess business holdings and the payout requirements of a private foundation. Thus, it can receive the large new assets generated by the conversion and, in time, turn these over to a sister organization, the California Endowment, a private foundation under Section 501(c)(3), for disbursal. However, the California HealthCare Foundation also operates its own grantmaking program. As a 501(c)(4) organization, it is an anomaly in the classification systems that the Foundation Center and others use for grantmaking foundations but is nonetheless an important grantmaker in the health field.

Overall, the twentieth century has been one of tremendous growth for the foundation field. More than that, it has been a century of innovation, seeing the emergence of the general purpose foundation, the community foundation, the corporate foundation, and most recently, whole new forms of institutional grantmaking. A legal and regulatory framework for the field has been created, and an infrastructure of organizations and associations to improve practice, advocate policy, promote public understanding, and study outcomes has grown up around it. The twenty-first century will, no doubt, see a great deal more change, as well as growth, but probably nothing that can rival the past one hundred years of foundation development.

Chapter 2

Where Foundations Fit in the Total Funding Picture

Patterns of Growth in the Foundation Field

The Center's analysis of trends since 1975 has examined three principal types of grantmaking foundations: independent, corporate, and community. These types of foundations are the most prolific in terms of amounts of giving and the most consistent in terms of patterns of growth. Grantmaking operating foundations are also included in the Center's trends analysis. However, they provide only a tiny percentage of overall giving and, since their principal activity is not grantmaking, their patterns of growth are far less predictable. According to the Foundation Center's 1999 edition of *Foundation Giving*, in 1997, there were 44,156 independent, corporate, community, and grantmaking operating foundations with a total of $329.9 billion in assets.

Independent foundations, which comprise the largest segment of this foundation universe (39,240 or almost 88.9 percent), experienced tremendous growth in 1997, with both assets and grants increasing at the fastest rate since the mid-1980s. The assets of independent foundations increased more than 24.7 percent in just one year, going from $226.6 billion in 1996 to $282.6 billion in 1997. Independent foundations made contributions of $12.4 billion, up nearly $1.66 billion or 15.5 percent from 1996.

Corporate foundations represent only one of many channels (direct cash and in-kind gifts, donations of staff time and expertise, etc.) that corporations use to make charitable contributions. However, corporate foundation giving is significant, comprising 12.9 percent of total foundation grants awarded in 1997. That year, corporate foundations paid out $2.1 billion in grants and contributions, up $230.5 million or 12.6 percent from 1995. Assets are not usually indicative of corporate foundation annual giving because companies frequently make annual gifts—based on profits—to their foundations for grantmaking purposes. However, assets of corporate foundations increased significantly from 1996 to 1997, growing from $9.5 billion to $10.9 billion, a 15.5 percent increase. Some of this growth can be attributed to increased value of stock held by the corporate foundations and some to new gifts to the foundation endowments.

Community foundations represent a relatively small, but extremely vital component of the foundation universe (403 or just under one percent (.9 percent) of foundations in 1997). The number of community foundations in the Center's foundations database has grown by three-quarters over the past decade. Asset values of community foundations increased 24 percent in 1997, growing from $15.9 billion to $19.7 billion. In 1997, community foundations distributed $1.2 billion in grants, up by $241 million or 25.3 percent from 1996.

Figure 1 provides a breakout of foundations by type, their aggregate assets, and their combined grant totals.

Figure 1. 1997 Aggregate Fiscal Data by Foundation Type (Dollars in Thousands)*

Foundation Type	Number of Foundations	%	Assets	%	Gifts Received	%	Qualifying Distributions[1]	%	Total Grants[2]	%	PRIs/ Loans	%
Independent	39,248	88.9	$282,618,485	85.7	$11,012,655	69.6	$13,591,237	74.4	$12,375,399	77.4	$117,702	80.2
Corporate	2,029	4.6	10,886,570	3.3	1,872,479	11.8	2,181,679	11.9	2,066,454	12.9	13,018	8.9
Community	403	0.9	19,699,826	6.0	2,223,753	14.0	1,242,913	6.8	1,192,301	7.4	12,585	8.6
Operating	2,466	5.6	16,705,416	5.1	724,068	4.6	1,254,215	6.9	351,277	2.2	3,515	2.4
Total	44,146	100.0	$329,910,297	100.0	$15,832,955	100.0	$18,270,044	100.0	$15,985,431	100.0	$146,820	100.0

Source: *Foundation Giving*, 1999.
*Due to rounding, figures may not add up.
[1]Qualifying distributions is the amount used in calculating the required 5 percent payout; includes total giving, as well as reasonable administrative expenses, set-asides, PRIs, operating program expenses, and amount paid to acquire assets used directly for charitable purposes.
[2]Includes grants, scholarships, and employee matching gifts.

Foundations, whether independent, corporate, or community, are located in every state, as well as in Puerto Rico and the Virgin Islands. However, the major concentration is in the Northeast. New York foundations alone account for 18.5 percent of all foundation assets, while foundations in New England and the Middle Atlantic states combined control 33.4 percent of assets (see Figure 2).

The unequal distribution of foundation assets across the country is rooted in past economic and industrial development patterns as well as in the personal preferences of the donors. This is offset to some extent by the funding policies of large national foundations, which give substantial amounts outside the states in which they are located. Moreover, since 1975, changing demographic patterns and relatively rapid economic and industrial growth in the Southeast and Pacific regions have stimulated a higher rate of growth in the number of foundations and foundation assets in those areas (see Figure 3). Pacific foundations, for example, have more than doubled their share of assets since 1975, up from 7 percent to 16.2 percent in 1997, and increased their portion of grants from less than 7 percent to 13.3 percent over the same period. California now ranks second to New York in foundation assets; it controls 14.2 percent of assets (versus New York's 18.5 percent) and provides 11 percent of grant dollars (compared with New York's 20.3 percent).

Foundation assets of the South Atlantic states grew from 8.3 percent in 1975 to 12.9 percent in 1997 and grants from 8 percent to 12.8 percent. Foundation growth in this area reflects the economic growth of the region: several established foundations received important additions to their endowments, large new foundations were formed, a few leading foundations relocated to the South, and corporate foundation activity increased.

Key Sources of Revenue for Nonprofits

While the distinctions among different types of foundations, the legal framework within which they exist, the evolution of foundations as philanthropic vehicles, and the scope of the foundation universe in terms of assets and giving are necessary building blocks for the funding research process, it is crucial for grantseekers to be able to distinguish between grants from foundations and other types of revenue nonprofit organizations receive. According to Lester M. Salamon's 1999 book *America's Nonprofit Sector: A Primer,* 2nd Edition, most of the income of nonprofit public benefit organizations comes from fees and service charges, with government a close second.

Figure 2. 1997 Fiscal Data of Grantmaking Foundations by Region and State*

Region[1]	Number of Foundations	%	Assets	%	Gifts Received	%	Expenditures	%	Total Grants	%
NORTHEAST	**14,840**	**33.6**	**$110,238,891**	**33.4**	**$ 4,651,613**	**29.4**	**$ 7,087,787**	**35.4**	**$ 5,771,957**	**36.1**
New England	**4,235**	**9.6**	**14,766,472**	**4.5**	**830,030**	**5.2**	**1,028,296**	**5.1**	**827,735**	**5.2**
Connecticut	1,060	2.4	4,639,461	1.4	240,809	1.5	338,319	1.7	275,853	1.7
Maine	286	0.6	377,443	0.1	36,714	0.2	28,337	0.1	22,128	0.1
Massachusetts	2,256	5.1	7,438,569	2.3	400,460	2.5	502,456	2.5	404,147	2.5
New Hampshire	219	0.5	708,696	0.2	43,936	0.3	47,480	0.2	33,404	0.2
Rhode Island	254	0.6	1,328,923	0.4	56,241	0.4	94,093	0.5	80,798	0.5
Vermont	160	0.4	273,381	0.1	51,870	0.3	17,611	0.1	11,405	0.1
Middle Atlantic	**10,605**	**24.0**	**95,472,419**	**28.9**	**3,821,583**	**24.1**	**6,059,490**	**30.2**	**4,944,222**	**30.9**
New Jersey	1,367	3.1	12,028,130	3.6	380,877	2.4	750,902	3.7	578,287	3.6
New York	6,454	14.6	60,868,617	18.5	2,683,045	16.9	3,977,255	19.8	3,237,288	20.3
Pennsylvania	2,784	6.3	22,575,672	6.8	757,661	4.8	1,331,333	6.6	1,128,647	7.1
MIDWEST	**11,810**	**26.8**	**83,518,485**	**25.3**	**3,731,246**	**23.6**	**5,016,240**	**25.0**	**4,112,590**	**25.7**
East North Central	**8,321**	**18.8**	**64,544,287**	**19.6**	**2,640,671**	**16.7**	**3,635,461**	**18.1**	**2,966,649**	**18.6**
Illinois	2,696	6.1	17,434,914	5.3	620,988	3.9	1,156,426	5.8	872,438	5.5
Indiana	928	2.1	14,642,502	4.4	253,288	1.6	487,238	2.4	420,346	2.6
Michigan	1,375	3.1	19,082,602	5.8	634,201	4.0	1,070,150	5.3	892,517	5.6
Ohio	2,196	5.0	10,178,280	3.1	921,232	5.8	660,159	3.3	562,180	3.5
Wisconsin	1,126	2.6	3,205,988	1.0	210,962	1.3	261,489	1.3	219,167	1.4
West North Central	**3,489**	**7.9**	**18,974,198**	**5.8**	**1,090,576**	**6.9**	**1,380,779**	**6.9**	**1,145,940**	**7.2**
Iowa	673	1.5	1,337,695	0.4	161,088	1.0	97,393	0.5	81,731	0.5
Kansas	511	1.2	1,208,245	0.4	71,207	0.4	98,748	0.5	83,975	0.5
Minnesota	860	1.9	7,998,198	2.4	346,532	2.2	540,981	2.7	466,211	2.9
Missouri	955	2.2	6,849,022	2.1	333,846	2.1	486,748	2.4	376,757	2.4
Nebraska	325	0.7	1,299,405	0.4	102,579	0.6	113,518	0.6	99,156	0.6
North Dakota	79	0.2	80,199	0.0	28,826	0.2	28,744	0.1	26,968	0.2
South Dakota	86	0.2	201,433	0.1	46,497	0.3	14,647	0.1	11,142	0.1
SOUTH	**10,574**	**24.0**	**72,644,644**	**22.0**	**3,341,624**	**21.1**	**4,420,869**	**22.1**	**3,488,864**	**21.8**
South Atlantic	**6,106**	**13.8**	**42,615,792**	**12.9**	**2,183,897**	**13.8**	**2,583,751**	**12.9**	**2,040,885**	**12.8**
Delaware	202	0.5	2,046,374	0.6	48,058	0.3	101,666	0.5	87,576	0.5
District of Columbia	314	0.7	3,802,028	1.2	109,866	0.7	296,610	1.5	192,673	1.2
Florida	1,842	4.2	7,761,443	2.4	492,416	3.1	559,193	2.8	425,076	2.7
Georgia	805	1.8	9,893,383	3.0	242,643	1.5	382,703	1.9	333,522	2.1
Maryland	846	1.9	6,535,807	2.0	661,193	4.2	384,139	1.9	316,819	2.0
North Carolina	793	1.8	6,962,238	2.1	307,772	1.9	387,081	1.9	318,184	2.0
South Carolina	253	0.6	775,331	0.2	42,069	0.3	52,605	0.3	42,834	0.3
Virginia	885	2.0	4,345,705	1.3	271,381	1.7	391,562	2.0	301,222	1.9
West Virginia	166	0.4	493,484	0.1	8,501	0.1	28,193	0.1	22,980	0.1
East South Central	**1,416**	**3.2**	**5,786,156**	**1.8**	**325,258**	**2.1**	**357,094**	**1.8**	**288,868**	**1.8**
Alabama	411	0.9	1,222,846	0.4	85,212	0.5	85,077	0.4	68,814	0.4
Kentucky	393	0.9	1,207,119	0.4	52,266	0.3	75,346	0.4	57,919	0.4
Mississippi	149	0.3	336,616	0.1	40,017	0.3	32,569	0.2	23,007	0.1
Tennessee	463	1.0	3,019,575	0.9	147,763	0.9	164,103	0.8	139,127	0.9
West South Central	**3,052**	**6.9**	**24,242,696**	**7.3**	**832,468**	**5.3**	**1,480,023**	**7.4**	**1,159,112**	**7.3**
Arkansas	183	0.4	895,055	0.3	52,377	0.3	132,803	0.7	121,043	0.8
Louisiana	278	0.6	967,761	0.3	64,072	0.4	55,444	0.3	40,733	0.3
Oklahoma	410	0.9	5,133,422	1.6	145,523	0.9	228,577	1.1	162,808	1.0
Texas	2,181	4.9	17,246,458	5.2	570,496	3.6	1,063,200	5.3	834,528	5.2
WEST	**6,915**	**15.7**	**63,474,481**	**19.2**	**4,106,743**	**25.9**	**3,520,819**	**17.6**	**2,609,532**	**16.3**
Mountain	**1,903**	**4.3**	**9,971,905**	**3.0**	**1,110,667**	**7.0**	**613,063**	**3.1**	**490,423**	**3.1**
Arizona	341	0.8	1,201,463	0.4	79,313	0.5	84,329	0.4	61,200	0.4
Colorado	610	1.4	3,136,586	1.0	204,122	1.3	214,797	1.1	169,472	1.1
Idaho	138	0.3	1,249,722	0.4	654,174	4.1	20,942	0.1	17,683	0.1
Montana	130	0.3	170,298	0.1	7,031	0.0	11,449	0.1	8,410	0.1
Nevada	218	0.5	1,407,929	0.4	66,410	0.4	130,399	0.7	117,098	0.7
New Mexico	119	0.3	771,995	0.2	12,066	0.1	49,677	0.2	31,613	0.2
Utah	239	0.5	1,620,154	0.5	67,755	0.4	79,426	0.4	68,156	0.4
Wyoming	108	0.2	413,758	0.1	19,797	0.1	22,044	0.1	16,791	0.1
Pacific	**5,012**	**11.4**	**53,502,575**	**16.2**	**2,996,077**	**18.9**	**2,907,755**	**14.5**	**2,119,109**	**13.3**
Alaska	43	0.1	44,591	0.0	7,632	0.0	6,885	0.0	4,337	0.0
California	3,646	8.3	46,752,854	14.2	2,659,798	16.8	2,430,126	12.1	1,754,106	11.0
Hawaii	191	0.4	1,214,827	0.4	22,064	0.1	71,245	0.4	41,283	0.3
Oregon	373	0.8	1,985,731	0.6	142,919	0.9	127,059	0.6	101,979	0.6
Washington	759	1.7	3,504,573	1.1	163,663	1.0	272,441	1.4	217,403	1.4
CARIBBEAN[2]	**7**	**0.0**	**33,796**	**0.0**	**1,728**	**0.0**	**3,107**	**0.0**	**2,487**	**0.0**
Puerto Rico	4	0.0	32,547	0.0	951	0.0	2,333	0.0	1,785	0.0
Virgin Islands	3	0.0	1,249	0.0	778	0.0	774	0.0	702	0.0
Total	**44,146**	**100.0**	**$329,910,297**	**100.0**	**$15,832,955**	**100.0**	**$20,048,822**	**100.0**	**$15,985,431**	**100.0**

Source: *Foundation Giving,* 1999.
*Dollars in thousands; due to rounding, figures may not add up.
[1]Geographic regions as defined by the U.S. Bureau of the Census.
[2]Private foundations in Puerto Rico and the Virgin Islands are not required to file IRS Form 990-PF. Only a few voluntary reporters are represented.

EARNED INCOME

While some large nonprofits, like universities, hospitals, and social service agencies, have always relied heavily on fees for services, more and more other nonprofits have turned to income-producing ventures and new dues and fee structures to help cover their operating costs. For many nonprofit organizations, this has meant simply establishing a fee structure for goods and services that they had previously supplied free of charge. Others have looked to capitalize on their existing resources by renting out unused office or meeting space; leasing computer time, services, or equipment; or offering consulting or information services to businesses and clients who can afford to pay. Still others have adopted a more ambitious approach to raising funds through ventures such as gift shops, publications, travel services, and the like. Fees, service charges, and other commercial income account for a whopping 54 percent of all nonprofit service organization revenues, according to Salamon (see Figure 4). Several books and articles on "nonprofit entrepreneurship" can be found in Appendix A.

GOVERNMENT FUNDING

Government funding is the second most important source of income for America's nonprofits. Government contracts, reimbursements, and grants account for 36 percent

Figure 3. Foundation Assets by Region, 1975 and 1997*

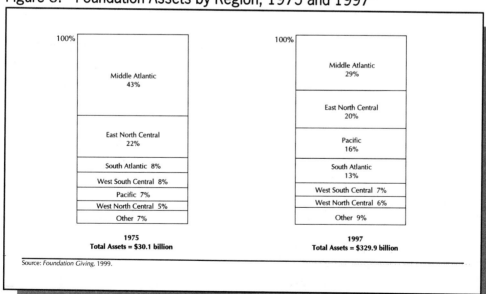

⌐. Sources of Nonprofit Public-Benefit Organization Income, 1996

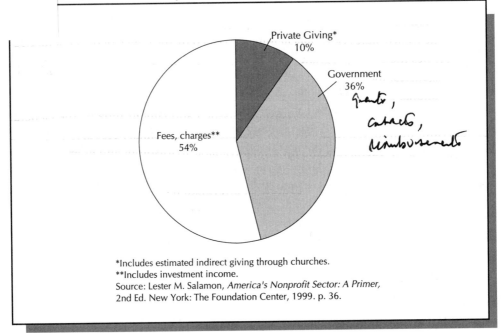

Private Giving*
10%

Government
36%

grants,
contracts,
reimbursements

Fees, charges**
54%

*Includes estimated indirect giving through churches.
**Includes investment income.
Source: Lester M. Salamon, *America's Nonprofit Sector: A Primer,*
2nd Ed. New York: The Foundation Center, 1999. p. 36.

of nonprofit service organization income, according to Salamon, reflecting a widespread pattern of partnership between government and the nonprofit sector in carrying out public purposes.

Due to the growth in government spending in recent decades and the prominence of government policies, Salamon asserts that while to some it may appear that the nonprofit sector has shrunk to insignificance, nothing could be farther from the truth. In addition to their social value, nonprofit organizations are a major economic force in U.S. life.

Most grantseeking nonprofits will want to become familiar with the activities and funding programs of the federal, state, and local government agencies with responsibility for their service areas. According to data provided by Independent Sector[1] in 1996, federal, state, and local governments were the source of more than half of the annual income of nonprofit organizations in the social and legal services field; 41

---

1. Independent Sector is a national forum promoting philanthropy, volunteerism, not-for-profit initiative, and citizen action.

percent of the income in the health services sector; 30 percent in civic affairs; 20 percent in education and research; and only 14 percent in arts and culture.

Information about federal government programs is available through a variety of sources. The *United States Government Manual*, issued by the Office of the Federal Register, describes the broad program responsibilities of all government departments and affiliated agencies, including the National Endowments for the Arts and Humanities and the National Science Foundation.

The *Catalog of Federal Domestic Assistance*, issued annually in June by the General Services Administration and updated in December, is the primary resource on federal funding, listing all federal funding programs available to for-profit and nonprofit institutions as well as to individuals.

There are two other important sources of information on federal funding: the *Federal Register*, which lists proposed and final rules and regulations developed by all federal agencies in addition to information on program deadlines and application procedures, and *Commerce Business Daily*, which publishes bid requests for federal contracts.

Information on these government publications, in addition to other useful guides and handbooks about government funding, is included in Appendix A.

In contrast to the wealth of information on federal government programs, information about funding by state and local governments is not always readily available. Most state and large municipal governments issue some type of guidebook or manual listing the addresses of departments and agencies along with brief descriptions of their program responsibilities. Sometimes the offices of state senators and congressional representatives may be able to guide you to appropriate sources of local funding information. You'll want to check with your local public library for the specific resources available in your area.

PRIVATE GIVING

In *America's Nonprofit Sector*, Lester Salamon also reports that private giving accounted for only 10 percent[2] of the total support for public-benefit nonprofit organizations in 1996. This compares with the previously cited 54 percent of revenues from fees, service charges, and other commercial income and 36 percent from government grants,

---

2. This excludes giving to religious organizations.

Loans/Program-Related Investments

In addition to grants, some foundations make loans to nonprofits, usually in the form of program-related investments (PRI). A PRI, broadly defined, is an investment by a foundation to support a charitable project or activity involving the potential return of capital within an established time frame. Unlike grants, PRIs must be repaid—generally with interest—and are governed by strict regulations that mandate greater administrative attention than conventional grants. In addition, foundations must prove to the IRS that PRI funds are spent only for the designated charitable purpose and that the loan recipient could not have secured funding through traditional financial channels. Despite these restrictions, a number of foundations report an interest in, or have a history of, making program-related investments.

According to a study conducted by the Foundation Center in 1997, there were approximately 250 active PRI funders in the United States. From 1993 through 1994, a sample of 116 leading PRI funders made 388 charitable loans and investments totaling $176.5 million. Seven out of 10 of these funders were independent foundations, and they accounted for 84 percent of all PRI dollars and 73 percent of PRIs. Community foundations made more PRIs than did corporate foundations, but the corporate foundations gave more dollars in the form of PRIs.

Although PRI funders represented all asset sizes, they tended to be among larger U.S. foundations. More than half of PRI funders held assets of

contracts, and reimbursements (see Figure 4). However, the average proportion of revenue received from private contributions varied widely among areas of nonprofit endeavor.

According to estimates in *Giving USA 1999*, published by the AAFRC Trust for Philanthropy, philanthropic contributions in 1997 totaled $157.7 billion (see Figure 5). The largest portion of these contributions—$135.6 billion or 86 percent—came from individual donors through gifts or bequests. Independent and community foundations accounted for $13.9 billion or 8.8 percent of this total, while corporations,

$50 million or over and they accounted for 85 percent of new charitable loans and investments.

The community development field—encompassing a wide range of activities from housing development to neighborhood revitalization in large urban centers to small business creation in rural communities—represents the largest single area of PRI-making. Nearly 66 percent of new investment dollars, but only about 33 percent of the total number of PRIs, financed community development and housing. Other PRI-financed projects and organizations were in the fields of the environment, arts and culture, education, health, churches and religious activities, human services, and international development.

While the Center's in-depth study of the PRIs of leading funders has not yet been updated, summary information on loans and other program-related investments is published annually in the Center's statistical yearbook, *Foundation Giving*. According to the 1999 edition of the yearbook, in 1997 foundations provided $147 million in low- or no-interest loans and other program-related investments. The total amount of PRI funding grew only slightly in 1997. Summary figures are based on data reported by foundations included in *The Foundation Directory* and *The Foundation Directory Part 2*.

For more information about PRIs, see the Center's publications *The PRI Index: 500 Recent Foundation Charitable Loans and Investments* (1997) and *Program-Related Investments: A Guide to Funders and Trends* (1995), as well as other titles in Appendix A.

through their foundations or direct giving activities, were responsible for $8.2 billion or 5.2 percent of total estimated private giving.

Individual Donors and Bequests

Giving by individuals, historically the largest source of private giving, has grown steadily over the past three decades, reaching $123 billion in 1997, according to *Giving USA 1999*. As can be seen in Figure 5, these gifts by individuals accounted for 78 percent of all private giving in 1997. Giving by individuals in 1997 represents an increase of 14.2 percent over *Giving USA*'s revised 1996 estimate of $107.7 billion, and again in terms of percentage of personal income. Over the previous three decades, individual giving ranged from a high of 2.1 percent of personal income to a low of 1.6 percent. The 1997 estimate of $123 billion is 1.8 percent of personal income.

Figure 5. Giving 1997: $157.7 Billion—Sources of Contributions

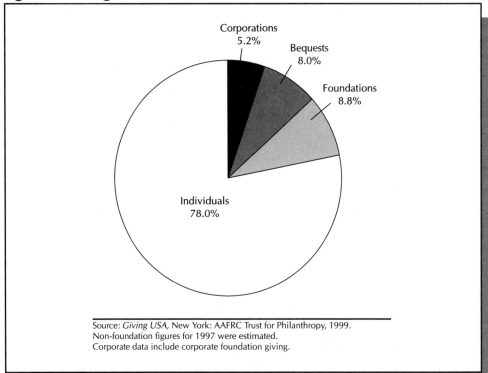

Source: *Giving USA*, New York: AAFRC Trust for Philanthropy, 1999.
Non-foundation figures for 1997 were estimated.
Corporate data include corporate foundation giving.

Bequests accounted for 8 percent, or $12.63 billion, of all private giving in 1997. Because a few large bequests can skew the figures, bequest giving appears erratic when viewed from year to year. From the longer perspective, *Giving USA* reports that bequest giving has increased almost 1,000 percent since 1967, indicating that this type of giving is growing.

Individual contributions range from a few pennies to millions of dollars and from used appliances and clothing to priceless art collections. Many individuals also contribute another priceless resource—their time—although volunteer time is not consistently reported by all nonprofits in terms of monetary value.

The list of techniques used by nonprofit organizations to raise money from individual donors is long and varied. It includes increasingly popular direct-mail appeals, door-to-door solicitation, membership programs, special fundraising events, and deferred giving programs. A good many guides and handbooks detailing these approaches have been published, and a number of them are listed in the bibliography in Appendix A.

Independent and Community Foundations

Independent and community foundation giving as a proportion of total private philanthropic giving grew during the 1960s from 6.4 percent in 1960 to 9 percent in 1970. During the 1970s the proportion of giving coming from foundations declined to a low of 5.2 percent in 1979. With a soaring stock market causing increases in foundation assets in the 1980s, foundation giving as a share of private contributions moved back up to 6.7 percent in 1989 and continued to rise in the 1990s as new foundations were created and existing ones received new assets. The 8.8 percent share captured in 1997 represents a slight increase over the previous year's 8.7 percent share and is the highest percentage level for independent and community foundations reported in *Giving USA* since 1970.

Corporate Giving

According to *Giving USA 1999*, corporate giving has represented between 5 and 6 percent of philanthropic giving throughout the 1990s, after a five-year period from 1984 through 1988 with between a 6 and 7 percent share. Corporate giving first outstripped independent and community foundation giving, according to *Giving USA* estimates, in 1983. The mid-80s were initially hailed as a turning point in corporate philanthropy, with predictions that it would continue to gain in relation to independent and community foundation giving. However, this new equilibrium did not last long. In fact, in the late 1980s, the Foundation Center noted a growing gap between grants paid out by corporate foundations and new gifts into these foundations, indicating that companies were eroding their foundation asset base to keep giving high. Starting in 1994, this pattern reversed, and corporations have been putting more into their foundations than they have paid out.

The *Giving USA 1999* estimates for corporate foundation grants and their direct giving activities puts these contributions to the nonprofit sector at $8.2 billion in 1997.

Just over $2 billion of that amount is estimated to have been distributed by corporate foundations, which are believed to be responsible for 20 to 25 percent of total corporate giving. While corporate foundation giving can be documented through the forms 990-PF that all private foundations must file with the IRS, corporate direct giving numbers, even historically, are based on estimates because no formal reporting is required and because corporate direct giving takes so many different forms. Corporate assistance expenditures, which include in-kind gifts, donated personnel, use of facilities, and below-market loans, make up about 20 percent of total corporate giving estimates and appear to be increasing more rapidly than outright grants and cash gifts.

Information on resources for corporate grantseeking will be found in Chapter 9 and in Appendix A.

Religious Funders

Churches, temples, and other religious organizations are usually thought of as recipients of charitable contributions, but many are also funding sources. According to Independent Sector's *Nonprofit Almanac 1996–1997* (San Francisco, CA: Jossey-Bass Publishers, 1996), approximately 24 percent of the expenditures reported by congregations in 1991[3] was spent on donations to organizations, both within and outside specific denominations.

While many religious institutions operate their own service programs, the same survey revealed that, on average, congregations contributed about one-fifth of their total donations to organizations *outside* their own denomination for activities they wished to promote. These activities include a range of direct social service programs, grassroots and advocacy activities, and education and research. According to the *1997–98 Religious Funding Resource Guide* (Washington, D.C.: ResourceWomen, 1997), grants from religious sources average between $1,000 and $10,000, with a few religious funders making larger grants of $35,000 and up.

While relatively little has been written about how best to approach religious institutions for funding support, a few directories and guides have appeared in recent years. Religious Funding Resource Guide, previously cited, states that seeking funding from religious bodies requires a different approach than seeking grants from foundations.

---

3. Because religious organizations do not have to report to the government, there is little information about their finances on a national scale. Independent Sector conducted the first national survey of the activities and finances of congregations in 1991.

The *Guide*, published annually, offers guidelines for identifying, approaching, and building relationships with religious groups. Information on religious funding sources is included in Appendix A.

Summary

As detailed in this chapter, foundations may be important sources of support for organizations, but their grants represent a relatively small proportion of the total philanthropic dollars received by nonprofit organizations. And government funding and earned income sources vastly overshadow the entire field of philanthropy in accounting for nonprofit revenue. While the most successful nonprofit organizations develop strategic fundraising plans that encompass a range of income sources, this guide focuses on strategies for securing information on funding from foundations and corporations. In future chapters, we provide step-by-step assistance in identifying those foundations and corporate giving programs that will be most likely to fund your project, program, or organization. Next, we will examine who gets foundation grants.

Chapter 3

Who Gets Foundation Grants?

The overwhelming majority of foundation grants are awarded to nonprofit organizations that qualify for "public charity" status under Section 501(c)(3) of the Internal Revenue Code. An organization may qualify for this tax-exempt status if it is organized and operated exclusively for charitable, religious, educational, scientific, or literary purposes; monitors public safety; fosters national or international amateur sports competition (but only if its activities do not involve the provision of athletic facilities or equipment); or is active in the prevention of cruelty to children or animals. These tax-exempt organizations must also certify to the IRS that no part of their income will benefit private shareholders or individuals and that they will not, as a substantial part of their activities, attempt to influence legislation or participate in political campaigns for or against any candidate for public office.

Under federal law, foundations are permitted to make grants to individuals and organizations that do not qualify for public charity status if they follow a set of very specific rules covering "expenditure responsibility." Essentially, the rules for expenditure responsibility involve submitting a number of financial and fiduciary reports certifying that the funds were spent solely for the charitable purposes spelled out in the grant agreement, and that no part of the funds was spent to influence legislation. As opposed to support for nonprofit organizations, provisions for grants to individuals require advance approval of the program by the IRS and prohibit giving to "disqualified persons"—a broad category covering contributors to the foundation and its relatives, foundation managers, and certain public officials. Although some foundations have instituted such giving programs, they represent a small segment of the foundation universe.

Nonprofit Organizations

Foundations award grants to a wide variety of nonprofit organizations. The majority confine their giving to nonprofits that provide services in the foundation's home community. Others restrict their grants to specific types of institutions or organizations active in a particular subject area, such as medical research, higher education, or youth services. Still others limit their giving to specific purposes, such as capital campaigns, providing seed money, or bolstering endowments. The research strategies outlined in the chapters that follow are designed to help nonprofits identify funders that are likely to fund organizations similar to their own.

HOW TO FORM A NONPROFIT CORPORATION

Virtually every grantmaker you identify through your research will want to know that your organization is recognized as a 501(c)(3) organization by the IRS, and most will ask to see a copy of your IRS exemption letter. Depending on the particular state in which your organization is located, the foundation may also wish to see that you've received the appropriate state certification for tax-exempt charitable organizations. If your organization has not yet received tax-exempt status, you'll want to read the IRS booklet *Tax-Exempt Status for Your Organization* (IRS Publication 557), which includes the actual application forms for Section 501(c)(3) organizations as well as for most other tax-exempt organizations. Copies of the booklet can be obtained by calling the tax information number listed under "United States Government, Internal Revenue Service" in the phone directory (1-800-TAXFORM). You may also order the booklet online at www.irs.ustreas.gov. The publication can also be downloaded from the Internet, but special software is needed. The help section of the IRS Web site will explain how to retrieve a free copy of the necessary software.

The process of incorporating as a tax-exempt nonprofit organization is regulated under federal, state, and sometimes local law. It is advisable to consult an attorney, preferably one with nonprofit experience, to guide you through the process. There are also a number of handbooks that explain the application procedures and examine the legal ramifications and issues involved in structuring your organization. Figure 6 outlines the basic steps involved in forming a nonprofit corporation. The bibliography in Appendix A lists publications on forming a nonprofit that can be examined free of charge at Foundation Center libraries.

A corporation is a legal entity that allows a group of people to combine their money, expertise, time, and effort for certain activities, which can be for-profit (has ability to issue stock and pay dividends) or nonprofit (cannot issue stock or pay dividends). State law governs the formation of corporations. Although most for-profit corporations can be formed for "any lawful purpose," state statutes usually require nonprofit corporations to be established to accomplish some specific purpose to benefit the public or a community. Only those nonprofit corporations formed for religious, charitable, scientific, educational, or literary purposes of benefit to the public are eligible for tax-exempt status under Section 501(c)(3) of the Internal Revenue Code.

Once a nonprofit organization has been incorporated in one of the fifty states and has obtained a federal Employer Identification Number (EIN), it can then apply for tax exemption from the IRS. The nonprofit organization may also have to file for separate exemption under the state's revenue regulations. Thereafter, the nonprofit must report income receipts and disbursements annually to the IRS and the state revenue department. Also, it will usually have to renew registration with the appropriate state agency on an annual basis.

BENEFICIARIES

The nonprofits that benefit from foundation grants are many and varied. As can be seen in Figure 7, education was the most popular subject category for grant dollars in 1997, followed by health (17 percent), human services (15 percent), arts and humanities (13 percent) and public/society benefit (12 percent). Those four areas also received the most grants, but in slightly different percentages, with human services receiving the largest number of grants (23 percent), followed by education (21 percent), arts and humanities (14 percent), health (13 percent), and public/society benefit (12 percent).

A look at beneficiaries by types of recipients (see Figure 8) shows that educational institutions, with 37.4 percent of the grant dollars distributed in 1997, were far and away the most likely nonprofits to receive foundation funding. Colleges and

Figure 6. How to Form and Operate a Nonprofit Corporation

	Steps	Applicable Form	Results
Articles of Incorporation	Reserve the name of your organization (optional).	File application for reservation of name with appropriate agency in your state. Obtain necessary consents for the name, where required.	Reserves your name so that no other organization can, for a limited period of time, incorporate under that same name in your state.
	Prepare Certificate of Incorporation. Includes: purposes and incorporators of the corporation and any other clauses that are required by your State Not-for-Profit Law.	File Articles of Incorporation with your Secretary of State.	The State recognizes your organization as an Incorporated Nonprofit Organization (i.e., one conducting nonprofit activities for charitable, educational, religious, scientific, literary or cultural purposes).
Federal Employer Identification Number	File with the Internal Revenue Service (IRS) as a nonprofit, even if you do not have employees.	IRS Form SS-4	Your organization has an identification number so the IRS can track your reports and IRS Form 1023 tax exempt application (see below).
Federal Tax Exemption	Determine the applicable section of the Internal Revenue Code.	IRS Publication 557 and IRS Forms 1023 or 1024.	Your organization is recognized by the IRS as exempt from paying income tax on most revenues related to your charitable functions.
	File with the IRS as a tax exempt organization, preferably within 27 months of the date of incorporation.	IRS filing fee is maximum of $500. See IRS Form 8718.	Donations made to your organization are tax deductible only if you are a 501(c)(3) organization.
State Registration and Reporting	Contact the Secretary of State (Corporate Division) and Attorney General (Charities Division).	Registration forms and fiscal annual reports (e.g., New York State NYCF-1 and New York State G750-497); fee will vary with size of your organization's operating budget.	Your organization is officially registered as a charity to solicit funds, do business or own property in your state.
			You may have to apply for a separate exemption under your state's regulations.
Reporting to the IRS	Report annually to the IRS.	IRS Form 990	Provides the IRS with a report of your organization's income and disbursements.

© 1998 The Nonprofit Connection, Inc., One Hanson Place, Brooklyn, NY 11243

Figure 7. Grants by Major Subject Categories*

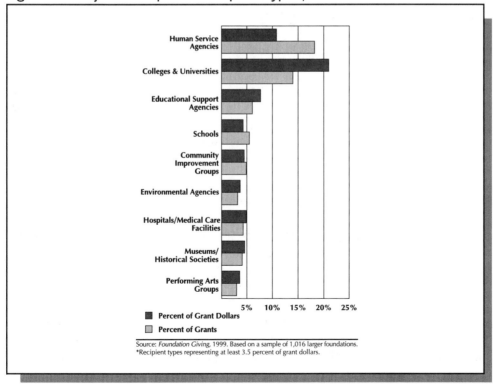

Source: *The Foundation Grants Index*, 1998. Based on a sample of 1,016 larger foundations.
*Due to rounding, figures may not add up.
[1]Includes civil rights and social action, community improvement, philanthropy and voluntarism, and public affairs.

Figure 8. Major Field-Specific Recipient Types, 1997*

Source: *Foundation Giving*, 1999. Based on a sample of 1,016 larger foundations.
*Recipient types representing at least 3.5 percent of grant dollars.

universities received most of these grants. Human service agencies with 10.8 percent of the 1997 grant amounts and hospitals and other medical care institutions with 4.9 percent came in second and third, respectively. The distribution of grants by field-specific recipient type has remained fairly consistent since 1992.

The major types of support provided to nonprofit organizations in 1997 were program funding, capital, general/operating expenses, research grants, and student aid. While there were differences between the percentage of grant dollars received and the number of grants received by category, the distributions remained consistent (see Figure 9).

Figure 9. Major Types of Support*

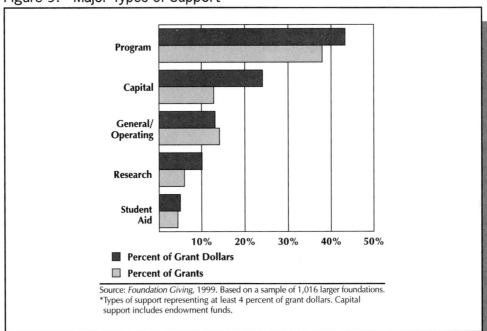

Source: *Foundation Giving*, 1999. Based on a sample of 1,016 larger foundations.
*Types of support representing at least 4 percent of grant dollars. Capital support includes endowment funds.

FISCAL SPONSORSHIP

Organizations that do not have tax-exempt status can still participate in the grant-seeking process. However, doing so may be difficult. You may receive funds, for example, by affiliating with an existing organization that already is eligible to receive foundation grants and is willing to assume fiscal responsibility for your project on a contract basis. Since grants would then be made directly to the sponsoring organization, you and the sponsor should have in advance a clear written agreement about the management of funds received and what fees (if any) may be subtracted by the fiscal sponsor. Since there is no master list of organizations willing to act as sponsors, you will need to investigate those with purposes similar to your own. *Fiscal Sponsorship: Six Ways to Do It Right* by Gregory L. Colvin is a useful resource on this topic. Many of the general fundraising and nonprofit management guides listed in Appendix A outline this and other options in detail.

Profit-Making Organizations

While foundations generally cannot award grants to profit-making groups, they are permitted under the Tax Reform Act of 1969 to make grants to organizations that are not tax-exempt, or have not yet received their exemption, for projects that are clearly charitable in nature, so long as the funders exercise "expenditure responsibility." Most foundations do not have the staff to provide the necessary oversight for expenditure responsibility and, therefore, are unlikely to fund profit-making organizations or other organizations that do not have tax-exempt status.

Those wishing to start their own for-profit businesses will find information at the local office of the Small Business Administration, the local Chamber of Commerce, business libraries at colleges or universities, or the business sections of large public libraries. Foundations do not provide funding for starting private for-profit businesses.

Individuals

Under the provisions of the Tax Reform Act of 1969, private foundations may make grants to individuals for "travel, study or similar purposes" if they obtain, in advance, approval from the IRS of their selection criteria and procedures. These procedures must ensure an objective selection process and usually involve extensive follow-up reports that demonstrate adequate performance and appropriate expenditures of the grant funds by the individual receiving the grant. Although foundations may make grants to individuals, only a small percentage do. In 1996, roughly one out of ten foundations listed in *The Foundation Directory* made grants to individuals. These grants totaled $195 million.

Individuals seeking foundation grants should first look at the programs described in *Foundation Grants to Individuals* published by the Foundation Center. It contains descriptions of approximately 3,800 foundations of all sizes that currently operate grant programs to individuals. Individual grantseekers should also examine the entries under "Grants to Individuals" in the Types of Support Indexes in the various Foundation Center directories, such as *The Foundation Directory* and the *National Guide* series (see Chapter 5 for complete descriptions).

There are, as well, a wide variety of funding sources other than foundations that make grants to individuals. Individual grantseekers should also consult *The National Directory of Grantmaking Public Charities*. This directory indexes public charities that provide grants to individuals, scholarships, fellowships, and student loans. Several general reference books (e.g., *The Annual Register of Grant Support*, *The Grants Register*, and *Awards, Honors and Prizes*) describe grant programs run by government agencies, corporations, associations, and nonprofit groups in such diverse fields as sports, religion, medicine, and the performing arts. Foundation Center libraries also maintain a selection of specialized funding guides for individuals interested in specific subject areas or from specific population groups.

STUDENTS AND ARTISTS

Many individual grantseekers are either prospective students or artists. Students seeking financial aid for their education should be sure to consult with the financial aid office at the school they plan to attend. Approximately 85 percent of the 3,800 foundations in the Center's publication *Foundation Grants to Individuals* fund programs for educational aid, including scholarships, fellowships, and loans. The Center's new CD-ROM, *FC Scholar*, which is being developed at the time this book goes to press, is a searchable database containing information on the more than 3,000 foundations making grants to individuals for educational purposes. There are a number of guides and directories that describe grant programs operated by local and state governments, corporations, labor unions, educational institutions, and a variety of trade associations and nonprofit agencies. A comprehensive bibliography of sources on individual scholarships and grants can be found in *Foundation Grants to Individuals*. Many high school and public libraries maintain, and make available free of charge, collections of funding information resources for students. There are a number of sites on the Internet that provide information on scholarships, fellowships, and loans, including CollegeNet (www.collegenet.com) and FINAID: Financial Aid Information page (www.finaid.org).

Individual artists should look in the "Arts and Culture" section of *Foundation Grants to Individuals* for potential funders. Fiscal sponsorship is another possibility for an artist (see the section below). Several Internet sites may prove helpful in the quest for funding:

- Art Deadlines List (www.xensei.com/users/adl): lists funding, residency and internship opportunities; updated monthly.

- Arts Over America (www.nasaa-arts.org/new/nasaa/aoa/ aoa_contents.shtml): links to state art agencies, many of which offer funding.

- Arts Wire (www.artswire.org): contains information on grants in weekly digest of news in the arts.

FISCAL SPONSORSHIP

Individuals seeking funds for research or special projects not related to their education may wish to do what organizations without tax-exempt status do: affiliate with a nonprofit organization that can act as a sponsor, sometimes called a "fiscal agent," for a foundation grant. Universities, hospitals, churches, schools, arts organizations, and theaters are just a few of the many types of nonprofits that have received and administered foundation grants for work done by individuals. The challenge to individual grantseekers is to identify those organizations with which they or their project have something in common. For more information about fiscal agents, see Appendix A, particularly *Fiscal Sponsorship: Six Ways to Do It Right* by Gregory L. Colvin.

Summary

Nonprofit organizations with tax-exempt status as public charities under Section 501(c)(3) of the Internal Revenue Code are the major recipients of foundation grants. The types of nonprofit organizations, the types of support they receive and the subjects they cover vary widely. Individuals and non-exempt organizations can receive grants from foundations and other nonprofits; however, these individuals and groups must perform more research and be more creative in their approach to fundraising. Seeking fiscal sponsorship from an exempt nonprofit is one such approach.

Nonprofits, as well as other organizations and individuals seeking grants, must plan their research strategies and learn about the resources available to help identify potential funders. The next two chapters outline a research strategy and introduce you to the vast array of resources in the field of fundraising research.

Chapter 4

Planning Your Funding Research Strategies

Grantmakers receive thousands of requests for funding every year, as the competition for foundation resources grows ever more intense. Many requests go unfunded because there are simply not enough resources to go around; others are denied because the proposal clearly falls outside the funder's interest. Proposals may also fail because they are poorly prepared or do not reflect a careful analysis of the applicant organization's needs, its credibility, or its capacity to carry out the project as proposed. (For detailed recommendations on proposal writing, see Chapter 10 or the Proposal Writing Short Course at the Foundation Center's Web site at www.fdncenter.org.)

The key to any successful fundraising effort is homework, beginning with a careful analysis of your organization, the formulation of a clear idea of where it's going, and the development of a concrete plan for getting there. Once you have completed this assessment, you're ready to begin tracking those foundations whose stated objectives and grantmaking priorities are directly related to your organization's goals and needs. All of this takes time.

Faced with this reality, some grantseekers look for ways around the funding research process. They mail copies of their proposal to such easily targeted groups as the largest foundations in the United States, to all foundations in their own geographic region, or to foundations whose names are well known. Rarely does this approach work. Funders are only too familiar with the mass-mailing technique, and groups that employ it may do their causes harm. Grantseekers are well advised, instead, to do their homework carefully and to be sure to let it show. Explore all the resources described in this guide, including primary source material. And, let the funders you approach know exactly why you believe your program matches their interests. It is helpful to use the grantmakers' own words from IRS returns, annual reports, Web sites, and other sources in describing how your program and their interests coincide.

The process is lengthy. Therefore, six months or a year prior to needing the money is not too early to begin your research. Many foundation boards meet only once or twice per year. You would not want to miss a prospect's deadline. As part of your plan, allow adequate time not only for your research at the beginning but also for the funder's review of your proposal at the end.

KNOW YOUR OWN PROGRAM

The importance of program planning cannot be overstated. Yet far too many nonprofit organizations get so caught up in their day-to-day tasks and immediate concerns that they give the process short shrift. Simply stated, there is nothing more important than the careful analysis and planning of your organization's programs and financial needs. Without such analysis, no amount of funding research will save the day. Scores of useful guides and handbooks on program planning and nonprofit management are available. Many of these publications are listed in Appendix A. Whatever procedures you adopt, however, there are several items you need to take care of before you can plot your research strategy:

1. Is your organization structured so that it is eligible to receive foundation and corporate grants? As noted in Chapter 3, most foundations limit their giving to organizations that have received 501(c)(3) tax-exempt status from the IRS. Many foundations require that grantees also be classified as "not a private foundation" as described in sections 509(a)(1) and 170(b)(1)(A)(vi) of the Internal Revenue Code. Individuals seeking grant support should refer to the resources mentioned in the previous chapter.

2. Can you transmit verbally and in writing a clear picture of the purpose of the program or project for which you are seeking support?

3. Can you delineate the type of support required, such as general operating, capital, or seed money? (See Appendix D for definitions of the different types of support.)

4. Do you have a formal budget indicating the costs of the project, the amount of money you hope to raise, and how you plan to cover other costs?

5. Have you carefully defined your project, goals, timeline, and budget to help you report successfully back to funders?

In preparation for planning your funding research strategies, complete the questions in "Know Your Program" (see Figure 10). This comprehensive outline will help you make a realistic appraisal of your project.

RESEARCH STRATEGIES

Once you have analyzed and pinpointed your organization's funding needs, you can begin to develop a strategy for identifying potential funders. Although there are a variety of approaches to uncovering appropriate funding sources, they all boil down to three basic steps:

1. Developing a broad list of prospects—that is, foundations and/or corporate grantmakers that have shown an interest in funding projects or some aspect of programs similar to your own.

2. Refining your list of prospects to eliminate those grantmakers that seem unable or unlikely to fund projects in your subject field or geographic area, or that do not provide the type or amount of support you need.

3. Investigating thoroughly the funders remaining on your list to determine which ones are most likely to consider your proposal favorably.

The key to success is doing your homework. Identifying potential funders requires serious, time-consuming research, but grantseekers often determine that it is well worth the effort.

Figure 10. Know Your Program

A successful funding research strategy must be based on a realistic appraisal of the types of funders that are most likely to be interested in your project. Your first step, then, is to get all relevant aspects of your own program clearly in focus.

1. Is your organization structured to receive foundation and/or corporate support? _____

_____

_____

2. What is the central purpose of the activity for which you are seeking funding? _____

_____

_____

(a) What is the *subject* focus of the activity? _____

_____

_____

(b) What *population groups* will benefit from the activity? _____

_____

_____

(c) What *geographic* area will be served by the activity? Will this project have an impact beyond that geographic area? _____

_____

_____

Figure 10. Know Your Program (continued)

3. How does this activity fit into the central purpose of your organization? __

_____

_____

4. What are the unique qualifications of your organization and/or staff to accomplish the proposed activity? _____

_____

_____

5. What is the total budget for the project? _____

_____

(a) What *type of support* (e.g., building funds, equipment, operating support) are you seeking? _____

_____

(b) How *much* grant support are you seeking? _____

(c) What *other sources* of income will be used to meet the project costs? __

_____

(d) How will the project be funded for the *long term*? _____

_____

6. Who has supported or expressed an interest in your organization's programs? (Note past and current funders, members of the board of directors, volunteeers, community leaders, etc.) _____

_____

_____

The Foundation Center

STEP ONE: DEVELOPING A BROAD PROSPECT LIST

The first step in funding research is to identify foundations and corporate grantmakers that have indicated in their statements of purpose or by their recent grantmaking activities an interest in funding programs or organizations similar to your own. In analyzing your organization and its funding needs, consider the subject fields in which your group is active, the geographic area it serves, and the type and amount of grant support you need. Our experience at the Foundation Center has led us to recommend three basic strategies when developing a broad list of funding prospects:

1. The **subject approach** identifies funders that have expressed an interest in your specific subject field or population group focus.

2. The **geographic approach** identifies grantmakers that fund programs in a specific city, state, or region.

3. The **types of support approach** identifies foundations that provide specific types of support to nonprofit organizations (e.g., construction or renovation funds, research funds, endowment money, program-related investments, and so on; see Appendix D for a complete list).

We'll examine each of these strategies in greater detail in Chapters 6, 7, and 8. If you use *FC Search: The Foundation Center's Database on CD-ROM,* you will be able to combine the above approaches in various ways. If you rely on print resources, you will need to work on each strategy independently or sequentially.

The Prospect Worksheet (see Figure 11) is the format the Foundation Center recommends to grantseekers. During the initial phase of your research you should focus on certain basic facts about the funders you uncover. While you may want to develop your own prospect worksheet, the contents should include the following elements: the funder's name and location; the subject and geographic focus of its grantmaking activities; any stated restrictions or limitations it places on its grants; the size and type of grant it typically awards; and its application procedures, if any.

STEP TWO: REFINING YOUR LIST

Once you have developed a broad list of funding prospects, you need to narrow it down to those grantmakers whose interests are similar to your own and therefore warrant further research. The Center recommends that you eliminate funders on your list that:

Figure 11. Prospect Worksheet

Date:	Funder	Your Organization
1. Name, Address, Contact Person		n/a
2. Financial Data Total Assets Total Grants Paid Grant Ranges/Amount Needed Period of Funding/Project		n/a n/a
3. Subject Focus (list in order of importance)	1. 2. 3.	1. 2. 3.
4. Population(s) Served		
5. Geographic Limits		
6. Type(s) of Support		
7. Type(s) of Recipients		
8. People (officers, donors, trustees, staff)		

Application information:
Does the funder have printed guidelines/application forms?
Initial approach (letter of inquiry, formal proposal):
Deadline(s):
Board meeting date(s):

Sources of above information:
❑ 990-PF (Year:)   ❑ Directories and grant   ❑ Funder's Web site
❑ Annual report (Year:)   indexes   ❑ Other
  ❑ Requested   ❑ Received   ❑ *FC Search*

Notes:

Follow-up:

The Foundation Center

1. do not fund projects in your geographic area, even though they may have an interest in your subject field;

2. do not fund projects in your subject field, even though they are located in your community or provide the type of support you are seeking;

3. do not provide the type of support you need (e.g., they do not fund general operating expenses or endowment campaigns).

If you follow the research strategies presented in this guide, you should be able to compile a manageable list of funders that merit in-depth investigation.

STEP THREE: FINDING YOUR MOST LIKELY PROSPECTS

The final phase of your research will focus on identifying those prospects that seem most likely to consider your proposal favorably. During this phase you will be gathering information on the funder's current financial status, its application procedures, and its most recent grantmaking activities. A foundation's 990-PF, Web site, and/or printed materials, such as annual reports and guideline brochures, can be particularly helpful at this stage. Background information on the donors to the foundation or its sponsoring company, financial and institutional history, current program interests, and future plans will not only help you to eliminate prospects that are unlikely to provide funding for your proposal but will also assist you with coming up with a more compelling case directed to that particular funder.

Learning More About Your Funding Prospects

In going through the process of identifying potential funding sources, you will gather names of grantmakers that, on the basis of the initial evidence, appear to have an interest in some aspect of your project. Next, you will eliminate those that, on closer examination, seem unlikely to consider your proposal favorably.

Finally, you will need to be sure you have up-to-date information on those grantmakers you consider to be your best bets. You'll want to confirm not only the funder's current address and officer and trustee names, but also funding guidelines, assets, gifts received, application procedures, and actual grants awarded in a recent time period. As you assemble these facts, you'll also be looking for answers to the following questions:

Does the funder accept applications? You may find it surprising that some do not. You'll want to find this out early in the research process so you don't waste your time. However, even when a funder says it gives only to pre-selected organizations, grantseekers should not completely disregard it as a prospect. For such grantmakers a different approach is necessary. The grantseeker must cultivate a relationship with the grantmaker who funds only pre-selected organizations, and this takes time.

Has the funder demonstrated a real commitment to funding in your subject field? You may have noted one or more grants by a particular foundation in your subject field. Upon examining the full grants list, however, you may find that these were the exceptions to their normal giving patterns. They may have been made for reasons other than a true commitment to the field, perhaps because of a special relationship between the recipient organization and a foundation board member, for example. Some foundations have historic and continuing relationships with particular institutions (due to a specified interest of the donor) that may cause them to fund activities that do not fall within their usual giving guidelines. In other cases, grants may have been awarded because the funder is committed to the recipient organization's location rather than to its primary field of endeavor.

Does it seem likely that the funder will make grants to organizations in your geographic location? Although it isn't necessary for a foundation to actually have made grants in your state or city to remain on your list, you should examine funding guidelines and grant records carefully for either explicit or implicit geographic restrictions. Be on the lookout for local or regional giving patterns or concentrations in rural or urban areas that might exclude your project. Corporate grantmakers, of course, generally restrict their funding to locales where they do business or have plants, subsidiaries, or corporate headquarters.

Does the amount of money you are requesting fit within the funder's typical grant range? Obviously you should not request $25,000 from a foundation that has never made a grant larger than $10,000. At the same time, look for more subtle distinctions. If a foundation's arts grants range from $10,000 to $20,000 and its social welfare grants are in the $3,000 to $5,000 range, consider what that says about its emphasis. About 50 percent of this weeding out process is common sense; the rest is intuition and luck.

Does the funder have a policy prohibiting grants for the type of support you are requesting? Many foundations will not make grants for operating budgets. Others will not provide funds for endowment, physical plant improvements, or equipment. Be sure the funder is willing to consider the type of support you need.

Does the funder like to make grants to cover the full cost of a project or does it favor projects where other funders have an opportunity to participate? Since it is unlikely that a first-time donor will fund an entire project, it is entirely appropriate to approach multiple funders for the same project, asking each to contribute to the whole.

Does the funder put limits on the length of time it is willing to support a project? Some foundations favor one-time grants, while others will continue their support over a number of years. It is rare to find grantmakers that will commit funding to an organization for an indefinite period of time, however. Be sure you can point to possible avenues of income or support for the future before approaching funders. Many funders will expect you to have thought through and be able to present a long-term funding plan for any project in which they might be asked to participate.

What types of organizations does the funder tend to support? Does it favor large, well-established groups such as symphonies, universities, and museums, or does it lean toward grassroots community groups? A funder's past recipients will give you an excellent feel for its focus. Look carefully at the mix of its recipients for clues that may not be stated explicitly in its printed guidelines.

Does the funder have application deadlines, or does it review proposals continuously? Note carefully any information you uncover about deadlines and board meeting dates so you can submit your proposal at the appropriate time. Since calendars fill up, and staff and/or board members have a limited amount of time to review and consider proposals, proposals should be sent well ahead of the stated deadline. Be aware, as well, that the time elapsed between the submission of your proposal and notification of actual receipt of a grant may be considerable—rarely less than three months and often up to six months or more. In planning your program, be sure to allow enough time to obtain the necessary funding.

Do you or does anyone on your board know someone connected with a potential funder? You'll want to gather background information on the foundation or corporate funder's sponsoring company as well as its current staff and trustees. In doing so, you may find some unexpected connections between your organization and a potential funder that will make it easier to approach the funder. Make a list of individuals that have supported or expressed an interest in your organization and its programs. Include past and current donors, board members, volunteers, and "friends." See if there are any obvious links between these individuals and the funder's board and/or staff. The savvy fundraiser is constantly working to establish these kinds of connections. While knowing somebody who is affiliated with a prospective funder usually is not enough to win you a grant, it does tend to facilitate the process.

FINANCIAL DATA

Carefully examine the available financial data. Although it's often mystifying to first-time grantseekers, data from foundation 990-PF forms, annual reports, and published directories generally include information on assets, grants awarded, and gifts received. Learning to interpret these figures can provide important clues about the funding patterns of a particular grantmaker. Has the foundation or corporation received any large contributions in recent years that might increase its grantmaking potential? Has there been an increase or decrease in the funder's assets in recent years? Might it be "going out of business?" These are the factors that can affect the amount of money available for grants, as well as the size and type of grants awarded. Of course, general economic conditions also affect a foundation's assets and gifts received (especially for corporate grantmakers), which in turn impacts the amount of money it has to give away.

Recording What You Do

You must keep careful records of your findings during the research process and especially once you have made contact with a potential funder. We call the first activity "data gathering" and the second activity "record keeping."

DATA GATHERING

Throughout the research process you should gather as many pertinent facts about your funding prospects as possible. Develop careful files, either in hard copy or electronically. Each record of a potential funder should include the information in the Prospect Worksheet shown in Figure 11.

These records should be updated on a regular basis to provide a dynamic, consolidated base of funding information for your organization. Developing such a system helps to compensate for one of the biggest problems nonprofits face—the lack of continuity in fundraising efforts resulting from staff turnover.

It is important to document your research at every step along the way. As you gather facts about a funder, note the source and date of the information so that later on, if you come across conflicting information, you can quickly determine which is more current. While such attention to detail at the outset may seem needlessly time consuming, careful data gathering is guaranteed to save you and your organization time and money in the long run.

RECORD KEEPING

You need to keep track of each and every contact between representatives of your organization and a staff or board member at a funding institution. Your profiles should include copies of your letters of inquiry, formal proposals, and supporting documents, as well as reports, press releases, and invitations to events. In addition, you should keep careful notes regarding informational and follow-up phone calls, and your written summaries of interviews and site visits. Each record should include the date and the initials of the individual who made the contact. Figure 12 is a sample all-purpose form for keeping track of contacts with potential funders. It can also serve as a "tickler" or reminder sheet to let you know when the next steps need to be taken. There are a number of commercially available record keeping software programs you can use, such as Raiser's Edge for Windows™ by Blackbaud (1-800-443-9441) or PledgeMaker® by SofTrek (1-800-442-9211).You can also develop your own from any versatile general data management software package, such as Microsoft Access. The Notepad feature of *FC Search: The Foundation Center's Database on CD-ROM* enables fundraisers to create a basic prospect tracking and tickler system as well.

Summary

Homework is your key to unlocking grants. Know your own program, and develop a clear idea of what you are trying to accomplish. Formulate a plan and a timetable and calculate what it will cost to carry out. Then you are ready to compile a broad list of prospects that will be interested in your subject, give in your geographic area, and/or offer the types of support your organization needs. The list of prospects you compile will need to be reviewed, and the grantmakers clearly not interested in your program or geographic location will be eliminated. Then you can begin in-depth research on the remaining names, trying to answer several key questions. During all this research, you will need to keep accurate records of your efforts and continue to do so after you have submitted a proposal. Chapter 10 will offer further suggestions about record keeping and the proposal writing process.

The next chapter will describe key resources for performing this funding research. After that, we will go into detail about the various research strategies.

Figure 12. Record of Funding Contacts

Funder (Name & Address): _____

_____

Principal Contact (name & title): _____

_____

Telephone Calls

Date(s): _____

Time(s): _____

Call from: _____

Spoke to: _____

Comments: _____

_____

MEETINGS	Date: Time: Outcome:	
PROPOSALS	Date submitted: Format: Signed by: Board meeting date(s):	For project: Amount requested:
TICKLER	Deadline: To do: Follow up:	By whom: By whom:
DECISION Notification date: Reason for rejection:		NEXT STEP Resubmit Cultivation: Special activities: Send report:
The Foundation Center		

Chapter 5

Resources for Foundation Funding Research

A wide range of materials is available to help you identify sources of support for your organization or project. The types and number of resources you use will depend upon the type of support you are seeking and the search strategy you adopt to identify appropriate funding sources. Before you can plan an effective search strategy, however, you need to become familiar with the basic resources available to you.

Materials that describe the grantmaking universe can be accessed electronically or in traditional print format. Regardless of format, the information usually falls into six general categories: (1) general reference directories; (2) indexes to grants awarded in the recent past; (3) specialized funding directories or guides; (4) original materials generated or published by grantmakers, including annual reports, brochures, information at their Web sites, and tax returns filed annually by foundations with the IRS; (5) secondary resources such as newspaper or journal articles; and (6) people.

General reference directories may be national or local in focus and can vary widely in the amount of information they provide. Many general reference directories are now in electronic format, with search engines that allow them to serve as specialized funding directories. In this chapter we focus on the national directories published by the Foundation Center, but refer to other directories and databases in Appendix A. When possible, your research should encompass all pertinent resources.

Indexes to foundation grants, in whatever format, provide listings of actual grants awarded, enabling you to determine the specific subject interests of a foundation, the types and locations of the organizations it funds, the size of the grants it makes, and the types of support it awards. Such indexes usually do not, however, list grants *available*. For information on grants available, you should refer to requests for proposal (RFPs), an increasingly popular (but still uncommon) vehicle for foundations to notify the public of grant programs. Links to recently posted foundation RFPs are a feature of *Philanthropy News Digest* at the Center's Web site (www.fdncenter.org).

Specialized funding directories or guides enable you to concentrate on a particular aspect of your fundraising needs, be it a specific field (e.g., the arts, health), population group (e.g., women, minorities), type of support (e.g., equipment, research), or type of grantmaker (e.g., corporations, community foundations). Some of the more specialized directories are listed in the bibliography in Appendix A, but you should check with your colleagues or local library to learn about others related to your field. A number of journals, periodicals, and newsletters, particularly those issued by professional, educational, and alumni associations, include features or columns on funding opportunities in specific fields. So be sure to look for such listings as well.

Materials issued directly by funders, such as annual reports or application guidelines in written format or at a Web site, can be used to secure detailed information about those grantmakers you have identified as potential funding sources for your project. However, only a small percentage of funders provide written or electronic information about themselves. The annual information returns filed by private foundations (Forms 990-PF) are often the only source of information on the grantmaking activities and interests of smaller foundations.

Secondary narrative sources, such as newspapers and magazines, can provide up-to-date information about grants awarded or changes in leadership or priorities within a foundation or corporation. Indexes to newspapers and other periodicals are your key to unlocking this resource. There are several resources on the Web that are particularly helpful in locating articles about specific donors and about philanthropy in general because they are searchable by keyword. The *Literature of the Nonprofit Sector Online* (www.fdncenter.org/onlib/lnps/index.html) and the Philanthropic Studies Index (wwwnt.ulib.iupui.edu/psi/) are two searchable bibliographic tools on the Web that cover periodicals from the philanthropic sector. *Philanthropy News Digest* (www.fdncenter.org/pnd/current/index.html), a weekly news service, is a compendium in digest form of philanthropy-related articles and features culled from print and electronic media outlets nationwide. Major newspapers in the U.S. often have searchable indexes at their Web home pages.

People you know can be either useful or somewhat unreliable sources of information. Rumor and innuendo will not be very helpful. However, a telephone chat with a foundation's grants officer or a face-to-face interview with a representative of a foundation can produce just the information you are seeking. Public forums where grantmakers speak openly about their interests and procedures can also prove quite helpful to the nonprofit grantseeker. All Foundation Center libraries host such forums, called either "Meet the Grantmakers" or "Dialogue with Donors." Some Cooperating Collections also sponsor similar forums for the public to hear grantmakers talk about their funding interests.

SOME IMPORTANT CONSIDERATIONS

Once you have a general overview of the available resources, we'll explore the ways you can put those resources to work for you. Most, if not all, of the materials described here can be consulted at the five Center-operated libraries or the more than 200 Cooperating Collections listed in Appendix F. Although some of the databases and publications described may be useful additions to your organization's library, we recommend that, initially, grantseekers invest their time rather than their money. Visit one of our libraries or Cooperating Collections and examine the materials relating to your area of interest before making a decision as to which publications to purchase.

An alternative way to compile fundraising information is the Foundation Center's Associates Program (www.fdncenter.org/about/associates.html). The Associates Program provides its members with an exclusive toll-free telephone number linking them directly to researchers who will access electronic databases, research publications, 990-PFs, and grantmaker files to answer questions for them.

When doing research yourself, pay attention to the quality of the information in the publication or electronic resource, as well as its relevance to your funding search. It is especially important to:

- note the date the book was published or database last updated and whether or not it contains the most current information available;

- read the introduction and any instructions on how to use the material, paying particular attention to how the information was obtained, how current it is, and what verification procedures, if any, were used in obtaining it;

- familiarize yourself with the format, indexes, and the kinds of information about potential funding sources contained in the book or database.

Taking the time to evaluate resources for their accuracy and thoroughness prior to using them can save you countless hours that might otherwise be wasted.

The Foundation Center's Databases

The Foundation Center implemented its computerized database in 1972. Since that time the database has grown in size, scope, and quality. Its nearly three million records provide detailed information on more than 1.2 million grants and 68,240 currently operating and terminated grantmakers, including: background data on the grantmaker; its purpose and programs; application procedures; the names of its trustees, officers, and donors; and its current financial data.

Information stored in this database is drawn primarily from one of three sources: (1) IRS information returns (Form 990-PF) filed annually by private foundations, received on a monthly basis by the Center from the IRS; (2) information voluntarily provided by foundations, including responses to questionnaire mailings, electronically transmitted grants lists, and grantmaker-issued reports and/or guidelines; and (3) the annual computer tape produced by the IRS covering all private foundations in a given period. Center staff verify and update the majority of the entries from the first two sources. The Center then makes the verified information available in print through its various publications, in Foundation Finder on the Center's Web site, on CD-ROM through *FC Search*, and as an online computer file through DIALOG Information Services.

The Foundation Center began to record and categorize grants in 1961 and established a computerized grants classification system in 1972. In 1989, following explosive growth in the number of grants indexed annually, the Center introduced a new classification system based on the National Taxonomy of Exempt Entities (NTEE). The NTEE is a comprehensive coding scheme developed by the National Center for Charitable Statistics that established a unified standard for classifying nonprofit organizations while permitting a multi-dimensional structure for analyzing grants. The Center's classification system provides a concise and consistent hierarchical method with which to classify and index grants and the nonprofit organizations receiving foundation funding. Therefore, hundreds of specific terms can be researched with consistent results, and grant dollars can be tallied to determine distribution patterns. (For more information about NTEE and the Center's Grants Classification System, see Appendix C.)

The Center makes the grantmaker and grants information in its databases available to the public electronically and in printed format. The electronic formats are comprehensive and flexible. You can combine several elements—for example, subject, type of support, geographic limitations, and intended population group—in one search. In a short amount of time, thousands of foundation profiles and grant records can be scanned and then downloaded and viewed with a few simple key strokes. In printed format, grantmaker information is either general, such as in the comprehensive *Guide to U. S. Foundations, Their Trustees, Officers, and Donors* or targeted by subject, such as in the *National Guide to Funding in Arts & Culture*; population served, such as *National Guide to Funding for Women & Girls*; or some other criteria, such as assets, annual giving, or geographic location.

FC SEARCH: THE FOUNDATION CENTER'S DATABASE ON CD-ROM

Since its introduction in 1996, *FC Search: The Foundation Center's Database on CD-ROM* has become a popular way to search the grantmaking universe for potential funders. *FC Search* is produced annually in the spring with an update six months later. It includes profiles of close to 50,000 U.S. foundations and corporate givers; the names and foundation affiliations of approximately 200,000 trustees, officers, and donors who make the funding decisions at these institutions; and descriptions of close to 200,000 grants reported recently. *FC Search* includes data found in: *The Foundation Directory; The Foundation Directory Part 2, The Foundation Directory Supplement*, the *Guide to U.S. Foundations, Their Trustees, Officers, and Donors*, the *National Directory of Corporate Giving*, and *The Foundation Grants Index. FC Search* allows the user to link directly to the Web sites of over 600 grantmakers and to the Center's own Web site. *FC Search* is available in all Foundation Center libraries and at most Cooperating Collections throughout the U.S.

FC Search has a browse feature that allows the user to scan the contents of the Grantmaker and Grants databases and to access individual records. The Basic Grantmaker Search option lets you search four of the most common criteria researchers use to target grant prospects as well as to do free text searching. The Advanced Search feature allows the researcher to use multiple criteria in searching both the Grantmaker database and the Grants database. Searching multiple fields (fourteen in the Grantmaker database and twelve in the Grants database) and using a range of Boolean operators allow the user to develop very sophisticated and very specific searches. The user can also readily navigate between the Grantmaker database and the Grants database within individual records.

FC Search: The Foundation Center's Database on CD-ROM allows you to accomplish the first two steps of the research process—developing a broad prospect list and then refining that list.

FC Search is configured so that you can scroll through the list of grantmakers or grant recipients using the browse feature, or you can adopt one of three search modes (Basic Grantmaker, Advanced Grantmaker, and Advanced Grants) to tailor a search to your specific criteria. The search modes allow you to choose multiple criteria and create customized prospect lists by choosing from among twenty-one search fields:

Grantmaker Name	Trustees, Officers, & Donors	Recipient Name
Grantmaker State	Text Search	Recipient State
Grantmaker City	Types of Support	Recipient City
Grantmaker Type	Total Assets	Subjects
Geographic Focus	Total Giving	Grant Amount
Establishment Date	Corporate Name	Authorization Year
Fields of Interest	Corporate Location	Recipient Type

The Main Menu Screen showing the choice of search or browse functions is illustrated in Figure 13.

Browsing

The Browse feature is a good introduction to the information in *FC Search*. Browsing the Grantmakers file (see Figure 14) or Grants file (see Figure 15) allows you to:

- Become familiar with the contents of the two files comprising the database;

- Find a specific grantmaker by name or the grants to a specific organization (grant recipient);

- Browse alphabetically through all grantmakers located in a specific state or browse alphabetically through all grant recipients located in a specific state or country;

- Link to a list of recent grants for a particular foundation, when available, directly from the grantmaker record.

Figure 13. Main Menu Screen from *FC Search: The Foundation Center's Database on CD-ROM*

Once familiar with the contents of *FC Search*, you are ready to use its search features to develop a broad list of potential funders that have interests in common with your organization's goals and activities.

Basic Search

The Basic Search mode for the Grantmaker file is designed for users new to *FC Search* or for those who wish to use the most common search criteria. Basic Search allows searching on the following five criteria:

- Grantmaker Name
- Grantmaker State

Figure 14. Browse Grantmaker File from *FC Search: The Foundation Center's Database on CD-ROM*

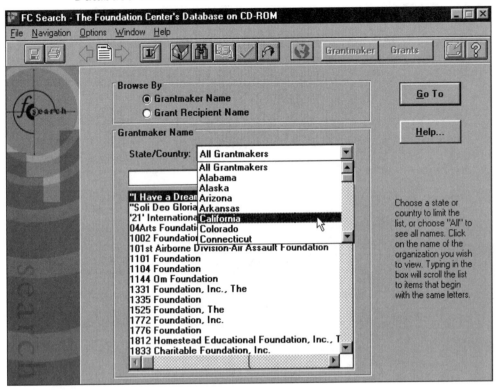

- Fields of Interest

- Trustees, Officers, and Donors

- Text Search

The first four of these search criteria have an associated index from which possible search terms can be selected. Searches performed using these criteria result in hits in particular areas of the grantmaker records; these specific areas are called fields. The Text Search criterion will search for words that appear anywhere within the grant-maker records.

To find a list of potential funders using the Basic Search process, you select search criteria (or fields), perform the search, and view the results. When designing a Basic Search, you may choose from one to all five of the default search criteria. An example

Figure 15. Browse Grants File from *FC Search: The Foundation Center's Database on CD-ROM*

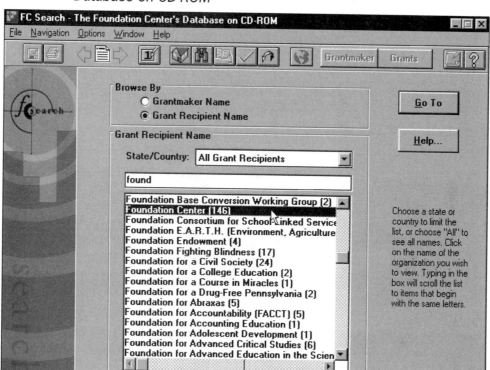

using two fields of a Basic Search is shown in Figure 16. In this instance, the grantseeker is conducting a search to identify foundations in three Southern states (Alabama, Georgia, or Tennessee) that are interested in environmental programs. As can be seen in the results box, sixty-six grantmakers fit the specified criteria.

The Text Search field, which does not have an index, can be used to find information that may or may not be indexed in other fields. When Text Search is used, the program will search all the words in the Grantmaker file for the terms you type into the search criteria entry box next to Text Search. For example, let's assume you want to identify as many grantmakers as possible in New York State that are interested in water conservation issues. If you fill in the Grantmaker State box with "New York" and the Fields of Interest box with "Environment, water resources" ("water conservation" is not an indexed term for the Fields of Interest field), you would get four hits. As an

Figure 16. Basic Grantmaker Search from *FC Search: The Foundation Center's Database on CD-ROM*

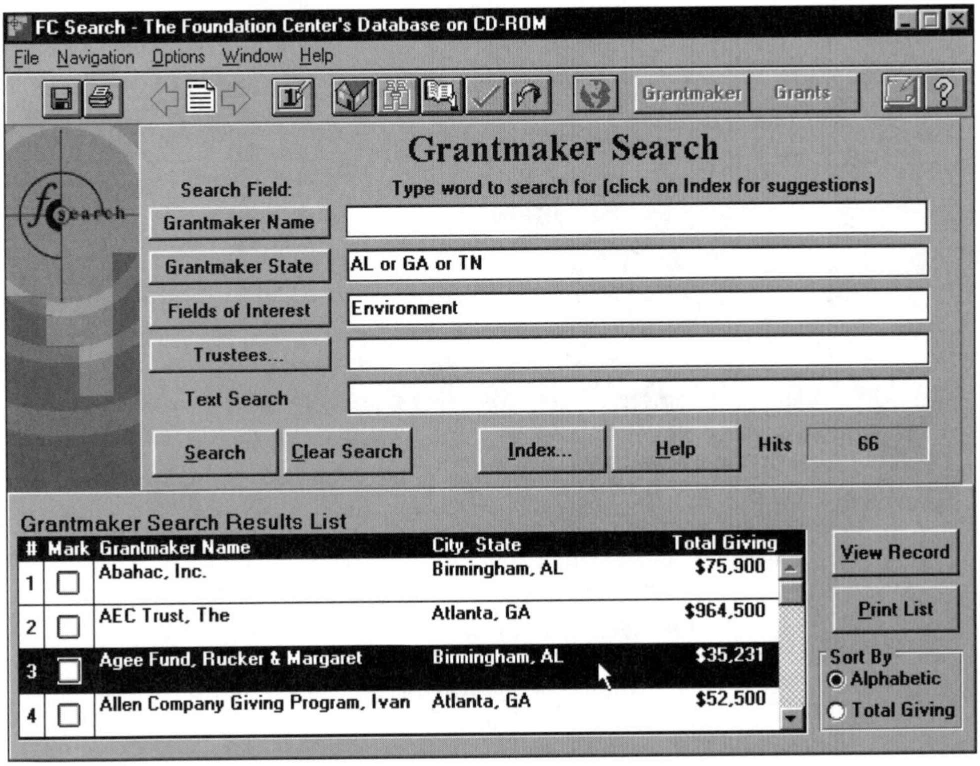

alternative search, you could delete the terms in the Fields of Interest box and enter the term "water" in the Text Search box. This search would yield fifteen hits. A couple of the these hits, such as the Prudential Securities Foundation and the Sherrill Foundation, would have no documented interest in the environmental issue of water conservation. They were picked up because their mailing addresses are on Water Street in New York; this is one of the caveats of text searching. However, the search did yield several foundations whose selected grants lists or purpose and activities statements indicate an interest in the subject.

Advanced Search

Advanced Search is available for two files, Grantmaker and Grants. Advanced Search mode for the Grantmaker file has additional capabilities beyond those offered in Basic

Search mode. It is designed for those with some experience using *FC Search* or for those who wish to search on fields that are not available in the Basic Search mode. In Advanced Search, you have fourteen different search criteria to choose from and you have a choice of Boolean operators that work among different search fields (see Figure 17).

The five default fields in Advanced Search are the same as in Basic Search: Grant-maker Name, Grantmaker State, Fields of Interest, Trustees. . ., and Text Search. However, in Advanced Search, you have nine additional criteria on which to search:

Corporate Location	Geographic Focus	Total Assets
Corporate Name	Grantmaker City	Total Giving
Establishment Date	Grantmaker Type	Types of Support

Five is the maximum number of search criteria you can use in any one search; however, you can organize them in any combination you wish. By clicking on the arrow in the search criterion box, the program will display a drop-down field list from which you can select the field in which you wish to search. As in Basic Search, in Advanced Search mode "AND" is the default Boolean operator when searching on multiple search criteria. However, in the Advanced Search mode, you have the option of changing the default selection to "OR" or to "NOT" by clicking on the arrow in the Boolean operator boxes and making the desired choice.

In the example shown in Figure 18, the grantseeker wants to identify grantmakers that: (1) provide funds for construction and renovation, (2) give in Georgia, (3) are interested in services to senior citizens, and (4) are capable of making large grants. The grantseeker also wants to be sure that the grantmakers who meet these criteria accept applications. In this case, ten grantmakers met all the criteria, including accepting applications, and are listed at the bottom of the screen. Figure 19 shows what a record for one of the selected grantmakers looks like. Each record will include most, if not all, of the following information: grantmaker name, address, phone and fax number, contact person, URL (address on the World Wide Web), donor, type of grantmaker, background, purpose and activities, fields of interest, application information, officers and trustees, financial data, and selected grants. For company-sponsored foundations or corporate direct giving programs, information about the company is also provided.

Figure 20 shows an Advanced Search in the *FC Search* Grants database. It is similar to the one performed in the Grantmaker database. The Grants file is searched in the

Figure 17. Advanced Grantmaker Search Screen Showing Boolean
Drop-Down Menu and Index Drop-Down Menu from *FC Search:
The Foundation Center's Database on CD-ROM*

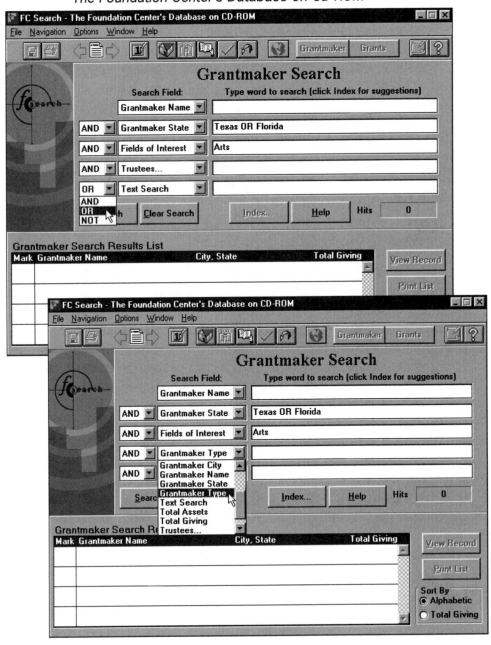

Figure 18. Advanced Grantmaker Search from *FC Search: The Foundation Center's Database on CD-ROM*

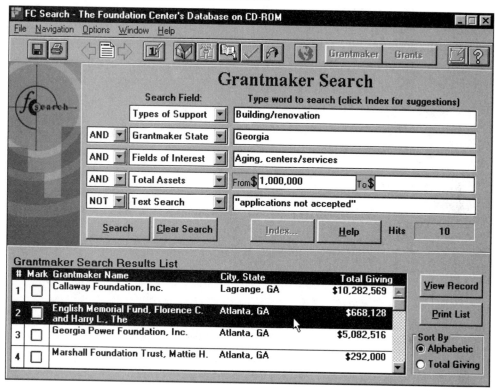

same general manner as the Grantmaker file. The Grants file gives you twelve different fields from which to choose:

Grant Amount
Grantmaker Geographic Focus
Grantmaker Name
Grantmaker State

Recipient City
Recipient Name
Recipient State/Country
Recipient Type

Subjects
Text Search
Types of Support
Year Authorized

The Advanced Grants Search function also allows you a choice of Boolean operators (OR, AND, NOT) that work between different search criteria (fields). The five default search fields that appear when first entering the Grants search screen are:

Figure 19. Sample Grantmaker Record from *FC Search: The Foundation Center's Database on CD-ROM*

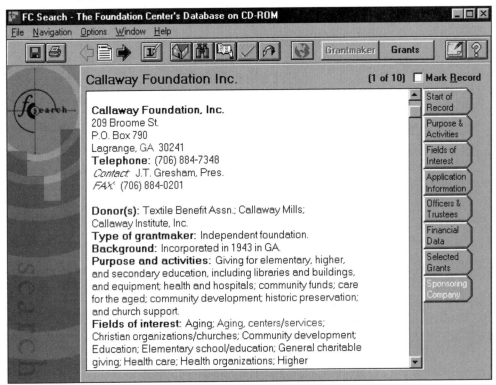

Recipient Name, Recipient State/Country, Grantmaker Name, Subjects, and Text Search. Changing the criteria to one of the other seven fields is simple: click on the arrow in the criterion box and select the new field from the drop-down window. The choices for Boolean operators between fields are in the boxes to the left of the field. Change these by clicking on the arrow within the box and making your choices.

You can develop an initial list of potential funders from the Grants file or research the actual grants of funders you have already identified. Reviewing grants that have been given by a foundation or corporation will help you identify funders with a demonstrated interest in your subject or geographic area.

In summary, *FC Search* is a versatile prospecting tool; however, grantseekers should further refine the list of potential funders they come up with this way by referring to other sources, such as annual reports, grantmaker guidelines, and so forth.

Figure 20. Sample Grants Search from *FC Search: The Foundation Center's Database on CD-ROM*

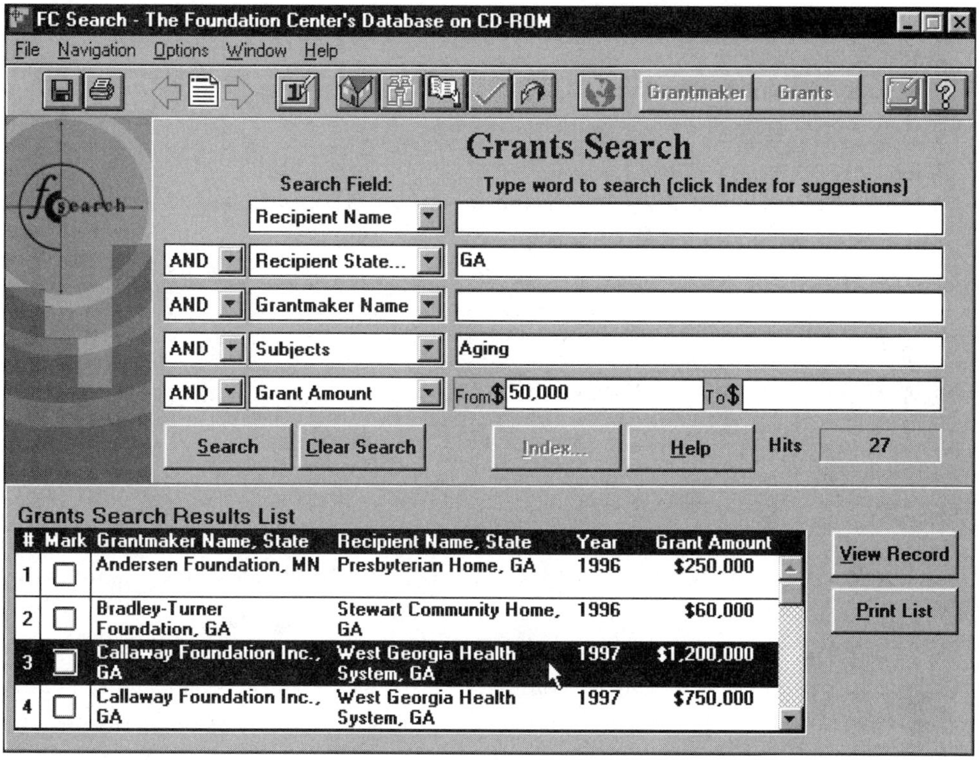

DIALOG

DIALOG, a commercial database available to the public by subscription or via the Internet, has provided access to the Foundation Center's databases since the 1970s. You can retrieve our recent data on foundations, corporate giving programs, and the grants they distribute via DIALOG on your own computer. The Center maintains two databases on DIALOG that are updated on an ongoing basis—one providing information on grantmakers (File 26), and the other on grants they distribute (File 27). With DIALOG, you design your own search for prospective funders. These databases provide an effective method of developing a targeted list of funding prospects, but there is a fee for using DIALOG, and some training and expertise in database research are necessary to reap the benefits of your investment.

For further information about online access to the Foundation Center's databases through DIALOG, visit the Dialog Corporation Web site (www.dialog.com) or call Dialog at 1-800-334-2564. The Center's *DIALOG User Manual and Thesaurus* is an essential companion to your online fundraising research, facilitating efficient and effective online searches for foundation and corporate grantmakers. The *User Manual* contains a fully revised and expanded list of subject terms and shows you how to retrieve facts from the Center's databases efficiently. The Center also offers a custom search service for a fee for those who want to have our information specialists conduct DIALOG searches on their behalf. Center libraries can provide further information on this custom search service.

General Grantmaker Directories

General grantmaker directories, whether national or local, provide information on the broadest possible selection of grantmakers. You may want to begin with general directories and work your way to those with more specific content.

The Foundation Center publishes several major directories that are general in content and well indexed: the *Guide to U.S. Foundations, Their Trustees, Officers, and Donors*, a two-volume annual publication; *The Foundation Directory* and *The Foundation Directory Part 2*, each published annually and updated semi-annually by the *Foundation Directory Supplement*; and *The Foundation 1000*, an annual publication in one volume. Please see Appendix A for a listing of general fundraising directories by other publishers.

GUIDE TO U.S. FOUNDATIONS, THEIR TRUSTEES, OFFICERS, AND DONORS

The Foundation Center's most comprehensive grantmaker directory is the *Guide to U.S. Foundations, Their Trustees, Officers, and Donors*. This annual reference book, in two volumes, is the only Center print publication that contains all active grantmaking foundations, more than 46,000 in 1999. Volume One is in two sections. Section 1 arranges independent, corporate, and community foundations by state and within each state in descending order by total giving. Section 2 lists operating foundations by state in descending order by asset amount. Volume Two consists of two indexes, an index of the foundation trustees, officers, and donors included in the edition, and a foundation name and locator index.

Entries in Volume One of the *Guide to U.S. Foundations* may contain any or all of the following: the foundation's name, address, and telephone number; separate application address(es) and contact person(s); fax number and e-mail and/or URL addresses; establishment date; donors; current financial data, including fiscal year-end date, total grants paid, total assets and asset type, total gifts received, total expenditures, qualifying distributions, loans to organizations, loans to individuals, and program amounts; geographic limitations; publications that the foundation makes available; a listing of officers, trustees, and/or directors; the IRS Employer Identification Number (EIN); and a series of codes that indicate: (1) the type of foundation; (2) its grantmaking status; and (3) other Foundation Center publications in which an entry for that foundation also appears (see Figure 21).

Volume Two is divided into two parts: the Foundation Trustee, Officer, and Donor Index and the Foundation Name Index and Locator. The first index is a comprehensive list of all the trustees, officers, and donors affiliated with the foundations in Volume One. Arranged alphabetically by individual or corporation name, it lists the individual, his/her foundation affiliation (in italics), the foundation's location by state, the foundation's sequence number in Volume One, and codes identifying other Center publications in which additional information can be found (see Figure 22). If an individual is both a donor and an officer or trustee of a foundation, his/her name will appear in the index only once for that particular foundation. An individual's name appears as a separate listing for each foundation affiliation, however, thus enabling grantseekers to quickly identify all foundations with which that individual is connected.

The second index in Volume Two is the Foundation Name Index and Locator (see Figure 23), an alphabetical listing of the foundations in Volume One with their state location and the codes indicating which Center publications contain additional information on that foundation (FD for *The Foundation Directory*, FD2 for *The Foundation Directory Part 2*, FM for *The Foundation 1000*, CD for the *National Directory of Corporate Giving*, and GTI for *Foundation Grants to Individuals*).

The *Guide to U.S. Foundations* is designed for preliminary research on funding sources. It is particularly useful in identifying newly established and smaller foundations, both of which are often good sources of local support. Listed below are five suggestions for using the *Guide* in your research:

Target local funding prospects. Use the *Guide to U.S. Foundations* as the first step in your search for local grant dollars. It includes more than 27,890 grantmakers not covered in other Foundation Center publications. Arranged by state, Volume One helps you identify both large and small foundations in your geographic area. You can also

Figure 21. Sample Entry from *Guide to U.S. Foundations, Their Trustees, Officers, and Donors*

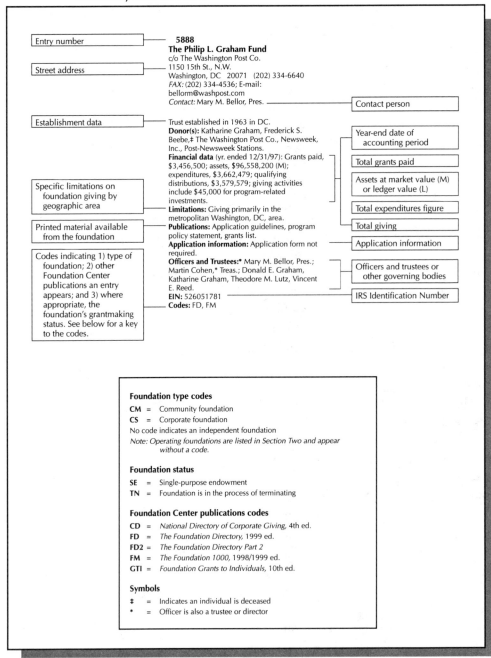

Figure 22. Foundation Trustee, Officer and Donor Index from *Guide to U.S. Foundations, Their Trustees, Officers, and Donors*, Vol. 2

FOUNDATION TRUSTEE, OFFICER AND DONOR INDEX

Morse, M. Sheila, *The Richard H. Morse Charitable Trust*, MA, 15804 (FD)
Morse, Marion M., *The Hearthstone Foundation*, NY, 22747 (FD)
Morse, Marjorie, *Rowe Historical Society, Inc.*, MA, 42196
Morse, Martha E., *Valentine Foundation*, PA, 32393 (FD)
Morse, Martha F., *The Pennsylvania Fund*, PA, 33134
Morse, Michael, *The Oliver Foundation*, NJ, 22003
Morse, Myrtle, *Colonel Daniel Putnam Association, Inc.*, CT, 5181
Morse, Peggy, *Christian Ministries International, Inc.*, SC, 43952
Morse, Peter C., *The JM Foundation*, NY, 22778 (FD)
Morse, Peter C., *The Pennsylvania Fund*, PA, 33134
Morse, Peter T., *The Tooth Fairy Foundation*, WA, 38535
Morse, Priscilla, *The Visiting Nurse Association of Rye, Inc.*, NY, 25739 (GTI)
Morse, Richard H., *The Richard H. Morse Charitable Trust*, MA, 15804 (FD)
Morse, Richard L.D., *Family Economics Trust*, KS, 13445
Morse, Richard P., *Richard P. & Claire W. Morse Foundation*, MA, 15186 (FD)
Morse, Roger H., *Frank A. Morse Nursing Scholarship Fund*, KS, 13340
Morse, Rosanne J., *W. Gerry and Reba H. Miller Foundation, Inc.*, FL, 7737
Morse, Rosanne T., *Ford Jeter Brown Foundation*, FL, 7575
Morse, Rose Marie, *Wheatland Foundation*, CA, 40958
Morse, Rosemary, *Hargis Daffodil Hills Foundation*, AL, 40414
Morse, Ruth, *Richard P. & Claire W. Morse Foundation*, MA, 15186 (FD)
Morse, Samuel, *The Clark Center for Japanese Art*, CA, 40570
Morse, Sarah D., *The Fred Harris Daniels Foundation, Inc.*, MA, 15154 (FD)
Morse, Stephan A., *The Bunbury Company, Inc.*, NJ, 21012 (FD)
Morse, Stephan A., *The Windham Foundation, Inc.*, VT, 44276 (FD, GTI)
Morse, Suzanne E., *W. C. English Foundation*, VA, 37724 (FD)
Morse, Terry, *The Aspen Foundation*, CO, 4228 (FD)
Morse, Timothy, *A. C. Ratshesky Foundation*, MA, 15229 (FD)
Morse, William A., *Byron L. Tennant Memorial Fund*, OH, 31142
Morse Living Trust, Bonnie Joy, *The Claire and Theodore Morse Foundation*, CA, 1933 (FD)
Morse-Diesel, Inc., *The Belle O. & Carl A. Morse Foundation*, NY, 24874 (FD2)
Morse-Karzen, Jerry, *Richard Karzen Foundation for Pancreatic Cancer Research*, IL, 10801
Morse-Lebow, Susan Lee, *The Adele Morse Platt Foundation*, CA, 2616
Morselli, Augusta Gianni, *The Richard Lippold Foundation*, NY, 43024
Morsh, Mari Christopherson, *W. & M. Christopherson Foundation*, IL, 10229
Morss, Everett, Jr., *Sailors' Snug Harbor of Boston*, MA, 15309 (FD)
Mortel, Cecilia, *Mortel Family Charitable Foundation*, PA, 34261
Mortel, Rodrigue, *Mortel Family Charitable Foundation*, PA, 34261
Mortensen, Joseph I., *Elsa U. Pardee Foundation*, MI, 17079 (FD, FM)
Mortensen, Trice D., *The William & Alice Mortensen Foundation*, CT, 4908 (FD)
Mortensen, William, *The William & Alice Mortensen Foundation*, CT, 4908 (FD)
Mortenson, Carl, *Evangel Mission*, IL, 41673
Mortenson, J.P., *Lewis M. Gabbe Foundation, Inc.*, NJ, 21362 (FD)
Mortenson, James G., *Lewis M. Gabbe Foundation, Inc.*, NJ, 21362 (FD)
Mortenson, Jerene, *Loomer-Mortenson Scholarship Foundation*, MN, 19139
Mortenson, R.S., *Philip B. Lowy Foundation, Inc.*, NJ, 22246
Mortenson, Robert S., *Aaron and Rachel Meyer Memorial Foundation, Inc.*, NJ, 21157 (FD)
Mortenson, Robert S., *The Robert M. Ellis Foundation*, NJ, 21324 (FD)
Mortenson, Robert S., *Lewis M. Gabbe Foundation, Inc.*, NJ, 21362 (FD)
Mortenson, Stephen D., *The Robert M. Ellis Foundation*, NJ, 21324 (FD)
Morter, Floyd, Jr., *Institute for Ethical Behavior*, NY, 27513
Mortgage Funding Corp., *If I Corporation*, MS, 19204
Mortimer, A. Chandler, *Ecesis Foundation*, CO, 4595
Mortimer, Averell H., *W. Averell and Pamela C. Harriman Foundation*, NY, 25321
Mortimer, Averill H., *Charles Jago Elder Foundation*, TX, 36487
Mortimer, Beatrice B., *Ecesis Foundation*, CO, 4595
Mortimer, Charles G., Jr., *Charles G. & Elizabeth A. Mortimer Foundation*, NY, 27373
Mortimer, Charles G. III, *Charles G. & Elizabeth A. Mortimer Foundation*, NY, 27373
Mortimer, David H., *Mary W. Harriman Foundation*, NY, 22798 (FD)
Mortimer, E. Laird III, *Barnabas Foundation, Inc.*, CT, 5377
Mortimer, Jason, *Ecesis Foundation*, CO, 4595
Mortimer, Kathleen H., *Mary W. Harriman Foundation*, NY, 22798 (FD)
Mortimer, Kathleen L.H., *W. Averell and Pamela C. Harriman Foundation*, NY, 25321
Mortimer, Mary Jane, *Ecesis Foundation*, CO, 4595
Mortimer, Mary S., *King-Bruwaert House*, IL, 41516
Mortimer, Pat, *Eccles-Lesher Memorial Library Association, Inc.*, PA, 43794
Mortimer, Peter, *Ecesis Foundation*, CO, 4595
Mortimer, Robert J., *Willard T. C. Johnson Foundation, Inc.*, NY, 22614 (FD, FM)
Mortimer, Sally, *Eccles-Lesher Memorial Library Association, Inc.*, PA, 43794
Mortimer, Virginia K., *Barnabas Foundation, Inc.*, CT, 5377
Morton, Annette, *New Bedford Home for Aged*, MA, 42201
Morton, Arlene Nazur, *Florida Care Foundation, Inc.*, FL, 7007
Morton, Carolyn, *Morton Foundation, Inc.*, MA, 42288
Morton, Clay, *Live Oak Gardens Foundation, Inc.*, NC, 43403 (FD)
Morton, Clay L., *The Tarrant Foundation, Inc.*, KY, 13598
Morton, Clay L., *Live Oak Gardens Foundation, Inc.*, NC, 43403 (FD)
Morton, Dan E., *Lynn B. and Dorothy Griffith Charitable Foundation*, TX, 36733
Morton, Dean O., *The David and Lucile Packard Foundation*, CA, 862 (FD, FM)
Morton, Dean O., *Monterey Bay Aquarium Research Institute*, CA, 40533
Morton, Diana H., *The Manton Foundation*, NY, 26811 (FD)
Morton, Eleanor, *New Bedford Home for Aged*, MA, 42201
Morton, George, *Community Foundation of Boone County, Inc.*, IN, 11637 (FD, GTI)
Morton, Glenn L., *Fitchett Foundation of Fort Lauderdale, Inc.*, FL, 7135
Morton, Gustel S., *Martin Salomon & Gustel Schrieber Morton Foundation*, MA, 17016
Morton, J.G., Jr., *Morton Foundation*, TN, 35175
Morton, James H., *The Maria John Nicholas Kelly Foundation*, WA, 39104
Morton, James M., Jr., *The Wolfe Family Charitable Foundation*, OH, 29514 (FD2)
Morton, James M., Jr., *The Weikel Family Charitable Foundation*, OH, 30392
Morton, James O'S., *Service League Foundation, Inc.*, MA, 42195
Morton, John, *The Good Works Foundation*, CA, 1231 (FD)
Morton, John K., *The Good Works Foundation*, CA, 1231 (FD)
Morton, John K., *The Travelers Foundation*, CA, 1548 (FD2)
Morton, Louis, *Michigan Association of the Blind and Visually Impaired, Inc.*, MI, 42403
Morton, Lynn S., *Automotive Museum, Inc.*, CT, 41132
Morton, Mark A., *Foundation Chapter of Theta Chi Fraternity, Inc.*, IN, 11783 (GTI)
Morton, Marshall N., *The Media General Foundation*, VA, 37957 (FD2, CD)
Morton, Mildred D., *The Morton-Kelly Charitable Trust*, ME, 14064 (FD)
Morton, Penelope Tarrant, *The Tarrant Foundation, Inc.*, KY, 13598
Morton, Preston D., *Mohr Foundation, Inc.*, TX, 36876
Morton, Richard A., *The Richard A. Morton Foundation*, VT, 37655
Morton, Richard M., *Student Communicant of St. Joseph's Church Trust*, ME, 41993
Morton, Ricky, *Conroe Area Youth Baseball, Inc.*, TX, 44148
Morton, S. Sidney, *The Northern California Scholarship Foundation*, CA, 1247 (FD, GTI)
Morton, Susan, *Branch County Community Foundation*, MI, 17555 (FD2)
Morton, Thomas C., *Sea Pines Coastal Conservancy*, SC, 34730
Morton, W. Alan, *Alan Morton Foundation*, NY, 43099
Morton, W. Hugh M., *David Greenewalt Charitable Trust*, MA, 15658 (FD2)
Morton, W. James, Jr., *Ressler Mill Foundation*, PA, 43697
Morton, Warren A., *Tom and Helen Tonkin Foundation*, WY, 40336 (FD)
Mortrel, Rodrique, *Health Alliance Charitable Foundation*, PA, 32589
Morua, Andrew, *Harris Bank Foundation*, IL, 9061 (FD, CD)
Mory, Gene, Jr., *Lagrange County Community Foundation, Inc.*, IN, 11578 (FD2)
Mosbacher, Barbara, *Mosbacher Foundation, Inc.*, TX, 35522 (FD)
Mosbacher, Diane, *Woman Vision*, TX, 44123
Mosbacher, Emil, *Mosbacher Foundation, Inc.*, TX, 35522 (FD)
Mosbacher, Emil, Jr., *Emil Mosbacher, Jr. Foundation, Inc.*, CA, 1494 (FD)
Mosbacher, Emil, Jr., *Mosbacher Foundation, Inc.*, TX, 35522 (FD)
Mosbacher, Gertrude, *Mosbacher Foundation, Inc.*, TX, 35522 (FD)
Mosbacher, Nancy Ditz, *Emil Mosbacher, Jr. Foundation, Inc.*, CA, 1494 (FD)
Mosbacher, Patricia R., *Emil Mosbacher, Jr. Foundation, Inc.*, CA, 1494 (FD)
Mosbacher, R. Bruce, *Emil Mosbacher, Jr. Foundation, Inc.*, CA, 1494 (FD)
Mosbacher, Robert, Jr., *Mosbacher Foundation, Inc.*, TX, 35522 (FD)
Mosby, Megan, *Liberty Wildlife Rehabilitation Foundation*, AZ, 40472
Moscahlaidis, Eric, *Moscahlaidis Foundation*, NY, 26314
Moscahlaidis, John, *Moscahlaidis Foundation*, NY, 26314
Moscaritolo, Patrick, *Celebrate Discovery, Inc.*, MA, 16916
Moschell, Robert S., *The Cunningham Foundation*, FL, 7576
Moschides, Elly, *Nancy L. Starr Memorial Research Foundation*, NJ, 21958
Mosco, John W., Jr., *The Aspire Foundation*, PA, 33523
Moscou, Dorothy Hill, *Urban Home Ownership Corporation*, NY, 43004
Moscow, David, *David & Linda Moscow Foundation*, IL, 10019
Moscow, Linda, *David & Linda Moscow Foundation*, IL, 10019
Moscowitz, Alvin, *Foundation for Hearing Aid Research*, NY, 43346
Moscowitz, Lisa Lynn, *The Moskowitz Family Foundation*, MO, 19759
Moscowitz, Marvin, *The Moskowitz Family Foundation*, MO, 19759
Moscowitz, Neva, *The Moskowitz Family Foundation*, MO, 19759
Moscowitz, Raymond, *Nixon Newspapers Benevolent Association, Inc.*, IN, 11877
Moseley, Alexander, *Flintridge Foundation*, CA, 1034 (FD)
Moseley, Bryan, *Flintridge Foundation*, CA, 1034 (FD)
Moseley, Carlos D., *The Charles A. Dana Foundation, Inc.*, NY, 22418 (FD, FM, GTI)
Moseley, Carlos D., *The Fan Fox and Leslie R. Samuels Foundation, Inc.*, NY, 22482 (FD, FM)
Moseley, Carlos D., *Eleanor Naylor Dana Charitable Trust*, NY, 22541 (FD, FM)
Moseley, Charlene O., *The O'Connor-Moseley Foundation*, KS, 13341
Moseley, Christine C., *Junick Foundation*, TX, 37016
Moseley, Colin, *Matlock Foundation*, WA, 38526 (FD, CD)
Moseley, Francis Loring, *Flintridge Foundation*, CA, 1034 (FD)
Moseley, Frank W., *Frank W. Moseley Foundation*, KS, 13276
Moseley, Frank W., Sr., *The O'Connor-Moseley Foundation*, KS, 13341
Moseley, Frank W., Jr., *Frank W. Moseley Foundation*, KS, 13276
Moseley, Frederick S. III, *Humane Society of the Commonwealth of Massachusetts*, MA, 15549 (FD)
Moseley, Huel, Rev., *Fresh Springs Foundation*, TN, 35173
Moseley, James B., *The Jockey Club Foundation*, NY, 22964 (FD, GTI)
Moseley, James B., *John G. Cavanagh Trust*, NY, 25310
Moseley, James E., *Mollie S. Moseley Eye Foundation Trust of Georgia, Inc.*, GA, 8479
Moseley, James F., Jr., *Jacksonville Community Foundation*, FL, 6175 (FD)
Moseley, Jean White, *Helen B. & Charles M. White Charitable Trust*, OH, 30635
Moseley, John D., *The Renewal Foundation*, TX, 37301
Moseley, John D., Jr., *The Renewal Foundation*, TX, 37301

724 **FD = *Foundation Directory*** **FD 2 = *Foundation Directory Part 2*** **FM = *Foundation 1000***

Figure 23. Foundation Name Index and Locator from *Guide to U.S. Foundations, Their Trustees, Officers, and Donors*, Vol. 2

FOUNDATION NAME INDEX AND LOCATOR

Robinson Foundation, Inc., J. William and Elizabeth S., GA, 8156 (FD)
Robinson Foundation, Inc., Jim A., The, FL, 6534 (FD2)
Robinson Foundation, John, The, CA, 40597 (FD)
Robinson Foundation, John M., The, ME, 14100
Robinson Foundation, Inc., Joseph R., The, MD, 14794
Robinson Foundation, Margaret Ann and Walter, The, TN, 35028 (FD2)
Robinson Foundation, Inc., Pearl, The, NY, 27630
Robinson Foundation, Stephanie & Michael, The, NY, 27468
Robinson Foundation, Stuart M. *see* 28476
Robinson Foundation for Hearing Disorders, Inc., CA, 1435 (FD)
Robinson Fund, Charles Nelson, CT, 5007 (FD)
Robinson Fund, Fred L., MT, 20246 (GTI)
Robinson Fund, Inc., Maurice R., NY, 23109 (FD)
Robinson Irrevocable Charitable Living Trust, Thomas E. & Patricia, OH, 43516
Robinson IV Foundation, George A., TX, 35808 (FD)
Robinson Mountain Fund, E. O., KY, 13514 (FD)
Robinson Scholarship Fund, Maud J., The, CA, 40663
Robinson Scholarship Trust, Florence M., KS, 13256 (GTI)
Robinson Scholarship Trust/Moeller High School, Jerry W., OH, 30749
Robinson Trust, MN, 18905
Robinson Trust, Agnes C., VA, 38209 (GTI)
Robinson Trust, Clara Stiles, WI, 40307
Robinson Trust, Harry W. & Virginia, CA, 1736 (GTI)
Robinson Trust, Lewis *see* 26841
Robinson Trust, Margaret L., MA, 16809
Robinson Trust, Mary H., MO, 19767 (GTI)
Robinson Trust, Robert, AZ, 628
Robinson Trust under paragraph 6A, L., NY, 26833
Robinson Trust under paragraph 6O, L., NY, 26841
Robinson Welfare Trust, John W., ME, 14097 (FD2)
Robinson-Broadhurst Foundation, Inc., NY, 22764 (FD)
Robinson-Costas Charitable Foundation, NY, 26741
Robinson-Newball Foundation, Luis Carlos, IL, 41626
Robinson, Illinois Elks Crippled Children Charitable Commission, IL, 41604
Robinson, Jr. Memorial Foundation, Inc., Angus, CT, 5176
Robison Charitable Trust, Rosalind, IN, 12301
Robison Foundation, Ellis H. and Doris B., The, NY, 22847 (FD)
Robison Foundation, Harold & Carolyn, MI, 17553 (FD2)
Robison Foundation, James E., NY, 23838 (FD2)
Roblee Foundation, Joseph H. and Florence A., MO, 19375 (FD)
Robonowitz Family Foundation, Mike & Sharon *see* 31369
Robowski Charitable Trust, John L., FL, 7293
Robsar Foundation, Inc., The, CT, 5198
Robson Foundation, Edwin O., IL, 11198
Robson Foundation, John & Margaret, CA, 1700 (FD2)
Robson Foundation, LaNelle, AZ, 449 (FD)
Robson Foundation, Nick and Alma, The, DE, 5770 (FD)
Roby Foundation, Sara, NY, 42990
ROC of Life Foundation, Inc., The, FL, 41405
Rocca, Jr. Foundation, B. T., CA, 1622 (FD)
Rocco Charitable Trust, Salvatore & Grace, MA, 42287
Rochat Foundation *see* 21825
Roche Foundation, James M. and Louise C., MI, 17692
Roche Relief Foundation, Edward & Ellen, NY, 23793 (FD)
Rochell Foundation, IL, 10416
Rochester Area Community Foundation, NY, 22552 (FD)
Rochester Area Community Foundation, Greater, MI, 17267 (FD2)
Rochester Area Foundation, MN, 18484 (FD)
Rochester Area Foundation *see* 22552
Rochester Female Charitable Society, NY, 24331 (FD, GTI)
Rochester Post Bulletin Charities, MN, 18686 (CD)
Rochester Telephone Corporation-Educational Fund *see* 25123
Rochetta-Wessies Scholarship Foundation, IL, 10456 (GTI)
Rochfort Foundation, Inc., GA, 8355
Rochkind Family Foundation, Inc., Max & Rebecca, MD, 42048
Rochlin Foundation, Abraham and Sonia, NV, 20579 (FD, FM)
Rochman Charitable Foundation, IL, 10828
Rochman Foundation, Inc., Morris & Rose, NY, 25876
Rochow Family Charitable Foundation, The, GA, 8289
Rock Creek Foundation, The *see* 37777
Rock Foundation, MT, 20265
Rock Foundation, NY, 42935
Rock Foundation, The, CA, 2297 (FD)
Rock Foundation, The, OH, 29478 (FD)
Rock Foundation, Milton L. and Shirley, PA, 32436 (FD)
Rock Foundation Charitable Trust, AK, 373
Rock Island Community Foundation, The, IL, 10408
Rock Island County Federation of Women's Clubs, IL, 10610
Rock Island Refining Foundation, IN, 11734 (FD, CD)
Rock of Ages Relief Organization, TX, 44202
Rock River Foundation, Inc., NY, 23589 (FD)
Rockbridge Area Educational Fund, Inc., VA, 38466
Rockbridge Historical Society, VA, 44362
Rockdale Foundation, Inc., The, GA, 8055 (FD)
Rockefeller Brothers Fund, NY, 22434 (FD, FM, GTI)
Rockefeller Charitable Trust, Laurance S., NY, 22861 (FD)
Rockefeller Foundation, The, NY, 22396 (FD, FM, GTI)
Rockefeller Foundation, Winthrop, The, AR, 704 (FD, FM)
Rockefeller Fund, Inc., David, The, NY, 23641 (FD)
Rockefeller Trust, Winthrop, AR, 707 (FD)
Rockette Alumnae Foundation, NY, 27862
Rockfall Foundation, The, CT, 5443 (FD)
Rockford Community Foundation, IL, 9034 (FD)
Rockford Community Trust, The *see* 9034
Rockford Health Careers Foundation *see* 10513
Rockford Products Corporation Foundation, IL, 9699 (FD2, CD)
Rocking Chair Foundation, NY, 26762
Rockland High School Golden Trust, MA, 16917
Rockland Trust Company Charitable Foundation, MA, 16165
Rockledge Institute, Inc., CT, 5119 (FD2)
Rockley Farm Corporation, GA, 8629
Rocks Family Foundation, CO, 4680
Rockwell Charities Fund, Amelia Silliman Rockwell and Carlos Perry, MA, 16047
Rockwell Foundation, The, PA, 32086 (FD)
Rockwell Foundation, Elizabeth Dennis, TX, 37107
Rockwell Fund, Inc., TX, 35317 (FD, FM)
Rockwell International Corporation Trust, PA, 31967 (FD, CD, FM)
Rockwell Museum, The, NY, 42942
Rockwood Fund, Inc., The, DC, 5980 (FD)
Rocky Foundation, NY, 24525 (FD)
Rocky Mountain Health Care Corporation Foundation, CO, 4262 (FD, CD)
Rocky Mountain Youth Leadership Foundation, Inc., CO, 41067
Rocque Family Foundation, IL, 9512 (FD2)
Rodale Family Foundation, Robert & Ardath, The, PA, 33541
Roddick Fund, OH, 30034 (FD2, GTI)
Roddis Foundation, Inc., Hamilton, WI, 39397 (FD)
Roddy Foundation, Inc., The *see* 34991
Roddy Foundation, Inc., Fred M., MA, 15146 (FD)
Roddy, Sr. Foundation, Inc., Kate Collins Roddy and J. P., TN, 34991 (FD2)
Rodeph Chesed Foundation, NY, 25141 (FD2)
Rodgers & Hammerstein Foundation, NY, 25326
Rodgers Family Foundation, Inc., The, NY, 22842 (FD)
Rodgers Foundation, The, CA, 1185 (FD)
Rodgers Foundation, J. B., AZ, 637 (CD)
Rodgers Foundation, James T. and Claudette M., TX, 36228
Rodgers Foundation, Inc., Leonard & Grace, CT, 5525
Rodgers Foundation, Mary & Christopher, The, NH, 20852
Rodgers Foundation, Richard and Dorothy *see* 22842
Rodgers Trust, Elizabeth Killam, MA, 15390 (FD)
Rodman Ford Sales Inc. Charitable Trust, MA, 15204 (FD)
Rodman Foundation, The, MN, 18601 (FD)
Rodney Fund, The, MI, 17122 (FD)
Rodricks Foundation, Inc., The, MD, 14826
Rodricks Foundation, Inc., Carol S., The *see* 14826
Rodriguez Family Foundation, Jorge and Guadalupe, The, TX, 36409
Rodstein Foundation, The, FL, 7334
Rodstein Foundation, Albert M. & Miriam, FL, 7674
Rodstein Foundation, Marc & Gail, The *see* 7334
Roe Family Foundation, Inc., NJ, 21476
Roe Foundation, The, SC, 34544 (FD)
Roe Foundation Charitable Trust, WA, 38726
Roebling Foundation, Inc., Mary G., NJ, 21974
Roeder Trust, Gertrude Dee, CA, 3145
Roehl Foundation, Inc., WI, 39459 (FD)
Roehr Family Foundation, Inc., MA, 15581 (FD)
Roelli Charitable Trust, Edwin and Anne, WI, 40089
Roemer-Elrod Trust Fund for the Handicapped, KY, 13705
Roemisch Research Foundation, OH, 30867
Roen Family Foundation, CA, 2077 (FD2)
Roerich Museum, Inc., Nicholas, NY, 28122
Roesch Vocal Scholarship Trust, Polly W., WI, 40090 (GTI)
ROFA Foundation, Inc., WI, 40263
Rofe Family Foundation, NY, 23484 (FD)
Roff Foundation, The, TX, 36124
Roffman Foundation, The, VA, 38076
Rogal Charitable Foundation, Helen & Sidney, MA, 15290 (FD)
Rogan Marymount Foundation, Mother Joseph, MO, 19762 (FD2, GTI)
Rogatz Memorial Foundation, Lillian, CA, 3355
Rogers Brothers Foundation, Inc., TX, 36406
Rogers Charitable Foundation, Wendell & Doris, MI, 18324
Rogers Charitable Trust, The, FL, 7878
Rogers Charitable Trust, Florence, The, NC, 28656 (FD)
Rogers Charitable Trust, Martha W., PA, 32783 (FD2)
Rogers Family Foundation, CA, 2293
Rogers Family Foundation, The, MA, 15147 (FD)

1364 **FD = *Foundation Directory*** **FD 2 = *Foundation Directory Part 2*** **FM = *Foundation 1000***

check for familiar family names in the Trustee, Officer, and Donor Index to learn more about the giving vehicles of wealthy individuals in your geographic region.

Find a foundation. Use the Foundation Name Index and Community Foundation Name Index in Volume Two to locate the entry for any foundation listed in Volume One. (See also Foundation Finder in the section entitled "The World Wide Web on the Internet" later in this chapter.)

Follow up giving leads with access to foundation facts. The foundation entries provide the data you need to decide whether or not to pursue a grant source you've heard mentioned, but on which you need more information. You can quickly determine the giving potential of a foundation by the current assets and grants listed under each entry. Many entries also list a grantmaker's stated geographic limitations, if any.

Find new philanthropic connections for your organization. The Trustee, Officer, and Donor Index can help you discover connections between your board members, donors, and volunteers and grantmakers that might be interested in supporting your organization. Using this index, you can determine if an individual has affiliations with other foundations and you can uncover the names of people who serve on grantmaking boards.

Locate even more information. A series of codes in each entry in Volume One and in the indexes in Volume Two shows you which Foundation Center directories include more detailed information on the grantmaker you're researching.

THE FOUNDATION DIRECTORY, THE FOUNDATION DIRECTORY PART 2, AND THE FOUNDATION DIRECTORY SUPPLEMENT

The Foundation Directory is the most authoritative and widely used directory of private foundations. It includes descriptions of grantmaking foundations in the United States with assets of $2 million or more or that award grants totaling at least $200,000 annually. The 21st edition of the *Directory*, published in 1999, includes more than 10,000 foundations, which together account for approximately 92.3 percent of the total assets owned by foundations and 90 percent of the total grant dollars awarded annually by private foundations.

Each *Directory* entry may include the following data elements: foundation name, address, and telephone number; separate application address(es) and contact person(s); fax number and e-mail and/or URL addresses; establishment data; donors; current financial data, including assets, gifts received, expenditures, qualifying distributions, grants to organizations, grants to individuals, matching gifts, loans or program-related investments, and foundation-administered program amounts; purpose and activities; fields of interest; types of support awarded; limitations on its giving program, including geographic limitations; application procedures; officers, trustees, and staff; the foundation's IRS Employer Identification Number (see Figure 24); and a list of selected grants (when available). The volume is arranged by state, then alphabetically by foundation name. The 21st edition of *The Foundation Directory* includes the following seven indexes to help you identify foundations of interest:

- an index of donors, officers, and trustees;

- a geographic index to foundation locations by state and city, including cross-references to foundations with identified giving patterns beyond the states in which they are located;

- an international giving index of countries, continents, or regions where foundations have indicated giving interests, broken down by the states in which the foundations are located;

- an index of types of support offered, broken down by the states in which the foundations are located;

- an index to giving interests in hundreds of subject categories, broken down by the states in which the foundations are located;

- an index listing foundations new to the current edition; and

- an index by foundation name.

In the geographic, subject, and types of support indexes, foundations with national, regional, or international giving patterns are indicated in bold type, while foundations restricted to local giving are listed in regular type. As you define the limits of your funding search, these indexes can help you to focus on locally-oriented foundations in your community as well as on national foundations that have an interest in your field of activity.

The Foundation Directory Part 2 is designed as a companion volume to *The Foundation Directory* and provides similar information on the second tier of U.S. foundations—those holding assets of $1 million to $2 million or those with total annual giving of at least $50,000, but not more than $200,000. The eighth edition of *The Foundation Directory Part 2*, published in 1999, includes entries for more than 5,700 foundations.

The Foundation Directory Supplement provides the latest information on *Foundation Directory* and *Foundation Directory Part 2* grantmakers six months after those volumes are published. The *Supplement* provides complete revised entries for foundations

Figure 24. Sample Entry from *The Foundation Directory*

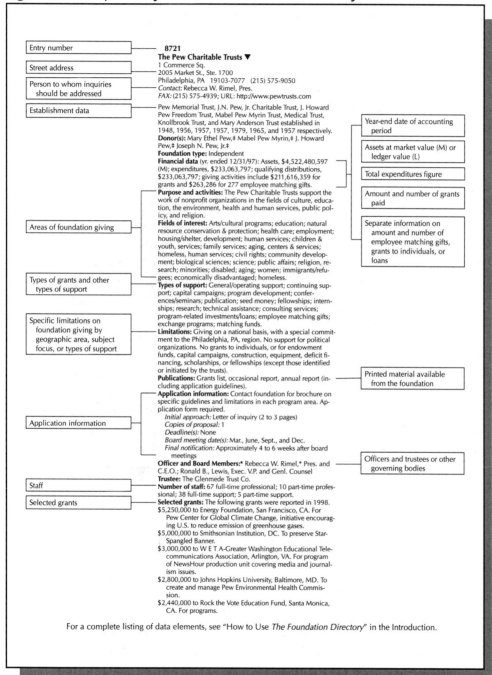

Entry number

Street address

Person to whom inquiries should be addressed

Establishment data

Areas of foundation giving

Types of grants and other types of support

Specific limitations on foundation giving by geographic area, subject focus, or types of support

Application information

Staff

Selected grants

8721
The Pew Charitable Trusts ▼
1 Commerce Sq.
2005 Market St., Ste. 1700
Philadelphia, PA 19103-7077 (215) 575-9050
Contact: Rebecca W. Rimel, Pres.
FAX: (215) 575-4939; URL: http://www.pewtrusts.com

Pew Memorial Trust, J.N. Pew, Jr. Charitable Trust, J. Howard Pew Freedom Trust, Mabel Pew Myrin Trust, Medical Trust, Knollbrook Trust, and Mary Anderson Trust established in 1948, 1956, 1957, 1957, 1979, 1965, and 1957 respectively. **Donor(s):** Mary Ethel Pew,‡ Mabel Pew Myrin,‡ J. Howard Pew,‡ Joseph N. Pew, Jr.‡
Foundation type: Independent
Financial data (yr. ended 12/31/97): Assets, $4,522,480,597 (M); expenditures, $233,063,797; qualifying distributions, $233,063,797; giving activities include $211,616,359 for grants and $263,286 for 277 employee matching gifts.
Purpose and activities: The Pew Charitable Trusts support the work of nonprofit organizations in the fields of culture, education, the environment, health and human services, public policy, and religion.
Fields of interest: Arts/cultural programs; education; natural resource conservation & protection; health care; employment; housing/shelter, development; human services; children & youth, services; family services; aging, centers & services; homeless, human services; civil rights; community development; biological sciences; science; public affairs; religion, research; minorities; disabled; aging; women; immigrants/refugees; economically disadvantaged; homeless.
Types of support: General/operating support; continuing support; capital campaigns; program development; conferences/seminars; publication; seed money; fellowships; internships; research; technical assistance; consulting services; program-related investments/loans; employee matching gifts; exchange programs; matching funds.
Limitations: Giving on a national basis, with a special commitment to the Philadelphia, PA, region. No support for political organizations. No grants to individuals, or for endowment funds, capital campaigns, construction, equipment, deficit financing, scholarships, or fellowships (except those identified or initiated by the trusts).
Publications: Grants list, occasional report, annual report (including application guidelines).
Application information: Contact foundation for brochure on specific guidelines and limitations in each program area. Application form required.
Initial approach: Letter of inquiry (2 to 3 pages)
Copies of proposal: 1
Deadline(s): None
Board meeting date(s): Mar., June, Sept., and Dec.
Final notification: Approximately 4 to 6 weeks after board meetings
Officer and Board Members:* Rebecca W. Rimel,* Pres. and C.E.O.; Ronald B., Lewis, Exec. V.P. and Genl. Counsel
Trustee: The Glenmede Trust Co.
Number of staff: 67 full-time professional; 10 part-time professional; 38 full-time support; 5 part-time support.
Selected grants: The following grants were reported in 1998.
$5,250,000 to Energy Foundation, San Francisco, CA. For Pew Center for Global Climate Change, initiative encouraging U.S. to reduce emission of greenhouse gases.
$5,000,000 to Smithsonian Institution, DC. To preserve Star-Spangled Banner.
$3,000,000 to W E T A-Greater Washington Educational Telecommunications Association, Arlington, VA. For program of NewsHour production unit covering media and journalism issues.
$2,800,000 to Johns Hopkins University, Baltimore, MD. To create and manage Pew Environmental Health Commission.
$2,440,000 to Rock the Vote Education Fund, Santa Monica, CA. For programs.

Year-end date of accounting period

Assets at market value (M) or ledger value (L)

Total expenditures figure

Amount and number of grants paid

Separate information on amount and number of employee matching gifts, grants to individuals, or loans

Printed material available from the foundation

Officers and trustees or other governing bodies

For a complete listing of data elements, see "How to Use *The Foundation Directory*" in the Introduction.

reporting substantial changes in personnel, name, address, program interests, limitations, application procedures, or other areas by the midpoint of the yearly *Directory*
cycle.

Each edition of the *Supplement* contains thousands of updated entries. The portions
of an entry that have changes are highlighted in bold type to aid you in identifying new
information quickly. The *Supplement* entries may also include a section called "Other
Changes" that provides additional information about the foundation, including significant growth in its asset base or grants awarded, or to highlight specific changes within
the entry, as when a foundation relocates to another state.

THE FOUNDATION 1000

Published annually, *The Foundation 1000* provides detailed descriptions of the nation's
1,000 largest foundations. Although it is confined to a somewhat narrower universe
than *The Foundation Directory*, it provides a more thorough description of these foundations' histories, giving programs, application procedures, and grants awarded. Each
Foundation 1000 profile provides the foundation's name, address, and telephone number; separate application address(es) and contact person(s); fax number and e-mail and/
or URL addresses; officers, governing board, and principal staff; purpose; current financial data; giving limitations; support and program areas; sponsoring company (if applicable); background history; policies and application guidelines; and publications. The
"Grants Analysis" section of each profile is what makes this resource unique. It presents statistical charts and analyses of grants awarded in the year of record for the following: subject area, recipient type, type of support, population group, and geographic
distribution. A listing of sample grants, selected to best represent the foundation's giving, follows the analyses. For a sample entry from this publication, see Figure 25.

Five indexes in *The Foundation 1000* provide access to the foundations profiled. The
indexes include:

- a name index of donors, officers, trustees, and principal staff;

- an index by subject/giving interests, broken down by the states where
  the foundations are located;

- an index by types of support offered by the foundations, broken down
  by the states where the foundations are located;

- a geographic index of foundation locations by state and city, with
  cross-references to foundations with identified giving patterns beyond
  the states in which they are headquartered; and

Figure 25. Sample Entry from *The Foundation 1000*

302

THE SHERMAN FAIRCHILD FOUNDATION, INC.

545 Wisconsin Ave., Ste. 1205
Chevy Chase, MD   20815-6901   (301) 913-5990
Contact: Bonnie Himmelman, Pres.

Purpose: Emphasis on higher education and fine arts and cultural institutions; some support for medical research and social welfare.

Support area(s): Types of support not specified.

Financial data (yr. ended 12/31/96):
Assets: $299,078,291 (M)
Gifts received: $4,346
Expenditures: $19,227,391
Grants paid: $16,143,904 for 49 grants (high: $2,500,000; low: $10,000)
Grants authorized: $3,428,812 for 13 grants
Outstanding commitments: $26,986,404

Officers and Directors:* Bonnie Himmelman,* Pres.; Patricia A. Lydon, V.P.; Walter Burke, Walter F. Burke III, Robert P. Henderson, Michele Myers, Paul D. Paganucci, Agnar Pytte, James Wright.

Number of staff: 1 full-time support, 1 part-time support.

Background: Incorporated in 1955 in NY. Funds donated by May Fairchild (deceased), Sherman Fairchild (deceased).

At his death in 1971, Mr. Fairchild was chairman of Fairchild Camera and Instrument Company, manufacturers of semiconductor devices in a wide variety of applications, and a director of International Business Machines, a company founded by his father. Mr. Fairchild attended Harvard College, but his formal education was interrupted by illness. He later studied engineering at Columbia University. He left Columbia during World War I to build an aerial camera for the War Department. The foundation's current name was adopted in 1974.

Policies and application guidelines: Application form not required. Applicants should submit the following:

1) detailed description of project and amount of funding requested
Initial approach: Proposal
Deadline(s): None

GRANTS ANALYSIS

Although the foundation provided financial information for 1996, the following grants analysis reflects grants authorized in 1995. During 1995, the foundation authorized grants totaling $9,159,255. This figure represents a 64 percent decrease from giving in 1994. The following analyses and the list of sample grants reflect grants authorized prior to cancellations. Contributions paid in 1995 totaled $19,800,775.

Subject Analysis:

Subject Area Distribution of Grant Numbers and Grant Dollars Authorized in 1995

Subject area	No. of grants	Dollar value	Pct.	General range of grants
Education				
Graduate & professional	2	$2,550,000	28	
Library programs	1	1,000,000	11	
Other	4	280,755	3	
SUBTOTAL:	7	3,830,755	42	$25,000–160,755
Youth development	2	2,800,000	31	
Science				
General science	4	1,262,500	13	
Other	1	10,000	<1	
Grants under $10,000	1	9,000	<1	
SUBTOTAL:	6	1,281,500	13	9,000–200,000
Human services— multipurpose	2	1,250,000	14	
TOTAL:	17	$9,162,255	100%	

High award of the year: $2,500,000, Boys Club of New York, NYC, NY; $2,500,000, California Institute of Technology, Pasadena, CA.

High single recipient: California Institute of Technology, Pasadena, CA (2 awards, totaling $2,570,000).

Top subject area by dollars: Education (also, largest by grant numbers)
Largest award in field: $2,500,000, California Institute of Technology, Pasadena, CA.
Second largest award: $1,000,000, Pierpont Morgan Library, NYC, NY.
Largest single recipient: California Institute of Technology, Pasadena, CA (2 awards, totaling $2,570,000).

Second largest subject area by dollars: Youth development
Largest award in field: $2,500,000, Boys Club of New York, NYC, NY.
Second largest award: $300,000, Police Athletic League, NYC, NY.

Third largest subject area by dollars: Science
Largest award in field: $750,000, Colby College, Waterville, ME.
Second largest award: $200,000, Gallaudet University, DC.

Recipient Type Analysis:

Analysis of Grants of $10,000 or More Awarded in 1995*

Recipient type	Dollar value	No. of grants
Colleges & universities	$3,993,255	7
Youth development organizations	2,800,000	2
Human service agencies	1,250,000	2
Libraries	1,000,000	1
Schools	60,000	3
Graduate schools	50,000	1

*Awards may support multiple recipient types, i.e., a university library, and would therefore be counted twice.

Top recipient type by dollars: Colleges & universities (also, largest by grant numbers)
Largest award in field: $2,500,000, California Institute of Technology, Pasadena, CA.
Second largest award: $750,000, Colby College, Waterville, ME.
Largest single recipient: California Institute of Technology, Pasadena, CA (2 awards, totaling $2,570,000).

Second largest recipient type by dollars: Youth development organizations
Largest award in field: $2,500,000, Boys Club of New York, NYC, NY.
Second largest award: $300,000, Police Athletic League, NYC, NY.

Third largest recipient type by dollars: Human service agencies
Largest award in field: $1,200,000, Salvation Army of Greater New York, NYC, NY.
Second largest award: $50,000, Salvation Army, DHQ, Northern Division, Brooklyn Center, MN.

Type of Support Analysis:

Analysis of Grants of $10,000 or More Awarded in 1995*

Support type	Dollar value	No. of grants
General support		
General/operating support	$4,050,000	4
Program support		
Program development	3,303,255	8
Capital support		
Endowment funds	1,000,000	1
Building/renovation	800,000	3
Equipment	200,000	1

*Awards may support multiple support types, i.e., seed money for research, and would therefore be counted twice.

Top support type by dollars: General support
Largest award in field: $2,500,000.
Second largest award: $1,200,000.

Second largest support type by dollars: Program support (also, largest by grant numbers)
Largest award in field: $2,500,000.
Second largest award: $200,000.

Third largest support type by dollars: Capital support
Largest award in field: $1,000,000.
Second largest award: $750,000.

Continuing support: 2 grants, totaling $1,210,000

73

Figure 25. Sample Entry from *The Foundation 1000* (continued)

302—Fairchild

Population Group Analysis:

Analysis of Grants Over $10,000 Designated for Special Populations*

Group	Dollar value	No. of grants
Children & youth	$2,985,755	4
Men & boys	2,500,000	1
Economically disadvantaged	1,275,000	3
Deaf & hearing impaired	200,000	1
Women & girls	137,000	1
Minorities, general	25,000	1

*Grants which support no specific population are not included; awards may support multiple populations, i.e., an award for minority youth, and would therefore be counted twice.

Top population group by dollars: Children & youth (also, largest by grant numbers)
  Largest award in field: $2,500,000, Boys Club of New York, NYC, NY (For general support).
  Second largest award: $300,000, Police Athletic League, NYC, NY (For general support).

Second largest population group by dollars: Men & boys
  Largest award in field: $2,500,000, Boys Club of New York (See above).

Third largest population group by dollars: Economically disadvantaged
  Largest award in field: $1,200,000, Salvation Army of Greater New York, NYC, NY (For general support).
  Second largest award: $50,000, Salvation Army, DHQ, Northern Division, Brooklyn Center, MN (For general support).

Geographic Analysis:

The geographic distribution of institutional awards of $10,000 or more is as follows. (Grants to individuals and with unknown locations are excluded.)

U.S. regional breakdown: Middle Atlantic, $5,200,500 (6 awards); Pacific, $2,570,000 (2 awards); New England, $1,107,755 (5 awards); South Atlantic, $225,000 (2 awards); West North Central, $50,000 (1 award).

GRANTS: The following is a complete list of grants authorized by the foundation in 1995.

Education

California Institute of Technology, Pasadena, CA — $2,570,000
  For Post-Doctoral Scholars Program, $2,500,000.
  For Hawking visit, $70,000.

Pierpont Morgan Library, NYC, NY — 1,000,000
  For endowment.

Yale University, New Haven, CT — 160,755
  For New Haven Teachers Institute fund.

Cambridge College, Cambridge, MA — 50,000
  For Urban Teacher Program.

Christchurch School, Christchurch, VA — 25,000
  For Brown Hall Restoration.

Prep for Prep, NYC, NY — 25,000
  For building renovation.

Youth development

Boys Club of New York, NYC, NY — 2,500,000
  For general support.

Police Athletic League, NYC, NY — 300,000
  For general support.

Science

Colby College, Waterville, ME — 750,000
  For renovations to Science Complex.

Gallaudet University, DC — 200,000
  For Scientific Equipment Program.

Colgate University, Hamilton, NY — 175,500
  For Summer Science Program.

Wellesley College, Wellesley, MA — 137,000
  For Summer Science Program.

Phillips Exeter Academy, Exeter, NH — 10,000
  For Exeter Mathematics Institute.

Council on Undergraduate Research, Tucson, AZ — 9,000
  For Summer Science Research Project.

Human services—multipurpose

Salvation Army of Greater New York, NYC, NY — 1,200,000
  For general support.

Salvation Army, DHQ, Northern Division, Brooklyn Center, MN — 50,000
  For general support.

Source(s): 1995 990

Employer Identification Number (EIN): 131951698

- an international giving index of countries, continents, or regions where foundations have indicated giving interests, broken down by the states where the foundations are located.

Like the indexes in *The Foundation Directory*, *The Foundation 1000* subject, types of support, and geographic indexes indicate foundations with a national, regional, or international focus in bold type, while locally-oriented foundations are listed in regular type.

The Foundation 1000 is useful for identifying potential funding sources among the nation's 1,000 largest foundations. It is especially helpful in the final stages of your research, when you should be gathering detailed information about the carefully selected group of foundations to which you plan to submit a proposal.

Foundation Grants

Indexes to foundation grants help you identify funders with a demonstrated interest in your subject or geographic area by listing the actual grants they have awarded. Studying listings of grants a foundation has recently awarded will give you a better understanding of a foundation's giving priorities in terms of the types of programs and organizations it likes to fund, the amount of money it awards for specific programs, the geographic area in which it concentrates its grantmaking activities, the population groups it serves through its grants, and the types of support it typically offers.

The Foundation Center currently maintains computer files on reported grants of $10,000 and more awarded by more than 1,300 major foundations. The Center's database currently contains more than 1.2 million grant records. Some 85,000 new records are added to the database every year. The information included in the database is made available to grantseekers in a variety of print, online, and CD-ROM formats designed to facilitate their individual funding searches.

Each grant record includes the name and state location of the grantmaker as well as that of the recipient organization, the amount of the grant and its duration, and a brief description of the purpose for which the grant was made. Where applicable, a statement outlining geographic, subject, or other restrictions on the grantmaker's giving program is also provided. Foundation Center editors analyze and index each grant by subject focus, type of recipient organization, population group served, and the type of support awarded (e.g., endowment, research, building/renovation, etc.).

There are two types of grant-based print publications produced from the Center's database: *The Foundation Grants Index* and the *Grant Guide* series. Each type of publication is designed to offer a different mode of access to the grants information in the database. As you become more skilled at foundation research, you'll be able to determine which of the print volumes will be most useful. In the beginning it's a good idea to use and become familiar with all of them.

THE FOUNDATION GRANTS INDEX

The Foundation Grants Index offers information on more than 50 percent of all grant dollars awarded annually by private foundations. The volume is divided into major subject fields, under which grants are arranged by state, then alphabetically by foundation name. Grants are listed alphabetically under the appropriate foundation by the name of the recipient organization. The volume's five indexes enable you to customize your search according to your needs:

- The **Recipient Name Index** helps you locate records of grants that have been awarded to specific organizations, making it possible to identify foundations that have funded organizations with missions or programs similar to yours. The index is divided into two sections: domestic (U.S.) and foreign recipients.

- The **Subject Index** identifies grants by keywords and phrases describing a specific subject focus (e.g., "Ballet," "Environment," "Physics"), the population group served (e.g., "Aging," "Hispanics," "Women"), and type of recipient organization (e.g., "Museum," "Boys clubs," "Hospital"), or the type of support (e.g., "Fellowships," "Endowments," "Publication"). Each grant may be indexed under a number of different keywords and phrases. An illustration will best demonstrate how the Subject Index works. In Figure 26, you will see that the subject "disasters" has been described by population group (e.g., "Aging," Children & youth," "Women"), and by type of support (e.g., "Equipment," "Research," "Technical aid").

- The **Type of Support/Geographic Index** is an alphabetical index by types of support and subject that is further broken down by the recipient organization's state or country, thereby providing access to grants made in broad subject fields to recipients in specific geographic areas. For instance, as seen in Figure 27, the Type of Support called

Figure 26. Subject Index from *The Foundation Grants Index*

SUBJECT INDEX

47973, 47974, 59255, 62506, 62715, 76951, 76954, 76958, 77903, 78070, 78174
Disabled, safety/disaster relief, 46279
Disabled, science, 2885, 23784, 37395, 38057, 38956, 58038, 58736, 61283-61285, 66621, 75769, 79815, 81825
Disabled, social sciences, 74922, 82493
Disabled, youth development, 23628, 56319, 63362, 76065, 83697, 83713, 83818, 83831, 83899, 84216, 84341, 85075, 85085, 85086, 85242, 85270, 85271, 85279, 85354, 85357, 85365, 85448, 85502, 85512, 85710, 85769, 85790, 86062, 86116
Disasters, aging, 64874, 79326, 79331
Disasters, blacks, 79238
Disasters, blind, 79398
Disasters, boys & young men, 79293
Disasters, building/renovation, 12454, 43432, 56456, 70402, 76941, 79207, 79208, 79213, 79215, 79262, 79272, 79276, 79280, 79289-79293, 79297, 79299, 79302, 79310, 79311, 79313-79316, 79318-79320, 79323, 79324, 79327, 79329, 79333, 79334, 79337, 79341-79347, 79349-79354, 79356, 79360, 79362-79368, 79372, 79373, 79377, 79379, 79429, 79433, 79447, 79483, 79490, 79872
Disasters, capital campaigns, 20161, 79251, 79278, 79302, 79305, 79355, 79358, 79370, 79382-79384
Disasters, children & youth, 20161, 22635, 62313, 79191, 79201, 79207, 79290, 79300-79302, 79312, 79320-79323, 79332, 79343, 79361-79363, 79368
Disasters, computer systems/equipment, 79357, 79440, 79453, 79457
Disasters, conferences/seminars, 79339, 79381, 79486
Disasters, crime/abuse victims, 79301, 79302
Disasters, deaf, 22635
Disasters, economically disadvantaged, 43432, 56456, 62083, 62313, 79198, 79201, 79225, 79229, 79257, 79265, 79279, 79280, 79327, 79331, 79348, 79355-79358, 79360, 79376, 79380, 79405, 79448, 79460, 79461, 79463, 79477, 79488
Disasters, equipment, 22635, 74041, 75289, 79194, 79196, 79204, 79206, 79221, 79270-79276, 79287-79290, 79296-79299, 79301, 79304, 79307-79309, 79312, 79313, 79315-79318, 79320-79323, 79325, 79326, 79328, 79329, 79333, 79334, 79337, 79338, 79343, 79346-79348, 79350, 79352, 79354, 79359, 79363, 79364, 79366-79368, 79371, 79372, 79375-79378, 79391, 79392, 79417, 79420, 79422, 79423, 79437-79439, 79450, 79451, 79455, 79456, 79478-79480, 79482, 79489
Disasters, exhibitions, 79250
Disasters, faculty/staff development, 79206, 79374
Disasters, film/video/radio, 41086
Disasters, fire prevention/control, 12454, 13268, 20161, 22635, 74041, 75289, 79195-79197, 79199, 79201, 79204, 79208, 79234-79240, 79250, 79252, 79253, 79260, 79267, 79269-79276, 79285, 79287, 79389, 79391-79394, 79412, 79413, 79415-79417, 79420, 79422, 79423, 79427-79429, 79432-79434, 79436-79440, 79443, 79447, 79451, 79454-79456, 79462, 79464-79474, 79478-79480, 79482, 79483, 79486, 79487, 79489-79491, 79494, 79499, 79500
Disasters, floods, 39629, 39688, 39693, 41074, 41080, 41081, 41086, 41087, 41094, 43432, 56456, 62083, 62313, 67945, 67946, 70402, 79192, 79193, 79198, 79202, 79209, 79210, 79213, 79215, 79222, 79224-79227, 79229, 79232, 79254, 79258, 79264, 79279, 79280, 79286, 79288-79382, 79404-79406, 79410, 79414, 79418, 79425, 79442, 79452, 79458-79461
Disasters, girls & young women, 79315
Disasters, Hispanics, 62905, 79402
Disasters, homeless, 79320
Disasters, mentally disabled, 79337
Disasters, migrant workers, 79198, 79336
Disasters, minorities, 79198
Disasters, preparedness & services, 58778-58780, 58956, 61515, 61516, 61541, 62344, 62905, 64874, 76941, 79190, 79191, 79207, 79214, 79220, 79223, 79228, 79245, 79251, 79255-79257, 79265, 79277, 79278, 79281, 79282, 79284, 79383, 79384, 79386, 79388, 79396-79402, 79407-79409, 79411, 79419, 79424, 79426, 79430, 79431, 79441, 79444, 79445, 79448, 79450, 79453, 79457, 79463, 79476, 79477, 79483, 79484, 79488, 79493, 79872
Disasters, publication, 41086, 79306
Disasters, research, 41094, 79369
Disasters, search & rescue, 45930, 74041, 79194, 79200, 79203, 79205, 79206, 79221, 79259, 79261, 79262, 79475, 79478
Disasters, seed money, 79484
Disasters, technical aid, 79226, 79369
Disasters, women, 79301, 79302
Disasters, youth, 62905, 79414
Diseases (rare), 54864
Diseases (rare) research, children & youth, 51645
Dispute resolution, 5481, 16271, 18192, 18271, 18273, 18274, 18276, 18277, 18280-18287, 18296, 18311, 18312, 18441, 18464, 18635, 18714, 18718, 18767, 18893, 18908, 18949, 19084, 19279, 19282, 19307, 19317, 19321, 19322, 19348, 19351, 19389, 19402, 19407, 19499, 19501, 19591, 20379, 39889, 39917, 41018, 41055, 42083, 47913, 56477, 68819, 68867, 73286, 79335, 83442
Dispute resolution, aging, 18270, 18675, 56209
Dispute resolution, Asian/Pacific islanders, 13373, 14467, 18181, 19286
Dispute resolution, blacks, 14467, 16885, 18275
Dispute resolution, boys & young men, 35671
Dispute resolution, children & youth, 1184, 3545, 6486, 9292, 13774, 14467, 17230, 18200, 18340, 18342, 18392, 18468, 18482, 18654, 18669, 18843, 18875, 18884, 18945, 19050, 19065, 19114, 19249, 19280, 19284, 19312, 19315, 19482, 19490, 19538, 19549, 19553, 19559, 19568, 19943, 21575, 22695-22697, 23008, 24211, 36831, 63503, 64493, 67004, 83802
Dispute resolution, collections management/preservation, 18279
Dispute resolution, computer systems/equipment, 18278
Dispute resolution, conferences/seminars, 18875, 19286, 19568
Dispute resolution, crime/abuse victims, 19065, 63503
Dispute resolution, curriculum development, 18207, 19280, 19316, 19566, 21575, 23294, 83802
Dispute resolution, economically disadvantaged, 13774, 16101, 18197, 18340, 18342, 18468, 18482, 18669, 18845, 18884, 19315, 19538, 64493, 64928
Dispute resolution, endowments, 18359
Dispute resolution, equipment, 18945
Dispute resolution, faculty/staff development, 18181, 19285, 23294
Dispute resolution, film/video/radio, 18850
Dispute resolution, girls & young women, 18813, 35671
Dispute resolution, Hispanics, 1184, 18342, 19342, 36831
Dispute resolution, homeless, 18813, 64928
Dispute resolution, immigrants/refugees, 13373, 18181
Dispute resolution, income development, 19453
Dispute resolution, internships, 19091
Dispute resolution, management development, 18262, 18263, 18375, 18382, 18873, 19000, 19453, 19456, 85808
Dispute resolution, minorities, 6486, 9292, 13774, 13871, 16101, 18207, 18261-18263, 18272, 18340, 18468, 18482, 18669, 18843, 18845, 19114, 19308, 19482, 19538, 64493, 85490, 85808
Dispute resolution, Native Americans, 18375
Dispute resolution, offenders/ex-offenders, 18197, 18391, 84318
Dispute resolution, program evaluation, 18269, 18340, 19249, 85808
Dispute resolution, publication, 16885, 19249, 40956
Dispute resolution, research, 13774, 18391, 19283, 68175, 68672, 84318
Dispute resolution, seed money, 18259, 18262, 18263, 19070
Dispute resolution, technical aid, 18986
Dispute resolution, women, 18846, 19487
Dispute resolution, youth, 13871, 18197, 18205, 18207, 18258, 19308, 84318, 85490, 85808
Domestic violence prevention, aging, 13801
Domestic violence prevention, Asian/Pacific islanders, 19059, 61389
Domestic violence prevention, blacks, 66637
Domestic violence prevention, boys & young men, 18346, 52234
Domestic violence prevention, building/renovation, 19008
Domestic violence prevention, children & youth, 18333, 18339, 18351, 18372, 18629, 18764, 18786, 18787, 18808, 18814, 18855, 18859, 18860, 18872, 18874, 18911, 18940, 18955, 18991, 18992, 19008, 19132, 19193, 19194, 19202, 19318, 19609, 44891, 52235, 52236, 52798, 58092, 58160, 59331, 61642, 62026, 62210, 62766, 62768, 62769, 64956, 66637, 66986, 67002, 78106
Domestic violence prevention, computer systems/equipment, 19346
Domestic violence prevention, conferences/seminars, 61963, 62251, 68105, 68944
Domestic violence prevention, crime/abuse victims, 1166, 13801, 14050, 18180, 18333, 18339, 18351, 18356, 18372, 18416, 18456, 18629, 18647, 18664, 18764, 18786, 18787, 18808, 18831, 18854, 18855, 18858-18860, 18862, 18872, 18874, 18890, 18894, 18911, 18917, 18940, 18955, 18970, 18977, 18978, 18989, 18991-18993, 19008, 19059, 19060, 19129, 19132, 19193, 19194, 19202, 19318, 19319, 19346, 19397, 19398, 19401, 19415, 19424, 19442, 19514, 19590, 19609, 44891, 47378, 52234-52236, 52321, 52798, 58092, 58160, 59049, 59250, 59331, 59679, 60180, 60351, 60621, 61389, 61642, 61963, 62026, 62043, 62210, 62226, 62227, 62251, 62264, 62766, 62768, 62769, 63428, 63624, 63700, 64804, 64817, 64956, 66637, 66947, 66986, 67002, 68105, 68507, 68944, 68954, 69012, 74595, 82147, 82665
Domestic violence prevention, economically disadvantaged, 14050, 18346, 18356, 18372, 18664, 19590, 74595, 82147
Domestic violence prevention, equipment, 18180, 18874
Domestic violence prevention, faculty/staff development, 63624
Domestic violence prevention, film/video/radio, 18854
Domestic violence prevention, gays/lesbians, 18369
Domestic violence prevention, girls & young women, 18346, 52234
Domestic violence prevention, Hispanics, 19060
Domestic violence prevention, management development, 18351
Domestic violence prevention, men, 18890, 18955, 62226
Domestic violence prevention, Native Americans, 18890
Domestic violence prevention, performance/productions, 19398
Domestic violence prevention, program evaluation, 67002
Domestic violence prevention, publication, 52234
Domestic violence prevention, research, 14050, 18346, 52236, 58160, 59331, 68954, 74595, 82147, 82665
Domestic violence prevention, seed money, 18940, 59250
Domestic violence prevention, single parents, 67002

FOUNDATION GRANTS INDEX 2051

Figure 27. Type of Support/Geographic Index from *The Foundation Grants Index*

TYPE OF SUPPORT/GEOGRAPHIC INDEX—ANNUAL CAMPAIGNS

ANNUAL CAMPAIGNS

Animals/wildlife

Texas 42939

Arts/culture

Arizona 923
California 1451, 1456, 6180
Connecticut 11632
District of Columbia 6238, 12253
Georgia 2893, 3230, 10441
Illinois 3645
Massachusetts 4740, 4742, 4744
Michigan 5206
Minnesota 5581
New Mexico 12316
New York 8180, 9923, 12231, 12232, 12297
North Carolina 22648
Ohio 10539, 10542, 10753, 10975, 10996, 33602
Pennsylvania 11276, 11631, 11655, 12142
Texas 12302, 12376, 12415
Vermont 4429
Wisconsin 13143, 13232

Civil rights

District of Columbia 59035

Community improvement/development

District of Columbia 15108

Education, elementary/secondary

Arizona 19821
California 19817, 19822, 43280
Connecticut 22973, 24336, 24342
Georgia 20935, 22650
Iowa 28390
Maryland 22653
Massachusetts 19916, 24331
Minnesota 22281
New Jersey 22649, 22651, 22657, 24330
North Carolina 22648
Oklahoma 24387
Pennsylvania 24339, 24706, 24761
Rhode Island 25001, 25002
Texas 25101, 25329
Virginia 25369

Education, higher

California 26375, 31146
District of Columbia 26958
Illinois 28038
Iowa 28390, 28393
Lebanon 31387
Maryland 31102
Massachusetts 34058
Michigan 29510, 29512, 29518
New Hampshire 26354
New York 28348, 32554
North Carolina 34446
Ohio 31114, 33317, 33455, 33456, 33602, 33695
Oregon 26378, 26380
Pennsylvania 33987
Rhode Island 33345
Virginia 29666, 32955, 33238, 33446, 35212

Education, other

New Jersey 24330
New York 36786

Environment

New York 41717, 42885
Texas 42939
Wyoming 42893

Food/nutrition/agriculture

California 43280

Health—general/rehabilitative

Connecticut 45475
Delaware 45563
Michigan 46869
New Jersey 22657

Health—specific diseases

Pennsylvania 55286

Human services—multipurpose

California 58083
District of Columbia 59035
Minnesota 62391, 62393
Ohio 64880
Pennsylvania 65604

Philanthropy/voluntarism

Arizona 70443-70446
California 70207, 70211
Colorado 70421, 70434, 70436, 70440
Connecticut 70458, 71945
Delaware 70529, 70532
District of Columbia 70852
Georgia 70664, 72412
Hawaii 70695, 70700-70702
Illinois 70786, 70787, 70792, 70837, 70850
Indiana 70567, 70884, 70920
Iowa 70925
Louisiana 72404, 72405
Michigan 71065-71068, 71108, 71109, 71112-71116, 71129, 71226, 71231, 71274, 71287, 71347, 71350, 71351
Minnesota 70416, 71376, 71438, 71459
Missouri 71531, 71605
Nebraska 71627
New Jersey 71707, 71708, 71720-71722
New York 71943, 71944, 71967, 71970, 72026
North Carolina 72498
Ohio 72416, 72429, 72430, 72452, 72495, 72550-72553
Oregon 70424, 70425, 70427, 72497
Pennsylvania 70531, 70533, 72657, 72680, 72722, 72725, 72743, 72759, 72760, 73110
Tennessee 70864
Texas 72882, 72952, 72953
Utah 70426
Virginia 73038
Washington 70420, 70423, 70433
Wisconsin 70793, 73145, 73159

Public affairs/government

District of Columbia 75233

Religion

California 76867
Maryland 77775
Minnesota 78153
Tennessee 77778

Youth development

Illinois 84228
Louisiana 85539

AWARDS/PRIZES/COMPETITIONS

Animals/wildlife

New York 51669
Pennsylvania 51731

Arts/culture

California 1343, 1346, 1347, 1349, 1909, 2103, 2888, 6291, 11911, 12043, 30934, 58426
Colorado 2406, 2417
District of Columbia 4512
Florida 20948
Hawaii 1342, 1345
Illinois 54399

Kansas 35050
Maryland 7282, 35063
Massachusetts 37853, 49209
Michigan 10547
Minnesota 5478
New York 5860, 5876, 6606, 6694, 7294, 9607, 10003, 12913, 13502, 14304, 41774
Ohio 10763
Oregon 11146
Pennsylvania 11724
Poland 2837
Russia 9065, 9076
Texas 12584, 12604, 37852
Vermont 6336
Virginia 11410, 12904, 54400

Civil rights

California 13435
Colorado 13482
District of Columbia 13505, 71277
Illinois 13656
Michigan 82458
New York 13502, 13946, 14304
Rhode Island 78959

Community improvement/development

California 15080
Colorado 14947
Florida 17675
New York 16673, 16682, 16693, 16695, 16736, 16738, 16740, 16743, 17658, 74410
Ohio 16386, 19338
Pennsylvania 11724

Crime/courts/legal services

California 13435, 18357
Florida 18826
Illinois 18681
North Carolina 19311
Ohio 19338
Texas 19584

Education, elementary/secondary

Arizona 20435
California 1909, 2103, 6291, 30934
Colorado 58627, 79967
England 24839
Florida 20948
Idaho 20436
Illinois 21316
Iowa 79965
Maryland 82290
Massachusetts 79799
Michigan 22099
Minnesota 20441, 22268
Montana 20428
New Jersey 22585, 73532, 73533
New Mexico 20439, 81336
New York 6694, 9607, 10003, 31406
North Carolina 22565
North Dakota 20445
Ohio 10763, 25416
South Dakota 20426
Tennessee 25039, 53508
Texas 25143
Utah 25349, 79962
Vermont 6336
Washington 79966
Wisconsin 79964
Wyoming 20429

Education, higher

Arkansas 54824
Brazil 31472, 82550
California 25940, 26049, 26505, 26520, 30934, 54822
Colorado 79967
Connecticut 26753, 54829
Georgia 27335
Indiana 28182
Kansas 35050

"Annual Campaigns" is broken down by subject (e.g. "Animals/ wildlife," "Arts/culture," "Education, higher") and within the subjects by geographic focus (e.g. "California," "Indiana," "Utah"). A listing of types of support and subject fields is included at the beginning of the index.

- The **Recipient Categories Index** provides access to grants by the type of recipient organization. Each recipient category is broken down by the type of support awarded (e.g., "Building/renovation," "Capital campaign," "Endowments") and the state location of the recipient organization. A listing of the thirty-six types of recipient organizations is included at the beginning of the index.

- The **Index to Grants by Foundation** allows you to access a foundation's grants list. The index is arranged alphabetically by foundation state, then by foundation name. For each foundation, grants are listed alphabetically by subject field.

The Foundation Grants Index ends with a foundation name and address list, which is alphabetical by foundation name. In addition to addresses, foundation telephone and fax numbers and e-mail and URL addresses are included when available. A limitations statement indicates geographic, program, and type of support restrictions on the foundation's giving. The 100 largest foundations are indicated in bold type.

The Foundation Grants Index can be used to get a broad overview of a specific foundation's giving priorities, to survey foundation giving within a state, to evaluate giving to a particular recipient or recipient type, and/or to identify the subject areas that currently are most attractive to private foundations.

GRANT GUIDES

Because many grantseekers want to focus their funding search on a particular subject, the Foundation Center publishes a series of books that lists grants from the annual *Grants Index* in a more specialized format. Each *Guide* is a "mini" *Grants Index*, listing grants of $10,000 and up arranged by foundation name and location, as well as by subject. *Grant Guides* are currently available in the following thirty-five subject areas or population groups:

Aging
Alcohol & Drug Abuse
Arts, Culture & the Humanities
Children & Youth
Civic Participation
Community/Economic Development, Housing & Employment
Crime, Law Enforcement & Abuse Prevention
Elementary & Secondary Education
Environmental Protection & Animal Welfare
Film, Media & Communications
Foreign & International Programs
Health Programs for Children & Youth
Higher Education
Homeless
Hospitals, Medical Care & Research
Human/Civil Rights
Information Technology
Libraries & Information Services

Literacy, Reading & Adult/Continuing Education
Matching & Challenge Support
Medical & Professional Health Education
Mental Health, Addictions & Crisis Services
Minorities
Physically & Mentally Disabled
Program Evaluation
Public Health & Disease
Public Policy & Public Affairs
Recreation, Sports & Athletics
Religion, Religious Welfare & Religious Education
Scholarships, Student Aid & Loans
Science & Technology Programs
Social & Political Science Programs
Social Services
Technical Assistance/Management Support
Women & Girls

Specialized Directories

Directories that specialize in a geographic area, a particular subject, or a specific type of funder can be extremely useful in identifying foundations that will support your program. These directories may be compiled by commercial publishers, state government agencies, libraries, associations of grantmakers, and other nonprofit groups. Many such directories are available, but they vary widely in the type, currency, and amount of information they provide. To identify specialized directories related to your subject or geographic area or some other criteria, look at the bibliographies in the *Guide to U.S. Foundations, Their Trustees, Officers, and Donors* and the various volumes in the

•

Foundation Center's *National Guide* series. The *Literature of the Nonprofit Sector Online* (www.fdncenter.org/onlib/lnps/index.html) can also be helpful in identifying specialized directories because it is keyword searchable. In addition, some Cooperating Collections compile directories for their geographic areas.

STATE AND LOCAL FUNDING DIRECTORIES

State and regional funding directories can be a very good source of information, particularly for smaller foundations not covered in depth in major reference works. Those state and regional directories that have a subject index may provide the only subject access to the giving patterns of smaller foundations. In addition, many of these directories list sample grants, which give you some indication of a funder's interests. Some directories also include information on corporations that support charitable programs in their geographic area, a very useful complement to foundation information.

The Foundation Center publishes three local funding directories: *New York State Foundations,* the *Guide to Greater Washington D.C. Grantmakers,* and the *Directory of Missouri Grantmakers.*

New York State Foundations is a comprehensive directory of foundations located in New York, as well as foundations located outside of the state that have documented giving interests in New York. The New York foundations are listed by the county in which they are located. In addition to indexes of the names of the foundations and their donors, officers, and trustees, the directory includes four indexes—geographic location, international giving interests, types of support awarded, and subject areas of interest. Out-of-state foundations are listed separately.

The Center's two other regional funding publications are produced in collaboration with regional associations of grantmakers: the *Guide to Greater Washington D.C. Grantmakers* is published with the Washington Regional Association of Grantmakers, and the *Directory of Missouri Grantmakers* is produced in collaboration with the Metropolitan Association for Philanthropy in St. Louis, Missouri. Both of these regional directories include corporate direct giving programs and public charities as well as foundations, and list grantmakers outside the specified region, if they have identified giving interests in the defined geographic area. Both publications include four indexes: donors, officers, and trustees; types of support; subject; and grantmaker name.

The Center's three regional funding publications and many other state and local funding directories are available for public reference in the Center's five libraries. Cooperating Collections generally have directories for their own state or region. There

81

is a comprehensive listing of state and local funding directories in the *Guide to U.S. Foundations* and in the Online Library at the Center's Web site.

NATIONAL GUIDE SERIES

The Foundation Center publishes a number of directories based on subject or population group targeted. This *National Guide to Funding . . .* series pulls information from the major grantmaker and grants directories and organizes it by topic for the convenience of the researcher. The *National Guides* are designed to facilitate grantseeking within specific fields of nonprofit activity. Books in the *National Guide* series are popular with grantseekers because they provide the facts needed to develop your list of funding prospects among foundations, corporate direct giving programs, and grantmaking public charities. Each entry provides address, financial data, giving priorities, application procedures, contact names, and key officials. Each volume also includes descriptions of recently awarded grants, and provides a range of indexes that will help you target funders by specific program areas.

Subjects and population groups covered by the *National Guide* series are currently available in the following areas:

Aging	Health
AIDS	Higher Education
Arts & Culture	Information Technology
Children, Youth & Families	Libraries & Information Services
Community Development	Religion
Elementary & Secondary Education	Substance Abuse
Environment & Animal Welfare	Women & Girls

The *Guide to Funding for International & Foreign Programs* is often listed as one of the *National Guide* topics because it is similar in format and content to the titles in the *National Guide* series. For detailed bibliographical information about each book, see Appendix E.

Additional Funding Information Resources

Beyond the resources already described in this chapter, Foundation Center libraries maintain collections of IRS information returns, annual reports, informational brochures, and newsletters issued by foundation and corporate grantmakers, in addition to files of news clippings, press releases, and historical materials related to philanthropy. Center libraries also provide public access to grantmaker information on the Internet. These supplementary materials are either primary, meaning that they were produced by the foundation itself, or secondary, meaning that they were produced by sources outside the foundation. Such resources can be particularly helpful in the final stages of your research as you gather detailed information about the grantmakers you have identified as the most likely funding sources for your program or organization.

THE WORLD WIDE WEB

The World Wide Web, an electronic information retrieval system with colorful graphics, sometimes sound and animation, and hypertext linking powers, is a valuable research tool for the grantseeker because it can provide the researcher with both primary and secondary resources from a very wide range of sources. Information on the Web is organized into content modules, often called pages. An organization's presentation, or content module, specifically developed for the Web is usually referred to as its home page. Pages are found by addresses called Uniform/Universal Resource Locators (URLs). The most helpful aspect of Web pages is the "hypertext transport protocol" (the "http" of a Web address). With hypertext, if you see an item of interest and it is highlighted (usually underlined and in a different color print), you can click on that item and you will automatically be taken to further information about that item.

Rather than relying on a specific address or word-of-mouth referrals, you can use a search engine to locate sites of interest to you. You may already be familiar with one or more of such popular search engines as:

- Google (www.google.com)

- Hotbot (www.hotbot.com)

- Infoseek (www.infoseek.com)

- Internet Sleuth (www.isleuth.com)

- Lycos (www.lycos.com)

- Mamma (www.mamma.com)

- Metacrawler (www.metacrawler.com)

- Yahoo (www.yahoo.com)

There are others. Try out each one to see which search engine is more to your liking. You will need to know the parameters of the specific search engine you may be using at the time. For instance, some engines search indiscriminately for every instance of the search term; other search engines utilize a selection process that reviews, classifies, and indexes Web sites for somewhat more focused searching. Also, as with any search, you need to choose the proper wording for your search query. Articles analyzing or recommending various search engines appear periodically in the popular press as well as in technology journals. Such articles can provide helpful tips for your research needs.

Using a search engine across something as large and diverse as the Web has its drawbacks, the major one being that you will likely find yourself sifting through long search results lists that contain a lot of irrelevant material. A "gateway" site or a "portal" is usually more helpful to the Web searcher than a search engine. A portal or gateway is a Web site offering a variety of services around a specific topic. A gateway or portal can be used as a home base for exploring the Web. The Foundation Center's Web site (www.fdncenter.org) is considered a gateway to the Web for many people in the nonprofit and philanthropic communities.

The Foundation Center's Web site (see Figure 28) is particularly useful to the grantseeker. From the Center's site, the grantseeker can, among other things: (1) link to information on nearly 900 grantmakers with a presence on the Web; (2) learn about the funding research process from the Center's *User-Friendly Guide,* the Online Orientation to the Grantseeking Process, or a Proposal Writing Short Course; (3) review highlights of the latest funding trends; (4) download a common grant application form and find out which grantmakers accept it; (5) read or download abstracts of the major philanthropy-related articles from national and weekly news sources in *Philanthropy News Digest*; and (6) search the *Literature of the Nonprofit Sector Online*, a bibliographic database accessing books and periodicals on philanthropy.

The Center's Web site also contains a free foundation look-up service called Foundation Finder. With all or part of a foundation name entered in the space provided, Foundation Finder will search a database of more than 48,000 foundations to provide you with the foundation's full name, address, telephone number, and contact person. Each record also provides a brief profile, such as type of foundation, assets, total giving, and Employer Identification Number (EIN) (see Figure 29). This is very much like having an online version of the *Guide to U.S. Foundations*, with the additional feature of being able to link directly to the Web sites of foundations with URLs.

For more in-depth information on mining the many Internet resources for grantseekers, see *The Foundation Center's Guide to Grantseeking on the Web*. This guide lists

Figure 28.   Home Page from the Foundation Center's Web Site

useful sites for grantseekers and provides the important "how-tos" of connecting to and effectively using the Internet for funding research.

Cautionary Note

The information on the Internet, and the tools used to search it, are constantly changing, and this information is often transitory in nature. That is, material that is available one day may be gone the next, addresses of Web sites may change, and the content of sites may be radically transformed overnight. Since anyone can post information on the Internet and since there is no publication or editorial process in place to screen the content, you must carefully evaluate the accuracy, scope, and currency of the material yourself. Some questions to ask include:

- Who wrote or published the information?

Figure 29. Foundation Finder

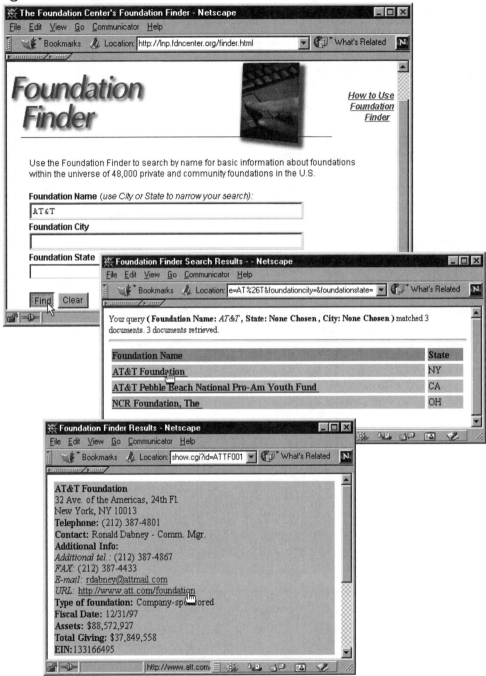

- Does the author or organization have a good reputation in the field?

- Is there biographical or publishing information, via a link to another document, that allows you to judge the credentials of the author or host?

- Is there a recognizable bias or agenda associated with the author or organization?

- How thorough is the information?

- Is the information appropriate for your needs?

- Is the information up-to-date?

- Is research methodology explained?

These and other questions related to your research will help you to critically evaluate the resources you uncover on the Web.

PRIMARY RESOURCES

Most foundations do not issue annual reports, giving guidelines, or other printed matter about themselves; and only a small percentage have as yet established sites on the Internet. However, if a foundation has produced such print or electronic resources, the grantseeker should review them for the most up-to-date picture of the potential funder's giving criteria.

Foundation Information Returns

One of the best and most comprehensive sources of information on a private foundation is its Form 990-PF. Foundations are required to file this form annually with the Internal Revenue Service (IRS). Federal law requires that these documents, unlike personal or corporate tax returns, be made available to the public by both the IRS and by the foundations themselves. This means that for all private foundations, regardless of size, basic facts about their operations and grants are a matter of public record. For many smaller foundations this information return is the only complete record of their operations and grantmaking activities. For larger foundations, 990-PFs supply important information about assets and investments, as well as a complete list of grants awarded in a particular year. See Figure 30 for the kinds of things you can find out by examining a foundation's Form 990-PF.

FOUNDATION FUNDAMENTALS

Figure 30. 1998 IRS Foundation Annual Return

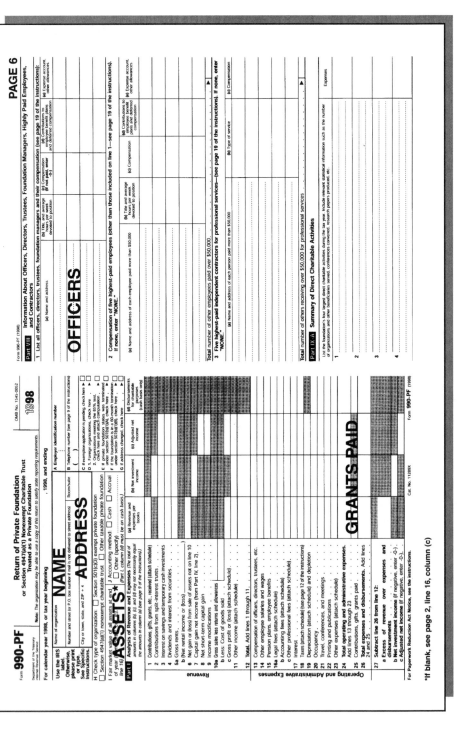

88

Figure 30. 1998 IRS Foundation Annual Return (continued)

PAGE 9

PAGE 10

GRANTS PAID

FUTURE GRANTS

APPLICATION INFORMATION

*Foundation does not accept unsolicited applications.

Since community foundations generally are classified as public charities and not as private foundations, they are not required to file a Form 990-PF with the IRS. They do file Form 990, however, which you can acquire from the community foundation itself or from the IRS. Most community foundations also issue separate annual reports or otherwise make available information about their activities. Keep in mind that many community foundations are actually engaged in soliciting funds as well as in grantmaking. Hence, it is in their self-interest to make their activities broadly known.

Where to Obtain Copies of IRS Information Returns

Form 990-PF: To comply with federal law, private foundations must make copies of their 990-PFs available to the public. They are allowed to charge a reasonable fee for copying and mailing a copy of the return. You may also order complete sets of foundation returns or copies of individual returns from the IRS for a fee. To request copies, use Form 4056A (available from the IRS at 1-800-829-8815), or write a letter including the full name of the organization, its Employer Identification Number (EIN), its address with city, state, and zip code, and the year(s) needed. You may either mail or fax your requests to:

> Internal Revenue Service
> Ogden Service Center
> P.O. Box 9941
> Mail Stop 6734
> Ogden, UT 84409
> FAX: 801-620-6671

The IRS generally takes four to six weeks to respond, and will bill you for all charges. The cost will vary, depending upon the number of pages involved.

Beginning in late 1998, the IRS began issuing 990-PF tax returns on CD-ROM, replacing the microfiche format of prior years. Returns filed from 1998 on are now available in all Foundation Center libraries in an electronic database utilizing Alchemy® software. (For years prior to 1998, the New York and Washington, D.C. libraries maintained complete sets of information returns, and the Atlanta, Cleveland, and San Francisco libraries had sets of IRS returns for foundations in their regions.) Cooperating Collections that have IRS returns for foundations in their own states are indicated by a symbol in Appendix F. For a historical perspective, older 990-PFs are archived as part of the Foundation Center's historical collection at Indiana University-Purdue University.

In most states, private foundations are required to file a copy of their 990-PF with the attorney general or charities registration office. You may be able to obtain a copy of a 990-PF by contacting the appropriate office in the state where the foundation is located. For a list of the appropriate offices in all fifty states, see Appendix B.

Form 990: The annual information return (Form 990) filed by community foundations and most nonprofit organizations with the IRS is also available to the public. However, unlike Form 990-PF for private foundations, these forms are not available in Foundation Center libraries. They can be inspected in the nonprofit organization's office, or the nonprofit will mail a copy of its return to you. The nonprofit organization may charge you a "reasonable" fee to cover copying, postage, and handling costs. These annual information returns can also be obtained by writing to the same IRS office from which you receive annual information returns for private foundations (Form 990-PF). See the previous paragraphs for address, fax number, and procedures.

Foundation Publications

Many foundations issue brochures, pamphlets, news releases, or newsletters that provide information on application procedures, specific grant programs or recent grants, and announcements regarding changes in foundation staff and trustees. Although such publications are most frequently issued by large, staffed foundations, there are any number of smaller foundations that publish descriptive brochures in lieu of more extensive annual reports. These documents are more than a source of facts about the foundation; they are also a good medium for determining its "personality."

The Foundation Center's libraries collect as many foundation-issued documents and news releases as possible. Many of the Center's Cooperating Collections also collect publications issued by area grantmakers and make them available to the public. If you have identified grantmakers active in your subject field or geographic area, you may even be able to have your name added to the foundation's mailing list by writing or calling the foundation directly.

The most common grantmaker-issued publication is the annual report. Approximately 1,300 foundations issue such reports. Usually a foundation will mail you an annual report upon request. Generally, a foundation's annual report will provide the most complete and current information available about that foundation. Annual reports usually include detailed financial statements, a comprehensive list of grants awarded or committed for future payment, the names of officers and staff members, and a definition of program interests. Most annual reports also indicate the application procedures grantseekers should follow, including any application deadlines and particular proposal formats the foundation may prefer. Some annual reports include information on the foundation's donors in addition to essays on the operating philosophy that influences its grantmaking decisions. All of this information is useful to the grantseeker preparing a proposal to the foundation.

Foundations are not required by law to compile a separately printed annual report. Those that do tend to be community foundations and foundations with assets of $1 million or more. Entries in the general reference directories published by the Foundation Center—the *Guide to U.S. Foundations, The Foundation Directory, The Foundation Directory Part 2,* and *The Foundation 1000*—indicate whether a foundation issues an annual report. Foundation Center libraries maintain collections of annual reports issued by foundations in their local communities and by national foundations located elsewhere. Since few foundations issue separate reports, it is wise to check *FC Search* or the print resources in your Center library or Cooperating Collection before requesting reports from foundations that don't publish them.

At this time, copies of 990-PFs filed by private foundations are not on the Internet. However, several sites provide some information from the 990-PFs. The Internal Revenue Service's site (www.irs.ustreas.gov) is based on the IRS print publication, *Cumulative List of Organizations.* It lists nearly 500,000 nonprofit organizations and indicates which are private foundations and which are public charities.

Foundation Web Sites

Only a few foundations and corporate giving programs, about 600 in 1999 (plus about 200 grantmaking public charities), have a presence on the Internet. Most of these grantmakers have established their own Web sites; but close to fifty use the Foundation Folder initiative provided by the Foundation Center. Because some foundations do not have the staff or expertise to set up an independent Web site, the Foundation Center provides a Foundation Folder service whereby it puts information on its own site about the foundation. The foundation provides the information, and the Center sets up a folder at its site that contains the foundation's information. The goal of this service, which is provided without charge, is: (1) to provide individual foundations with an immediate presence on the World Wide Web and (2) to put more foundation information in front of a wider audience. Any domestic private, community, or company-sponsored foundation may make use of the service.

Those foundations that do maintain Web sites provide much of the information grantseekers have come to expect from print sources, such as annual reports, grants lists, application guidelines, and so forth. A few foundations provide their annual reports *only* on the Web, and this may be a growing trend.

Whether a foundation establishes and maintains its own site or asks the Foundation Center to establish a folder on its behalf, the Center helps the grantseeker identify foundations and corporate giving programs with Web sites by two means. First, *FC Search: The Foundation Center's Database on CD-ROM* allows you to link directly from a grantmaker record to its Web site. Second, the Center's own Web site (www.fdncenter.org) has links to the home pages or folders of foundations and corporate giving programs. Since grantmaker Web sites contain the most up-to-date information directly "from the horse's mouth," grantseekers should be sure to explore these resources. These Web sites are likely to become increasingly important information resources in the future.

SECONDARY RESOURCES

Secondary sources include information produced by some source other than the foundation or corporate giving program. Newspaper and periodical articles are the most often referred to secondary sources. From time to time, you may have seen articles about foundations in local newspapers and observed that while a few foundations seem to receive a great deal of press coverage, most are never mentioned. Occasionally, national magazines print articles on individual grantmakers or on foundations in general. One of the grantseeker's challenges has been to locate such articles. The Foundation Center utilizes clipping services and electronic search services to identify and locate relevant articles. This information is available free to the public at the Center's Web site.

Philanthropy News Digest

Philanthropy News Digest (*PND*), a weekly news service of the Foundation Center that appears at the Center's Web site, is a compendium, in digest form, of philanthropy-related articles and features culled from print and electronic media outlets nationwide. Articles most likely to be summarized in *PND* include notices of large grants, profiles of grantmakers, trends in philanthropy, and obituaries of philanthropists.

Each abstract summarizes the content of the original article. An abstract may include a "FCnote," which provides information from the Foundation Center's database regarding grantmakers mentioned in the original article. The information supplied in the FCnote at the end of the abstract is the most current available, and may represent information not yet published in print form that is subject to additional verification procedures. Each abstract also includes a citation of the source, which can help you find a copy of the original article through a library or document delivery service (see Figure 31).

In addition to summaries of searchable articles, *PND* also provides links to other Web sites relevant to the articles; reviews of books, CD-ROMs and other Web sites; and announcements of requests for proposals (RFPs).

Literature of the Nonprofit Sector

Since 1988, when a retrospective conversion of all the Center's library holdings was completed and a new bibliographic service unit was created, the Foundation Center has sought to increase public access to information on philanthropy and the nonprofit sector by identifying, indexing, and abstracting relevant books, periodical articles, and non-print resources such as CD-ROM and audiovisual materials. To this end, the Center established a computerized database and began issuing annual printed volumes of the *Literature of the Nonprofit Sector.*

The first volume of the *Literature of the Nonprofit Sector* was published in 1989 and annual supplements were published through 1996. All eight print volumes are available for reference in Foundation Center libraries and Cooperating Collections.

In lieu of printing a ninth volume, the Center released at its Web site the *Literature of the Nonprofit Sector Online,* a comprehensive searchable database that includes all the citations that would have appeared in print in the ninth volume and also cumulates the citations from the eight preceding volumes. The *Literature of the Nonprofit Sector Online* contains citations to materials collected by the Center's five libraries as well as selected literature from other sources. This authoritative, regularly updated bibliography of works in the field of philanthropy contains more than 17,000 bibliographic entries, of which approximately 60 percent (more than 10,000) have abstracts. The "New Acquisitions" section contains the latest additions to the database by subject category.

The ease with which one can search *Literature of the Nonprofit Sector Online* is its major advantage. All nine volumes can be searched simultaneously by subject, author, title, journal name, year of publication, and keyword.

Philanthropic Studies Index

Another resource that helps you locate secondary sources about foundations and fundraising is the Philanthropic Studies Index, compiled and maintained by the Special Collections Department of the Indiana University-Purdue University Indianapolis University Libraries. The Index is a reference to literature, primarily periodicals and research

Figure 31. Sample *Philanthropy News Digest* Entry with FCnote

PND (5/18/99) -- Report on Racial Discrimination Suggests Public Support for Remedies

CURRENT ISSUE . REVIEWS . RFPs . JOB CORNER . SEARCH PND . ARCHIVES . SUBSCRIBE . FC HOME

PND
front page

PHILANTHROPY NEWS DIGEST
Vol. 5, Issue 20
May 18, 1999

Headlines

Kellogg Foundation Launches
Service-Learning Project

America's Promise Releases *Report to the Nation 1999*

Goldman Fund Supports Campaign for
Tougher Gun Control Laws

Pew Charitable Trusts Give $2.4 Million for
Grassroots Activism Documentary Project

National Film Preservation Foundation
Announces Film Preservation Grants

Pew Environmental Health Commission to
Help Track Health Problems Linked to the
Environment

Commonwealth Fund Report Finds Racial
Disparities in America's Health Care System

Report on Racial Discrimination Suggests
Public Support for Remedies

Silicon Valley Donors Help Replace Lost
United Way Funding

Growth of "Alternative Funds" Provide
Choice in Workplace Giving

American Online's Steve Case Pledges $1
Million for Oklahoma Tornado Victims

Coca-Cola Foundation Expands "First
Generation" College Scholarship Program

Other Links

· · · · · ·

Search

The Foundation Center

Report on Racial Discrimination Suggests Public Support for Remedies

Remedies for Racial Inequality: The Public's Views, a new national study conducted for the Southern Regional Council and funded by the Charles Stewart Mott Foundation, finds that an overwhelming majority of Americans favor an array of policies to reduce racial inequality.

According to the report, people across the U.S. say that race relations are less than ideal, that racial inequality persists, and that reducing the gaps between racial and ethnic groups in schools, workplaces, and the political arena should be a national objective. While white and black respondents differ in their perception of the degree of discrimination that exists, both groups agree that inequality persists in employment, education, housing, and methods of electing public officials. The study also reveals strong support for anti-discrimination policies and for educational efforts to promote interracial cooperation, and indicates that young people feel more hopeful about the future of race relations than their elders.

"The Southern Regional Council will pursue these threads of hope through our Partnerships for Interracial Unity program," writes Wendy S. Johnson, executive director of the SRC, and Ellen Spears, project director, in their commentary on the report. "We hope that a clear understanding of public opinion about remedies for racial inequality will encourage elected and civic leaders at both the national and local levels to build on this public concern and support to advance policies that lead to an America 'as good as its promise.' "

FCnote: The **Charles Stewart Mott Foundation** (MI) had assets of $1,963,825,032 and made grants totaling $77,539,282 in the year ending 12/31/97.

"Seeking an America as Good as Its Promise — Remedies for Racial Inequality: the Public's Views." Southern Regional Council Announcement 5/99.

FC002702

http://fdncenter.org/pnd/990518/002702.html [7/22/1999 10:39:12 AM]

reports, on nonprofit organizations and the issues and topics concerning the nonprofit sector. It is available on the Internet (wwwnt.ulib.iupui.edu/psi/) and can be searched in a variety of ways, including by author, title, subject, or name headings. While the Index does not include abstracts, it is a resource for students of philanthropy.

Organization Files

Don't overlook your own organization's files. As stated in Chapter 4, data gathering and record keeping are essential components of fundraising. All information about donors—potential, past, present—should be kept in written files or electronically in a format that facilitates retrieval. If you have received letters from a foundation in the past, such communication should be noted in your database, and the letters should be kept in your fundraising files. Records of phone conversations are also important.

PEOPLE

People can be both primary and secondary sources. You can talk to grantmakers or their staffs directly or to people who know the grantmaker or know something about the grantmaker. Someone from your board may know someone on the board of the foundation you wish to approach. Personal contacts help—if for no other reason than to get information—but their impact varies.

It makes sense that foundations with staff and explicit guidelines and formal procedures are unlikely to require contacts, while foundations with no staff and no formal guidelines or procedures are more likely to be amenable to personal contact. However, this is not always the case. If you have contacts, use them judiciously. If you do not have contacts, begin the cultivation process.

Grantseekers without personal contacts need to build relationships and establish a local presence. Write a letter of introduction to the appropriate contact person at the targeted foundation; in this letter describe your program and express your interest in arranging a meeting. Ask if you should send a preliminary letter of inquiry or a full proposal. Whether or not you hear back from the foundation, occasionally send printed literature and articles about your program. Also, invite foundation decision makers to see your organization in action or to attend special events. Stay in touch, but don't be a nuisance. Establishing credibility and rapport with a funder takes time; cultivation is a long-term effort.

Public Forums

Formal, group information sessions are another possibility for obtaining donor information from people. Some foundations, such as the Kresge Foundation and the Community Foundation for Greater Atlanta, hold periodic forums for the grantseeking public. At these programs, the foundations present their mission and guidelines and respond to questions from the audience. Foundation Center libraries sponsor such information programs, usually gathering several grantmakers interested in a particular subject or type of support for a panel discussion, followed by a question and answer session. Such programs, called "Meet the Grantmakers" or "Dialogue with Donors," are held with varying degrees of frequency, but dates, times, and topics are announced in the library newsletters and on the Center's Web site. Some Cooperating Collections and some nonprofit resource centers also sponsor such forums.

Summary

In summary, there are many sources of information in many formats about the interests, limitations, policies, and procedures of independent and community foundations. You will want to become familiar with as many of them as possible to enable you to sift through the mass of information in order to compile your prospect list and to narrow that list to the most appropriate potential funders. The next three chapters are devoted to techniques for using these resources to compile your prospect list.

Chapter 6

Finding the Right Funder:
The Subject Approach

$\mathbf{A}$s indicated in Chapter 4, the first step to finding a funding partner is to develop a broad prospect list. You can do this by identifying foundations that are interested in your subject (subject approach), that give in the geographic area(s) served by your organization (geographic approach), and that award the type(s) of support your organization needs (type of support approach). You may employ all three approaches simultaneously when using an electronic database such as *FC Search: The Foundation Center's Database on CD-ROM*, or sequentially using a variety of print resources.

The subject approach to funding helps a nonprofit organization identify foundations with a common interest in: (1) its field of activity, (2) the population group it serves, and/or (3) the type of agency or organization it represents. A church providing services to children with AIDS, for example, would look for funders with these same interests.

Grantmaker interests generally are indicated in two ways: by the foundation's own description of its purpose and activities and by the giving priorities reflected in the actual grants it makes. Statements of purpose are often left deliberately broad by foundations to allow for future shifts in emphasis. Although they may provide important information about funders' giving priorities, they should not be taken as gospel. Instead, you should compare them to actual giving records. Statements such as "general charitable giving" and "to promote human welfare" don't really mean a foundation will support every imaginable type of charitable activity. Your best indication of what a foundation will support is often that which it has supported in the recent past. The databases, directories, annual reports, newsletters, Web sites, and other resources described in Chapter 5 will help direct you to both statements of purpose and to records of actual grants awarded.

Step One: Developing a Fields of Interest Prospect List

Before you begin to develop your prospect list of funders potentially interested in your subject area, take a few minutes to think about all the fields related to your organization's general mission or to the particular program or project you're trying to fund. For example, if you're working for a day care center that is planning a special program for parents on child nutrition, your list of subject terms might include day care, children, food, nutrition, boys, girls, and parental education. Scanning the subject indexes of publications such as *The Foundation Directory, The Foundation Grants Index,* and the subject headings appendix in the *FC Search User Manual* may suggest other applicable terms.

In developing your initial list, keep the focus broad. This is not the time to concentrate your search too narrowly. Remember, it is rare, and not necessarily desirable, to find a recently awarded grant that precisely matches your needs: a funder may not want to make a grant for a project that so closely duplicates one it just funded. If you restrict yourself to looking for exact matches, you'll end up overlooking potential funders interested in activities similar, although not identical, to your own.

As you research each foundation interested in your subject, focus on the basic facts outlined in the Prospect Worksheet (see Figure 11). Check to see that your organization operates in the geographic area where the foundation makes grants and that the foundation gives the type of support your organization needs. This will save time later. Subsequent chapters discuss in greater detail the geographic and types of support approaches to funding research.

USING REFERENCE SOURCES EFFECTIVELY

You may use several types of reference books, as well as electronic databases on CD-ROM and/or the Internet, to develop your initial prospect list. You will refer to indexes of foundation grants, national and state directories describing foundation giving interests and guidelines, and specialized funding guides in your subject field. All grantseekers develop their own research strategies; with experience, you will find the procedures and sequence that work best for you.

To avoid duplication of information from various reference sources, take time to read the introductory material explaining the coverage of each directory or database. Knowing, for instance, that *Grant Guides* are subsets of *The Foundation Grants Index* may prevent you from researching the same grants information twice.

GRANTS APPROACH

Indexes to foundation grants provide listings of actual grants awarded, enabling you to determine the specific subject interests of a foundation, the type and location of the organizations it has funded in the past, the size of the grants it has awarded, and the types of support it favors. The four indexes we discuss below are derived from the Foundation Center's database, which was described more fully in Chapter 5. This database tracks grants of $10,000 or more awarded by about 1,300 major foundations. Because many of these foundations make relatively large grants for programs that have a national focus, the indexes will be most helpful to grantseekers whose projects are of a size and scope to attract the interest of national or regional foundations.

If you have access to *FC Search*, its Advanced Grants file, containing approximately 200,000 grants for about 1,300 of the largest U.S. foundations, is the place to start. A foundation's grants for multiple years are usually included to help indicate funding patterns. The subject field is one of twelve criteria that can be searched in the Advanced Grants file. There is a pop-up index to help you select appropriate terms. You can also search for multiple subjects simultaneously. You can make your search broad by using "OR" as your Boolean operator, or narrow the search by using "AND" as the connector between subjects (see Figures 32 and 33). For instance, if you were trying to raise money for an art museum that caters to children, you would obtain a very broad list by searching for "arts" OR "children," as this would yield all grants covering the subject of art and all grants covering the subject of children. If you entered your subject search as "arts" AND "children," the resulting much smaller grants list would be composed of only those grants covering both arts and children.

Figure 32. Advanced Grants Search from *FC Search: The Foundation Center's Database on CD-ROM*

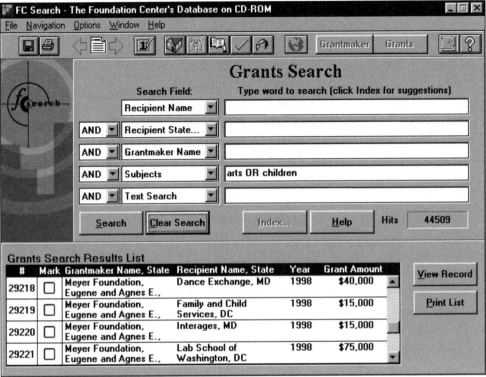

Several other search fields can be helpful in locating grants by subject: recipient name, recipient type, and text search. Foundations that have given grants to organizations that are similar to your own can be searched by organization name (Recipient Name) or by organization type (Recipient Type). If, for instance, you were interested in starting a club for children ages six to twelve years that emphasizes environmental awareness, you might look at who has been giving grants to the Boy Scouts or Girl Scouts (Recipient Name) or you might search for grants that have been awarded to "Boys & girls clubs" or to "Youth development, centers/clubs" (Recipient Types). To avoid spelling errors or incorrect names, use the index to select recipient names and recipient types rather than typing them in the box yourself.

If you do not have access to *FC Search*, you may want to begin your research into foundation grants by looking at the *Grant Guide* that is most applicable to your program.

Figure 33. Advanced Grants Search from *FC Search: The Foundation
Center's Database on CD-ROM*

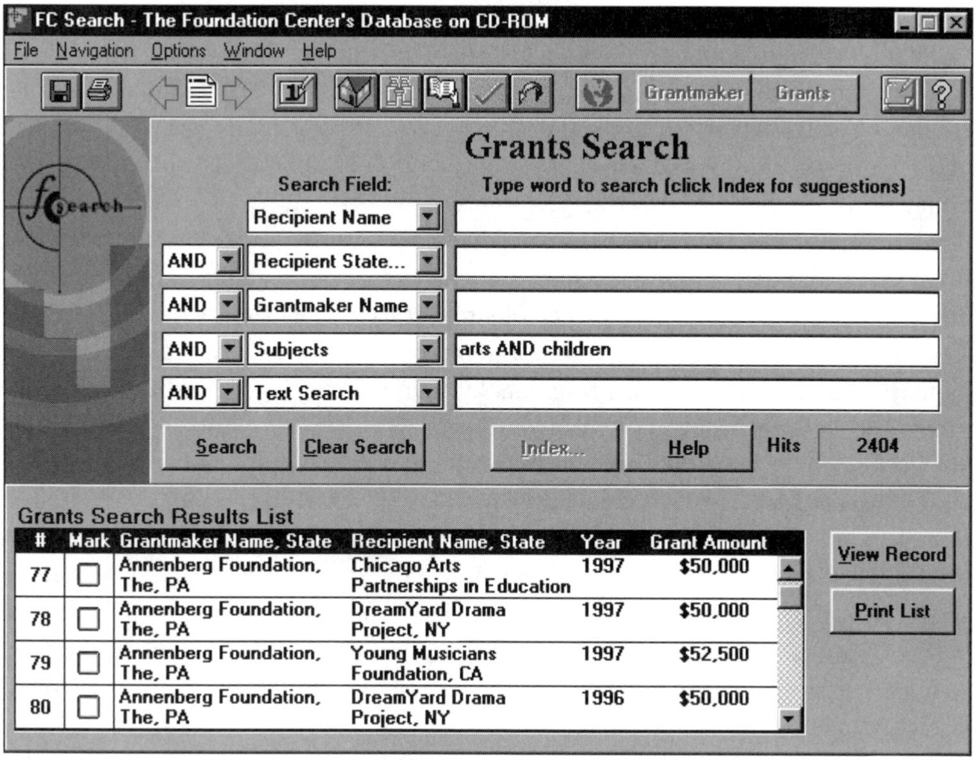

The thirty-five *Grant Guides,* published annually, are arranged alphabetically by foundation state and name. Each includes a list of foundations with their addresses and giving limitations, a subject index of keywords, an index of recipients organized by state, and an index of recipients organized by name.

Begin with the alphabetical list of foundations provided in the back of each book. This listing includes the foundation's address and a brief statement of any restrictions on its giving program. This will help you eliminate foundations that do not award grants in your geographic area. To complete your prospect worksheet—types of grant recipients, types of support awarded, and so on—scan the grants listed under foundations whose restrictions do not seem to prohibit them from funding your proposal.

The *Grant Guide* series will help you locate funders for your specific project, discover the grantmakers that favor your geographic area, and target foundations by grants awarded to other nonprofits, but you should bear in mind that these directories are not comprehensive. They cover recently awarded foundation grants of $10,000 or more. These grants are culled from a database of about 1,300 foundations.

Another path to foundations with a history of making grants in your subject area is *The Foundation Grants Index*. The *Grants Index* lists grants of $10,000 or more reported by about 1,300 foundations in the preceding year. It is particularly useful if your program or organization falls under a variety of subject fields, or if there is no appropriate *Grant Guide* for your subject area.

The *Grants Index* is divided into major subject fields, under which grants are arranged by foundation name and state. It includes indexes to grants listings by recipient name, specific subject focus, type of support categories subdivided by the state location of the grant recipient, type of recipient organization subdivided by the type of support awarded, and an index to grants by foundation. First, you should scan the grants lists of foundations located in your state. Then, check grants in your specific subject field in the Subject Index and Type of Support/Geographic Index. You will find the Subject Index to be very detailed. Not only will you find the topic "Children & youth," you will also find "Children & youth, *arts/culture/humanities*," and "Children & youth, *crime/abuse victims*," "Children & youth, *mentally disabled*," "Children & youth, *scholarships*," and many, many more. The Type of Support/Geographic Index will provide a list of more than thirty types of support. Finally, look for grants awarded to organizations similar to your own in the Recipient Name Index and the Recipient Category Index.

Again, you will want to check the size and nature of the grants the foundation typically makes in addition to the type and location of the organizations it supports. Note any giving-limitation statement provided immediately under the foundation's name.

GRANTMAKER DATABASES AND DIRECTORIES

At this point you may have developed a fairly long list of prospects. However, because the *FC Search* grants file and the Center's grants publications cover only 1,300 of the nation's major foundations, you've just gotten started. To expand your prospect list, turn to the grantmaker directories and databases. Include local foundation directories as well as national ones, and be especially alert to specialized subject directories in your field. As indicated previously, you'll find that indexes to foundation grants provide far more specific subject references than foundation directories, which usually employ a very general terminology to describe foundation program interests; as a result, the terms provided in their subject indexes are equally non-specific. For instance, the 1999 edition of *The Foundation Grants Index* lists more than forty-five variations of the subject "Music," whereas *The Foundation Directory* for the same year lists only three variations of "Music" (see Figures 34 and 35).

We suggest you begin with *FC Search* to identify grantmakers with relevant subject interests. The Grantmaker file on *FC Search* can help you identify the subject interests of nearly 50,000 foundations and corporate donors. On *FC Search*, there is both a Basic Grantmaker Search mode, which has five pre-selected means of searching the Grantmaker file, and the Advanced Grantmaker Search mode, which includes nine search criteria in addition to the defaulted fields. In both grantmaker modes, the subject field is called Fields of Interest. This field lets you select grantmakers who have a stated interest in a specific subject (art, health, religion, etc.) or who have shown an interest in a particular subject by the grants they have made. You can locate the fields of interest used, and the frequency with which the fields of interest appear in the database just by clicking on the pop-up index button. As with searching the Grants file, you can broaden or narrow your subject search by using "OR" or "AND."

If you prefer to work with books rather than with a computer, or if you do not have access to *FC Search*, we usually recommend that you begin your field of interest approach with the Foundation Center's *Foundation Directory*. The 21st edition of the *Directory* covers almost 10,000 foundations with at least $2 million in assets or grant programs totaling $200,000 or more annually, and includes a subject index subdivided by state to help you identify foundations that have expressed an interest in your subject field. Foundations with national or regional giving patterns appear in bold type under the state in which they are located; foundations that are restricted to local giving appear in regular type. As you check the references in your subject category, you should add to your prospect list foundations in your own state as well as those foundations in other states indicated in bold type. Make a note of the foundation's state and entry number so that you can refer back to the full entry later. Again, the full entry will provide the additional information you need to complete your prospect worksheet—that is, program interests, giving limitations, and the grant amounts typically awarded.

If your project is regional or national in scope, or of broad enough appeal to attract a major funder, your next stop should be *The Foundation 1000*, an annual publication that provides detailed analyses of the nation's largest foundations. *The Foundation 1000* includes a subject index that lists foundations under the subject fields expressed in the "Purpose" section of their entries. Once you have noted foundation names from the appropriate index categories, you should examine the actual foundation profiles to

Figure 34. Subject Index from *The Foundation Grants Index*

SUBJECT INDEX

7299, 7330, 7354, 7355, 7376, 7640, 7661, 7730, 7759, 7806, 7810, 7961, 7964, 7981, 8034, 8390, 8398, 8422, 8441, 8450, 8457-8459, 8555, 8582, 8644, 8677, 8877, 9011, 9216, 9217, 9410, 9593, 9607, 9633, 9641, 9665, 9671, 9906, 9935, 9958, 10013, 10046, 10097, 10099, 10207, 10325, 10362, 10482, 10515, 10548, 10556, 10568, 10569, 10582, 10685, 10698, 10742, 10800, 10803, 10804, 10859, 10873, 10967, 10969, 11269, 11277, 11413, 11423, 11585, 11590, 11595, 11620, 11654, 11664, 11795, 11801, 11841, 11898, 12034, 12045, 12054, 12055, 12099, 12171, 12172, 12284, 12316, 12474, 12758, 13069-13071, 13166, 13203

Music, equipment, 932, 999, 1021, 1035, 1681, 1985, 2947, 3161, 4486, 5159, 5172, 6318, 6358, 6362, 8045, 8046, 8156, 11058, 11083, 12429, 12474, 12723, 12848, 22648, 30501, 78222, 79321

Music, exhibitions, 3238, 6967, 10048

Music, faculty/staff development, 1982, 2391, 4310, 4363, 7631, 11590

Music, fellowships, 1434, 4003, 4019, 5397, 6881, 8095, 8783, 8784, 8790, 8887, 9093, 9225, 9374, 9556, 10158, 10162, 10178, 10182, 10183, 10189, 10190, 10205-10207, 10210, 11541

Music, film/video/radio, 995, 996, 1042, 1304, 1307, 2054, 2058, 2068, 2249, 3320, 3859, 4344, 8574, 9148, 10196, 10407, 10742, 10971, 11909, 11914, 12319, 12814, 68789

Music, gays/lesbians, 7286

Music, girls & young women, 974, 1418, 1560, 1622, 1895, 2212

Music, Hispanics, 7273, 11421, 11680, 11809, 11872, 11922, 84711

Music, immigrants/refugees, 13140

Music, income development, 1556, 1561, 1752, 1935, 2212, 2550, 3533, 3550, 3652, 4490, 5435, 5889, 6272, 6334, 7204, 7209, 7224, 9010, 9903, 10190, 10207, 10482, 11577, 11816, 12192, 12485

Music, internships, 9011, 9019

Music, management development, 1943, 2019, 2067, 3512, 5422, 7115, 7126, 7153, 7196, 7224, 7614, 8377, 8426, 9641, 10742, 11604, 11809

Music, mentally disabled, 50132

Music, minorities, 932, 1549, 3652, 3661, 4748, 5192, 6309, 6318, 6691, 6907, 6972, 7134, 7161, 7276, 7286, 7295, 7299, 7594, 8046, 8783, 8784, 8790, 9351, 9359, 9422, 9481, 10182, 10186, 12547, 12877, 13140

Music, performance/productions, 995, 996, 1003, 1396, 1561, 1778, 2055, 2068, 2178, 2217-2219, 2332, 2489, 2550, 2949, 4271, 4593, 4910, 5045, 5072, 5394, 5847, 6181, 6195, 6263, 6277, 6746, 6747, 6786, 6796, 6798, 6837, 6907, 6941, 6959, 6972, 6984, 7150, 7286, 7299, 7302, 7406, 7419, 7981, 8117, 8875, 8880, 8901, 9244, 9351, 9361, 9378, 9384, 9385, 9388, 9410, 9422, 9444, 9468, 9481, 9558, 9581, 9592, 9633, 9774, 10058, 10162, 10173, 10178, 10182, 10183, 10186, 10189, 10190, 10205-10207, 10210, 10315, 10469, 10513, 10548, 10556, 10568, 10569, 10571, 10578, 10641, 10642, 10659, 10722, 10776, 10844, 10873, 11153, 11168, 11338, 11388, 11392, 11577, 11595, 11669, 11854, 11883, 12054, 12298, 12306, 12429, 12514, 12547, 12597, 13039, 13203

Music, physically disabled, 7281, 28754

Music, professorships, 10640

Music, publication, 6795, 9083, 77793, 77854

Music, research, 1041, 4490, 6303, 9481, 77793, 77854

Music, scholarships, 1370, 1550, 1560, 1563, 3187, 3195, 4019, 4157, 4178, 4218, 4273, 5169, 7160, 7970, 10605, 10766, 11099, 12339, 12349, 13175, 28843, 33311, 33312, 33978

Music, seed money, 1558, 3187, 7522, 8877, 11413, 12171, 12547

Music, student aid, 2177, 4027, 4175, 9925, 11461, 11604, 11748, 13176, 32767

Music, women, 11392

Music, youth, 1549, 1612, 1985, 2420, 3985, 4015, 4273, 4607, 5192, 6023, 6200, 6824, 6984, 7145, 7286, 7640, 10003, 10099, 11654, 12390, 12474, 12758, 13166, 21512, 23747

Mutual aid societies, aging, 13553

Mutual aid societies, alliance, 13553

Mutual aid societies, association, 13553

Mutual aid societies, children & youth, 70081, 70091, 70092

Mutual aid societies, conferences/seminars, 70097

Mutual aid societies, economically disadvantaged, 70081, 70091, 70092

Mutual aid societies, formal/general education, 70097, 70098

Mutual aid societies, management/technical aid, 70082

Mutual aid societies, public education, 70062

Mutual aid societies, research, 70082

Mutual aid societies, women, 70062, 70081, 70091, 70092

Mutual aid societies, youth, 70097

Namibia, arts/culture/humanities, 9121

Namibia, civil rights, 9121, 68821

Namibia, community improvement/development, 41676, 68821-68824, 68895

Namibia, crime/courts/legal services, 41620

Namibia, education, 31461, 31535

Namibia, environment, 41620, 41676, 68822, 68823

Namibia, food/nutrition/agriculture, 68822-68824

Namibia, international affairs/development, 68714, 68821-68824, 68895, 68957

Namibia, public affairs/government, 68714

Namibia, religion, 77406

Namibia, social sciences, 68957

Native Americans, animals/wildlife, 5, 14065, 40056

Native Americans, arts/culture/humanities, 878, 1061, 1630, 1774, 2419, 2460, 2465, 2505, 2566, 2571, 2733, 2770, 2794, 3150, 3186, 3190, 3284, 3289, 3549, 3766, 3775, 3808, 4235, 4302, 4319, 4332, 4333, 4476, 4893, 5194, 5199, 5203, 5254, 5333, 5408, 5527, 5651, 5730, 5734, 6459, 6558, 6572, 6598-6600, 6624, 6633, 7271, 7272, 7557, 7569, 7601, 8669, 8730, 8907, 9349, 9354, 9360, 9369, 9411, 9420, 9453, 9464, 10026, 10062, 10152, 10170, 10184, 10405, 10816, 11183, 11186, 11229, 11746, 13097, 13816, 14065, 16014, 16883, 20234, 20827, 22095, 29404, 36949, 40073, 40720, 40721, 40746, 40751, 40752, 40757, 40853, 41753, 43258, 44870, 46932, 54461, 58767, 61765, 62020, 62305, 63125, 76167, 81120, 82113, 82289, 82408, 82456, 82775, 83421

Native Americans, civil rights, 5194, 9453, 13328, 13477, 13585, 13749, 13785, 13788, 13816, 13901-13905, 13925, 13999, 14038, 14053, 14065, 14154, 14280, 16883, 29393, 40059, 40065, 41499, 43962, 57429, 57979, 65484, 73552

Native Americans, community improvement/development, 5, 5734, 7557, 9453, 14053, 14584, 14630, 14674, 14716, 14947, 14962, 14968, 14986, 14988, 15198, 15223, 15382, 15503, 15992, 16014, 16032, 16190, 16198, 16199, 16212, 16241, 16291, 16435, 16570, 16571, 16794, 16804, 16805, 16831, 16838, 16849, 16850, 16876, 16883, 16889, 16942, 16949, 16969, 16970, 17224, 17355, 17404, 18116, 29411, 29937, 29961, 29984, 31470, 31490, 31491, 31519-31521, 39905, 40065, 40102, 40229, 40231, 41021, 41099, 41554, 41651, 41855, 42001, 43869, 59433, 62020, 63125, 84702, 84716

Native Americans, crime/courts/legal services, 13901-13903, 14053, 14154, 18189, 18375, 18567, 18865, 18866, 18890, 18902, 19063, 40005, 40079, 40819, 58072

Native Americans, education, 2571, 2733, 3190, 5203, 13816, 16942, 19938, 20234, 20478, 20484, 20827, 21436, 22064, 22093, 22095, 22105, 22193, 22194, 22200, 22201, 22205, 22220, 22227, 23030, 24750, 25750, 25751, 26328, 26331, 26333, 26560, 26639, 26900, 27118, 27247, 27346, 28042, 28244, 29214, 29280, 29372-29374, 29376, 29385, 29389, 29391, 29393, 29395, 29400-29402, 29404, 29407, 29409, 29411, 29419, 29484, 29614, 29635, 29638, 29642, 29652, 29653, 29661, 29682, 29722, 29728, 29937, 29961, 29984, 30410, 30681, 30847, 30851, 30853, 30855, 30979, 31075, 31221, 31228, 31439, 31462, 31470, 31490, 31491, 31519-31521, 31846, 31856, 31866, 31874, 31878, 31938, 31977, 31978, 31980, 32031, 32356, 32909, 33477, 33523, 33917, 34146, 34567, 35005, 35524, 35935, 36160, 36533, 36535, 36762, 36949, 37452, 37880, 40143, 40152, 40153, 40169, 40863, 40897, 40913, 41428, 42041, 45091, 45652, 58763, 62032, 62057, 74675, 77008, 78741, 80715, 81313, 81314, 81543, 84842

Native Americans, employment, 14986, 36762, 38517, 38520, 38523, 38543, 38574, 52263, 62369

Native Americans, environment, 7272, 13328, 13788, 14053, 14065, 14280, 14674, 14988, 16889, 39542, 39605, 39735, 39740, 39803, 39808, 39905, 39915, 40005, 40013, 40043, 40044, 40056, 40059, 40065, 40073, 40074, 40079, 40088, 40089, 40102, 40143, 40152, 40153, 40169, 40229, 40231, 40303, 40341, 40480, 40720, 40721, 40746, 40751, 40752, 40757, 40773, 40819, 40853, 40863, 40897, 40913, 41021, 41099, 41322, 41328, 41329, 41428, 41429, 41459, 41499, 41554, 41651, 41662, 41686, 41753, 41855, 41992, 41993, 42001, 42021-42023, 42041, 42127, 42426, 42475, 42493, 43258, 43424, 43497, 43962, 73552, 76167, 80715, 81872

Native Americans, food/nutrition/agriculture, 16838, 16970, 40089, 43424, 43497, 43869, 43960, 43962, 44191, 66939

Native Americans, health—general, 15992, 31866, 40043, 42493, 44190, 44191, 44208, 44209, 44372, 44374, 44375, 44433, 44441, 44536, 44810, 44825, 44870, 45091, 45652, 45745, 46008, 46161, 46886, 46932, 46946, 47075, 47093, 47136, 47138, 47621, 47658, 47935, 48533, 48876, 49777, 49778, 52800, 53841, 54447, 54763, 57492, 61765, 66939, 73552

Native Americans, health—specific diseases, 47075, 52800, 53760, 53841, 54422, 54447, 54448, 54454, 54460, 54461, 54763

Native Americans, housing/shelter, 18865, 55588, 55792, 55840, 55912, 56458, 56490, 56491, 56510, 56521, 56543, 56544, 56547, 56977, 62003

Native Americans, human services—multipurpose, 13749, 14584, 15382, 18567, 18890, 22093, 22193, 44433, 47136, 47138, 47621, 52263, 52797, 52800, 54448, 56521, 56543, 56544, 57359, 57409, 57429, 57492, 57979, 58072, 58461, 58661, 58763, 58767, 59433, 60220, 61744, 61765, 61864, 61947, 61988, 62002, 62003, 62015, 62018, 62020, 62032, 62056, 62057, 62067, 62069, 62070, 62077, 62079, 62111, 62115, 62125, 62149, 62160, 62217, 62233, 62285, 62286, 62291, 62305, 62339, 62367, 62369, 62398, 63125, 63873, 63964, 64328, 65484, 66939, 67124, 73310, 74164, 82408, 84843

Native Americans, international affairs/development, 40005, 40059, 41662, 59433, 70807, 73552

Native Americans, mental health/substance abuse, 18890, 22205, 22220, 52263, 52326, 52556, 52754, 52797, 52800, 52922, 52924, 52929-52931, 52937, 52975, 53001, 53010, 53020, 54422, 62057

Native Americans, philanthropy/voluntarism, 16032, 29374, 39542, 70339, 70807, 72060

Native Americans, public affairs/government, 5194, 7569, 13999, 14038, 14280, 14716, 16014, 16032, 16291, 16849, 16850, 22105, 26639, 29400, 29407, 29638, 38520, 40074, 40341, 42022, 42023, 73223, 73310, 73552, 74043, 74135, 74156, 74164, 74185-74187, 74327-74329, 74675, 76167, 82408

Native Americans, recreation/sports/athletics, 2566, 16883, 22095, 54461, 61988, 75627, 76167

2172 FOUNDATION GRANTS INDEX

Figure 35. Subject Index from *The Foundation Directory*

SUBJECT INDEX—Museums (history)

Florida: **Knight 1976**
Illinois: **Appel 2515, Knapp 2810**
Indiana: Blaffer 3105
Iowa: Kinney 3333
Maryland: Kay 3715, Stone 3797
Massachusetts: McDonough 4100
Michigan: Wilkinson 4625
Missouri: Uhlmann 5113
Nebraska: Kimmel 5187
Nevada: **Adelson 5231**
New Jersey: Todd 5610
New York: Davis 5991, Eig 6067, Gant 6180, Robbins 6974
Ohio: Fleischmann 7803
Oklahoma: Gaylord 8195, Oklahoman 8231
Oregon: Kuck 8305
Pennsylvania: Farber 8486, Fox 8505, RAF 8739
Rhode Island: Felicia 8927
Texas: Klein 9478
Vermont: Alcyon 9811

Museums (marine/maritime)

California: Grosvenor 548, Ingold 627
Florida: Kislak 1971, Palmer 2043
Hawaii: Alexander 2421
New York: **Silverburgh 7117**

Museums (natural history)

Colorado: **Marlon 1268,** Thomas 1311
Florida: **Knight 1976**
New York: Ellsworth 6073, Pauley 6851
Oregon: Kelley 8303
Washington: Ferguson 10042

Museums (science & technology)

Arizona: Dorrance 94
California: Ishiyama 634
Connecticut: Vance 1531
Florida: **Darden 1837, Knight 1976,** Saunders 2090
Illinois: Lake 2819
Massachusetts: McDonough 4100
New York: Hebrew 6330
Ohio: Rosenberry 8048
Texas: Kelley 9468, Lay 9486
Virginia: Holt 9893, Pauley 9956
Washington: Green 10055

Museums (specialized)

California: Witherbee 1150
Florida: Kislak 1971
Georgia: Staton 2390
Indiana: Met 3219
Massachusetts: DeMoulas 3933
Missouri: **Newman 5052**
New York: Gurwin 6284
Ohio: Smith 8096
Oklahoma: Morgan 8226
Texas: **Catto 9269,** Schissler 9627

Museums (sports/hobby)

Colorado: Ackerman 1172
Indiana: **Indiana 3184**
North Carolina: Ebert 7511

Music

Alabama: **Vulcan 75**
Arizona: Morris 112
California: Anderson 198, Arques 211, Bonner 271, Booth 273, **Bull 300,** Christensen 346, Colburn 350, Community 357, Copley 366, Disney 406, Femino 452, Firks 457, Fleishhacker 458, Fox 469, Getty 509, Gold 529, Gumbiner 556, Heller 584, Hewlett 595, Jewett 650, Knapp 678, Lurie 735, Lyons 739, Masserini 752, Murdy 811, **Nakamichi**

817, Osher 850, Pacific 859, **Packard 862, Pattiz 872,** Robinson 927, San Diego 945, **Seaver 971,** Skaggs 1004, Sonora 1022, Thornton 1071, Turk 1089, Weingart 1126, Whitelight 1140, Wood 1157, Zellerbach 1167, **Zimmer 1170**
Colorado: Bancroft 1179, Bernstein 1184, Boettcher 1188, El Pomar 1225, Gates 1232, Levy 1260, Schermer 1294, Shwayder 1297, Summit 1308
Connecticut: Carstensen 1352, Evans 1381, Heathcote 1412, **Kossak 1431, Lilybelle 1443, Perkin 1479,** Preston 1484, Schiro 1500, Smilow 1508
Delaware: Buckner 1557, Crystal 1566, Shrieking 1615
District of Columbia: Appleby 1624, Beech 1630, Beekhuis 1631, Bernstein 1638, Cafritz 1645, Carozza 1647, Delmar 1653, Dimick 1656, Nef 1721
Florida: Adams 1752, Beattie 1775, **Darden 1837,** Davis 1844, Holmes 1942, **Kapnick 1961,** Morningstar 2027, Russek 2082, Schultz 2095, **Shapiro 2103,** Thoresen 2137, Wiseheart 2169
Georgia: Arnold 2189, Exposition 2257, Georgia 2271, Jackson 2312, Schwob 2380, Zeist 2420
Hawaii: Frear 2439
Illinois: Abelson 2492, Allocation 2499, Bere 2535, **Dunard 2653,** First 2670, Goldberg 2706, Gray 2716, Grossinger 2724, Harris 2743, Hunter 2774, Kaplan 2796, Kemper 2805, Lederer 2826, Lill 2830, Mason 2848, McFarland 2859, Negaunee 2892, Sara 2973, Seid 2986, Shapiro 2990, **Shifting 2994,** Steigerwaldt 3015, Wilemal 3074, Wurlitzer 3088, Wyne 3089
Indiana: Clowes 3120, Griffith 3162, Honeywell 3178
Iowa: **Fisher 3318,** Hall 3321, Principal 3362, Siouxland 3367
Kansas: Brown 3385
Kentucky: Miller 3490, Opera 3494, Sutherland 3507
Louisiana: Powers 3567
Maryland: Adalman 3621, Blaustein 3641, Columbia 3659, First 3686, Freeman 3688, Gordon 3693, Hecht 3701, Lime 3734, Mulford 3755, Procter 3771, Rosenberg 3778, Rothschild 3782, Unger 3806
Massachusetts: Babson 3838, **Cabot 3877, Clark 3893,** Daniels 3927, Filene 3966, Goldberg 3984, Harvard 4002, High 4014, Little 4080, **One 4130,** Overly 4134, Pechet 4146, Phillips 4155, Prouty 4164, Ratshesky 4173
Michigan: Berrien 4313, Community 4342, Earl 4385, Eddy 4386, Shapero 4562, Shelden 4563, Welch 4613, Westerman 4615
Minnesota: Adams 4638, Andersen 4645, Baker 4654, Bush 4672, Carlson 4678, Duluth 4698, General 4712, Heilmaier 4730, Honeywell 4734, Jerome 4737, Musser 4774, O'Shaughnessy 4787
Mississippi: Hearin 4883
Missouri: Bloch 4912, Carter 4931, Garvey 4966, Gateway 4967, Gaylord 4968, General 4970, Kauffman 5002, Pulitzer 5074, Silva 5089, Sosland 5093, Stern 5100
Nebraska: Baldwin 5151
Nevada: **Buck 5238,** Hall 5252, Wiegand 5285
New Hampshire: **Penates 5311,** Smyth 5316
New Jersey: Bunbury 5358, Dodge 5388, Greenblatt 5421, Holzer 5437, Maneely 5500, **Merrill 5511,** Public 5547, Sunfield 5598
New Mexico: McCune 5653, Santa Fe 5660
New York: **AT&T 5721, Augustine 5727,** Bagby 5740, Baird 5744, Barker 5756, Barrington 5759, Bayne 5766, Berlin 5783, Bezalel 5792, Blum 5810, Bravmann 5823, Burns 5845, Cary 5865, **Chazen 5891,** Chernow 5894, **Cintas 5905,** Clark 5917, Combe 5936, Constans 5945, **Copland 5950,** Cowles 5958, Cremona 5964, Diamond 6011, Diker 6016, Earle 6048, Eckert 6054, **Edmonds 6059,** Ferkauf 6110, Fifth 6115, **Ford 6135,** Gilliam 6196, **Gilman 6197,** Goldsmith 6229, Good 6239, Gramercy 6253, Greene 6262, Hackett 6291, Harrison 6313, **Hauser 6319, Heineman 6333,** Henfield 6337, Herbert 6339, **Hermione 6340,** Hillman 6356, Kaplan 6461, Kellen 6478, **Koussevitzky 6529,** Kranes 6532, Krimendahl 6538, Liberman 6589, Loewe 6610, **MacDonald 6634,** Marcus 6648, Martinson 6663, Mercy 6709,

Merlin 6710, **Metropolitan 6714,** Millard 6721, Morse 6741, Moses 6744, Netter 6766, **Newhouse 6781,** Noble 6788, Olive 6814, Orvis 6821, **Paul 6850,** Phaedrus 6874, Pines 6884, Pope 6896, Reed 6936, Rhulen 6954, Samuels 7048, Scaturro 7057, Scherman 7065, Schneider 7074, **Schwartz 7086,** Sharp 7103, Smith 7141, Springate 7178, **Sullivan 7225,** Thompson 7257, Thomson 7258, Tisch 7266, **Trust 7284,** Tuch 7286, Tully 7288, U.S. 7291, Ungar 7293, Vidda 7314, **Wallace 7325,** Weiler 7344, **Weill 7346,** Western 7369, Wilson 7388, Wilson 7391, Zesiger 7428
North Carolina: Biddle 7451, Bryan 7462, Covington 7492, Ficklen 7516, Gambrell 7526, Gambrill 7527, Ginter 7531, Halton 7539, Rogers 7623, Triangle 7648
Ohio: Alms 7680, Bares 7695, Callahan 7728, Drinko 7777, Franklin 7813, **Goodrich 7834,** Gund 7843, Iddings 7878, Ireland 7881, Kulas 7908, Muskingum 7980, Nippert 7991, Northrup 7995, Reinberger 8034, Schwebel 8070, Simmons 8093, Smith 8096, Soo 8101, Standard 8106, Thendara 8123, Van Wert 8139, Youngstown 8174
Pennsylvania: Arcadia 8350, Aristech 8352, Arronson 8356, Bergen 8378, Bristol 8400, Campbell 8415, Day 8452, Dietrich 8460, Dolfinger 8462, **First 8495,** Greenfield 8530, Kardon 8595, Miller 8682, **Pew 8721, Presser 8733,** Roberts 8752, Rockwell 8758, Ross 8765, Saunders 8776, Smith 8810, Steinman 8831, Stockton 8837, Superior 8844, Teleflex 8850, **Whitaker 8886,** Willis 8893, Wyomissing 8900
South Carolina: Central 8988, Magill 9013, Symmes 9036
Texas: Bass 9227, Brochstein 9246, Cain 9262, Constantin 9297, Dougherty 9332, Fikes 9366, Harvey 9421, Huthsteiner 9453, McQueen 9529, Oppenheimer 9556, Pangburn 9564, Rockwell 9609, Rowan 9615, Rupe 9616, **Scaler 9624,** Schissler 9627, Shell 9637, **Starling 9659,** Stemmons 9661, **Tobin 9685**
Utah: Bastian 9755, Huntsman 9781
Virginia: Fralin 9875, Portsmouth 9960
Washington: Archibald 10015, Bishop 10020, Johnston 10071, **Kongsgaard 10078,** Kreielsheimer 10080, Matlock 10091, Norcliffe 10101, Wasmer 10146, Wenatchee 10148, Wright 10154
West Virginia: Clay 10162
Wisconsin: Oshkosh 10330, Pick 10339, Schoenleber 10367, Shattuck 10373, Wisconsin 10412
Wyoming: Hirschfield 10424

Music, choral

New York: Phaedrus 6874, **Potamkin 6901**
Ohio: Stranahan 8114
Pennsylvania: Ryan 8770

Music, ensembles & groups

Minnesota: Musser 4773

Native Americans

Alaska: **CIRI 83,** Rasmuson 85
Arizona: DeGrazia 93
California: **American 192,** California 316, Community 357, **Handsel 571,** Stern 1039
Colorado: **U S WEST 1316**
Connecticut: Culpeper 1364, Dibner 1371, **Educational 1376, Ettinger 1380,** Huisking 1419, Woodward 1545, **Xerox 1547**
Delaware: **Raskob 1608**
District of Columbia: Delmar 1653, Szekely 1737
Florida: Bush 1803, Thoresen 2137
Illinois: Fel-Pro 2666
Iowa: Siouxland 3367
Maryland: **Hughes 3710**
Massachusetts: Community 3902, High 4014, Hyams 4035, **Kendrick 4056**
Michigan: Grand Rapids 4420, India 4447

complete your prospect worksheet. Note especially the giving restrictions printed in bold type under each foundation entry.

As we noted in Chapter 5, state and local foundation directories issued by a wide range of publishers are another good resource, although they do vary in content and coverage. When using them, you should examine the most current edition of each relevant directory and identify potential funding sources through the subject index, where provided, or by scanning the entries themselves.

NATIONAL GUIDES

The Foundation Center publishes a number of directories focusing on the major funders and giving trends in a specific subject area or population group. Drawing on information gathered in *The Foundation Directory, The Foundation Directory Part 2, The Foundation Grants Index*, and the *National Directory of Corporate Giving*, the *National Guides* combine descriptive financial information with grants records for foundations operating in selected fields. They also include introductions, indexes, and specialized reading lists prepared from the Center's bibliographic database. They bring together in one convenient format information from various other Center publications. The subjects and population groups covered by the *Guides* are listed in Chapter 5. Appendix E provides annotations for each volume, including coverage, edition, etc.

SPECIALIZED FUNDING GUIDES

The final step in developing your subject prospect list is to examine specialized funding guides and Web sites devoted to your field. For instance, if you need funds for a hospital, cancer research, or health services for women, you may want to refer to the *Directory of Health Grants*, published by Research Grant Guides, Inc. of Loxahatchee, Florida. If your interest is the arts, you may find appropriate funding information on the Web at the Arts Over America site (www.nasaa-arts.org/new/nasaa/aoa/aoa_contents.shtml) or the Arts Wire site (www.artswire.org). A listing of some of the major specialized funding guides available in Foundation Center libraries is provided in Appendix A. Professional journals in your field may include information about other guides. While these guides vary tremendously in their currency and content, they can be helpful in identifying additional prospects.

Step Two: Refining Your List

You should now have a lengthy list of foundations that might possibly be interested in funding your project or program. Now is the time to refine the list to a reasonable number of grantmakers who would probably look favorably on your program. You should review your subject prospect list to eliminate those foundations that do not give in your geographic area and that do not award the type of support your organization needs. If you used *FC Search* to construct your list, you probably used multiple search criteria, thereby completing this step already. Completing the prospect worksheet for each potential funder enables you to quickly discard those least likely to fund your project.

Now that you have determined that the funders on your list have demonstrated a real commitment to funding in your subject field and geographic area and providing the type of support your organization needs, you are ready to scrutinize your list further to determine those potential funders who are most likely to be interested in your organization or program or project. You'll want to do as much research on all aspects pertaining to these grantmakers as time and resources permit. Posing the questions raised in Chapter 4 is a good place to start:

- Does the funder accept applications?

- Does the amount of money you are requesting fit within the funder's typical grant range?

- Does the funder put limits on the length of time it is willing to support a project?

- What type of organizations does the funder tend to support?

- Does the funder have application deadlines, or does it review proposals continuously?

- Do you or does anyone on your board know someone connected with a potential funder?

Most of these questions can be answered by referring to any one of several resources. *FC Search: The Foundation Center's Database on CD-ROM* will answer many of them. Directories such as *The Foundation Directory* or *The Foundation 1000* or some of the state and local directories will also provide many of the answers you need. For application deadlines and the names of trustees, officers, or donors, Center directories and databases are excellent sources.

On occasion you will need to refer to primary sources such as the IRS Form 990-PF, and annual report or application guidelines. Although grantmakers may say they are interested in a particular subject, if they have not made grants in that field for several years, their commitment may not be very strong. Look at the grantmaker's most recent list of grants awarded. Then compare it with the lists from the past two to three years to provide the most comprehensive analysis. For the larger foundations, you can get a fairly comprehensive look at their grants on *FC Search* and in *The Foundation 1000*. A foundation's annual report, if it publishes one, will usually provide a comprehensive list of grants awarded. Because the IRS requires a foundation to list all of its grants on the 990-PF, that tax return is your best source for comprehensive information about grants awarded, particularly for smaller grantmakers and those that do not publish an annual report. Annual reports and 990-PFs can be found in Center libraries and in many Cooperating Collections. If you are a member of the Foundation Center's Associates Program, Center reference staff members will look up information on a foundation's 990-PF and either read it to you over the phone or fax the appropriate page to you. Some information taken directly from the 990-PFs can be found at GuideStar (www.guidestar.org) or at the Internal Revenue Service's site (www.irs.ustreas.gov/prod/bus_info/eo/eosearch.html).

On still other occasions, secondary sources such as articles in newspapers and journals will provide the answers you need. *Philanthropy News Digest* (*PND*), the Foundation Center's weekly online summary of the news of the world of philanthropy, is a searchable database that allows you to seek recent information about foundations and their philanthropic efforts. *PND* summaries will also inform you of changes in leadership, very recent major grants, and other such information. You may wish to employ *PND's* search engine to enter the name of the foundation in question and see what, if anything, has been reported about this funder's recent gifts. Another source of information on recently awarded grants is the "Guide to Grants" at the *Chronicle of Philanthropy's* Web site (www.philanthropy.com/grants/). This database puts the grants lists published in the *Chronicle of Philanthropy* during the previous two years into a searchable format.

A review of the resources described in Chapter 5 will help you to decide which directory, annual report, IRS return, application guidelines, etc. will best assist you in answering the specific questions necessary to refine your list to the most likely prospects. When you have answered these questions about the funders on your broad prospect list, you will have narrowed your list to the few that you should approach.

Summary

A grantmaker's fields of interest are indicated by its own description of its purpose and activities and by the giving priorities reflected in the actual grants made. There are a variety of materials available to the grantseeker to develop a broad prospect list based on common subject interests. Once you have developed a list of potential funders interested in your subject, it is very important to find out if those funders give in your geographic area and if they provide the types of support your organization needs. The next two chapters will further explore the geographic and types of support approaches.

Chapter 7

Finding the Right Funder: The Geographic Approach

The phrase "charity begins at home" sums up the most typical pattern of foundation funding: philanthropy focused on the funder's home base has been a reality since its earliest days. Of the nearly 16,200 foundations tracked by the Foundation Center in the 1999 editions of *The Foundation Directory* and *The Foundation Directory Part 2*, approximately 80 percent restrict their giving to a specific state or multi-state region. Although some of the larger, better known foundations tend to break out of this pattern, most have a strong commitment to funding local nonprofits that serve their communities.

For these reasons, nonprofits interested in attracting foundation funding should learn as much as possible about the funders in their own backyard, both large and small. This is particularly important if you are seeking relatively small grants or funds for projects with purely local impact. Often, it will be possible to build a funding structure calling upon a variety of components. For example, you might approach local foundations for small grants in the $100 to $5,000 range for continuing operating support, while approaching larger foundations in your field when introducing a special project.

You are likely to discover that many small foundations give to the same organizations year after year and rarely make grants to new recipients. Don't let this fact deter you from investigating all local sources. Some of your work with potential funders—what professional fundraisers call "cultivation"—can and should be viewed as a learning experience. Making local grantmakers aware of the services you are providing and the ways in which your organization enhances life in their home community can only benefit you in the long run.

Step One: Developing a Geographic Prospect List

Developing a list of foundations that are either located in or fund projects in your city or state is relatively easy. The resources available include electronic databases, grantmaker directories, and indexes of foundation grants. Keep in mind, however, that simply sharing the same zip code is not reason enough to request funds from a foundation. Once identified, each foundation must be fully researched to see if its grantmaking activities match up in other ways with your program or project. Whether you are focusing on large or small foundations, you'll want to begin your search with local or state directories. (See the bibliography of state and local directories in the most recent edition of the *Guide to U.S. Foundations, Their Trustees, Officers, and Donors*.) If there are several directories for your area, use them all until you are able to determine through your research which are more current and/or comprehensive.

If your organization is located in New York State, Washington, D.C., or Missouri, consult the Foundation Center state directories covering those three states. *New York State Foundations* (6th edition, 1999) includes more than 6,000 foundations currently active in New York, plus more than 1,000 out-of-state grantmakers with a documented interest in New York. It is arranged and indexed by county, providing an additional point of access to foundations headquartered in your immediate area. *Guide to Greater Washington D.C. Grantmakers* (3rd edition, 1998) provides grantmaker portraits of 1,200 foundations, public charities, and corporate giving programs in the D.C. area. The *Directory of Missouri Grantmakers* (3rd edition, 1999) provides information on approximately 1,000 foundations, corporate giving programs, and public charities in Missouri.

As you add foundation names from state or local directories to your prospect list, be sure to fill in the appropriate information on your prospect worksheet. Note, in particular, any restrictions on a foundation's giving program that would prevent it from funding your project. Some of the smaller foundations are restricted by will or charter to giving to only a few designated or "preselected" organizations. Others may not fund projects in your subject area or may not be able to offer the type or amount of support you need.

GRANTMAKER DATABASES AND DIRECTORIES

Once you have investigated relevant state or local directories, you will want to search the more comprehensive grantmaker directories, such as *FC Search: The Foundation Center's Database on CD-ROM*, or the Center's print directories *The Foundation 1000*, *The Foundation Directory*, and *The Foundation Directory Part 2*.

If you have access to *FC Search*, it is the place to begin because it is comprehensive and because you can conduct searches using multiple points of entry, such as fields of interest and geographic focus. If you simply want to identify those foundations located in the state where your organization is based or where your program takes place, use the Basic Grantmaker Search mode in the Grantmaker file on *FC Search*; one of the default search fields is Grantmaker State. To locate grantmakers in your geographic area, you can also search by zip code in the Basic Grantmaker Search mode. Enter the state in the Grantmaker State field and the zip code in the Text Search field (see Figure 36). It is also possible to search by telephone area code in the Text Search field (see Figure 37). See the *FC Search User Manual* for instructions on using the Text Search field.

In the Advanced Grantmaker Search mode, you can perform all the searches above, and you also have additional options. You can search by the city in which the grantmaker is located and/or by the states in which the grantmaker has a stated interest in giving or a history of giving. Searching by Grantmaker City can be of great assistance in locating foundations in your home town. Be aware, however, that a foundation's headquarters may well be located in a suburban municipality of an urban area. For instance, if the organization for which you seek funding is located in Atlanta and you conducted a search for grantmakers actually located in Atlanta, you would miss out on some potentially good prospects that give in the greater Atlanta area, but are physically located in the suburbs of Tucker or Norcross or Roswell.

Geographic Focus is the field that notes the states in which the foundation indicates it is interested in giving. In addition to the names of all fifty states, the Geographic Focus field has two generic terms that can be helpful—national and international. Grantmakers who designate "national" as their geographic focus are interested in funding projects in many states. Grantmakers who designate "international" as their geographic focus give both to U.S.-based nonprofits that are concerned with international issues and/or to nonprofits that provide services outside the United States.

Figure 36. Basic Grantmaker Zip Code Search from *FC Search: The Foundation Center's Database on CD-ROM*

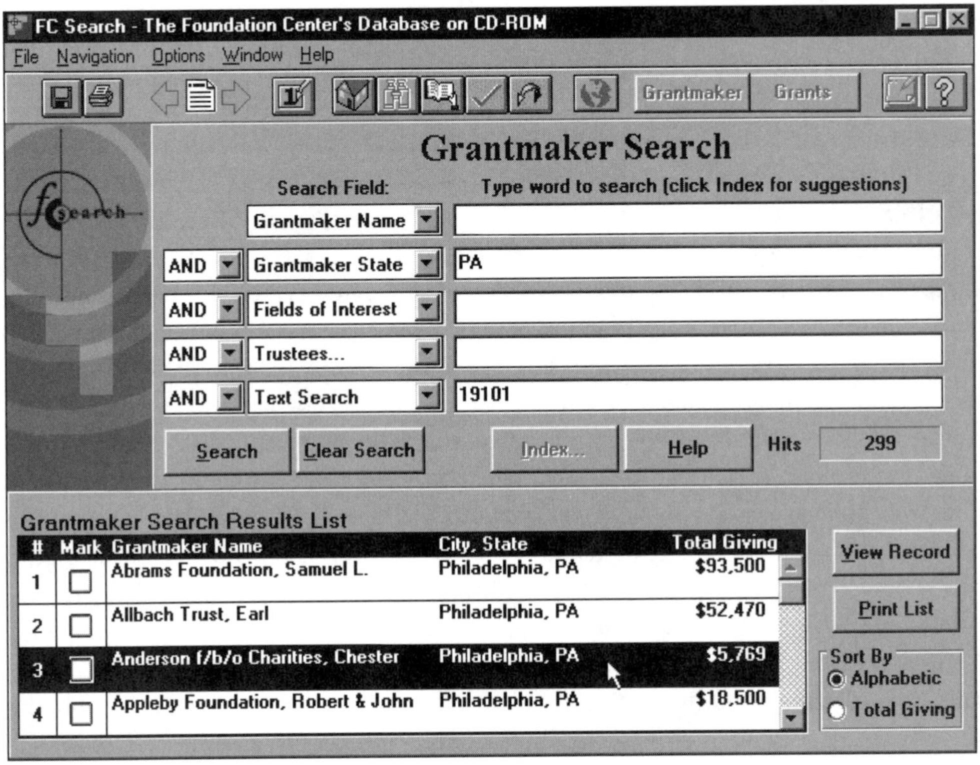

Because geographic focus is not available for all foundations, it is a good idea to conduct two geographic searches, one using Grantmaker State and the other using Geographic Focus (see Figures 38 and 39), and then compare your results.

The print directories—*The Foundation 1000*, *The Foundation Directory*, and *The Foundation Directory Part 2*—have indexes that group foundations by the state and city in which they maintain their principal offices. The names and entry numbers of foundations that make grants on a regional, national, or international basis appear in boldface. For these funders you can adopt an approach based on subject interest rather than geography (see Figure 40). Those foundations that give locally or in a few specified states are listed in regular type. Users interested in local giving within their state should check the series of "see also" references at the end of each state section. These

Figure 37. Basic Grantmaker Telephone Area Code Search from *FC Search: The Foundation Center's Database on CD-ROM*

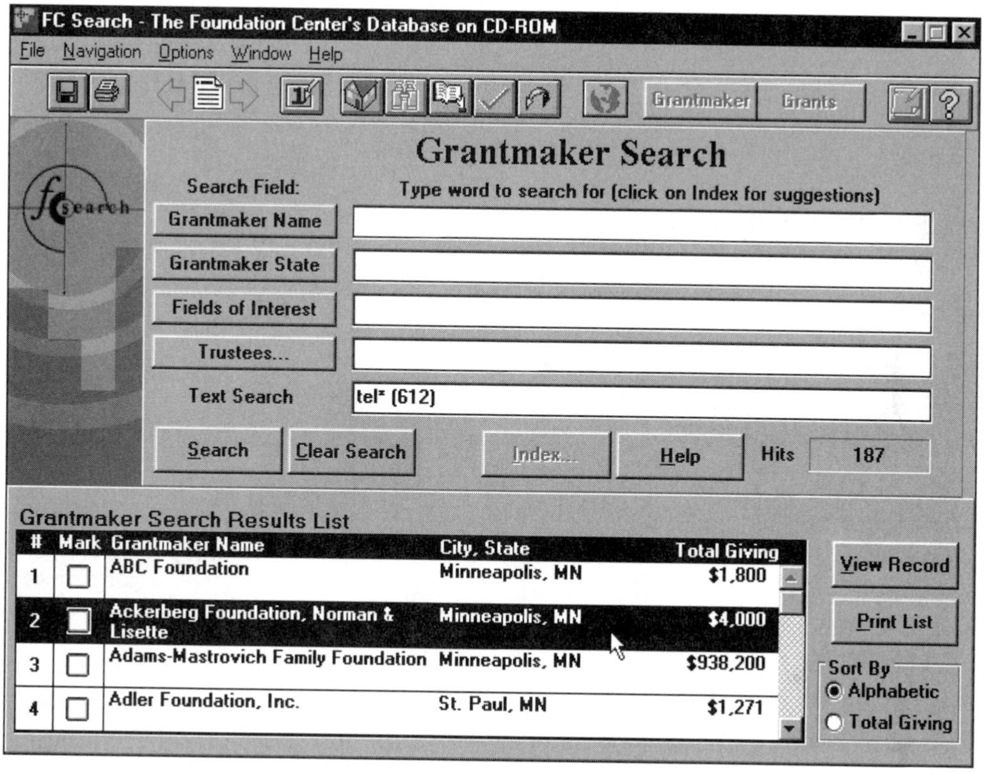

cross-references identify foundations that may be located elsewhere but have a history of grantmaking in your state.

If your search focuses on smaller foundations in your local area, your next stop should be the *Guide to U.S. Foundations, Their Trustees, Officers, and Donors*, the only Center print directory that offers access to the more than 46,000 active grantmaking foundations in the United States. The *Guide to U.S. Foundations* is arranged by state and, in descending order within states, by annual grant totals. Although the information presented in the *Guide to U.S. Foundations* is abbreviated, it does allow you to make some preliminary determinations about each foundation based on its size, location, and principal officer.

When you identify foundation prospects from the *Guide to U.S. Foundations*, be sure to note the Employer Identification Number (EIN). This number will help you locate

Figure 38. Advanced Grantmaker/Grantmaker State Search from *FC Search: The Foundation Center's Database on CD-ROM*

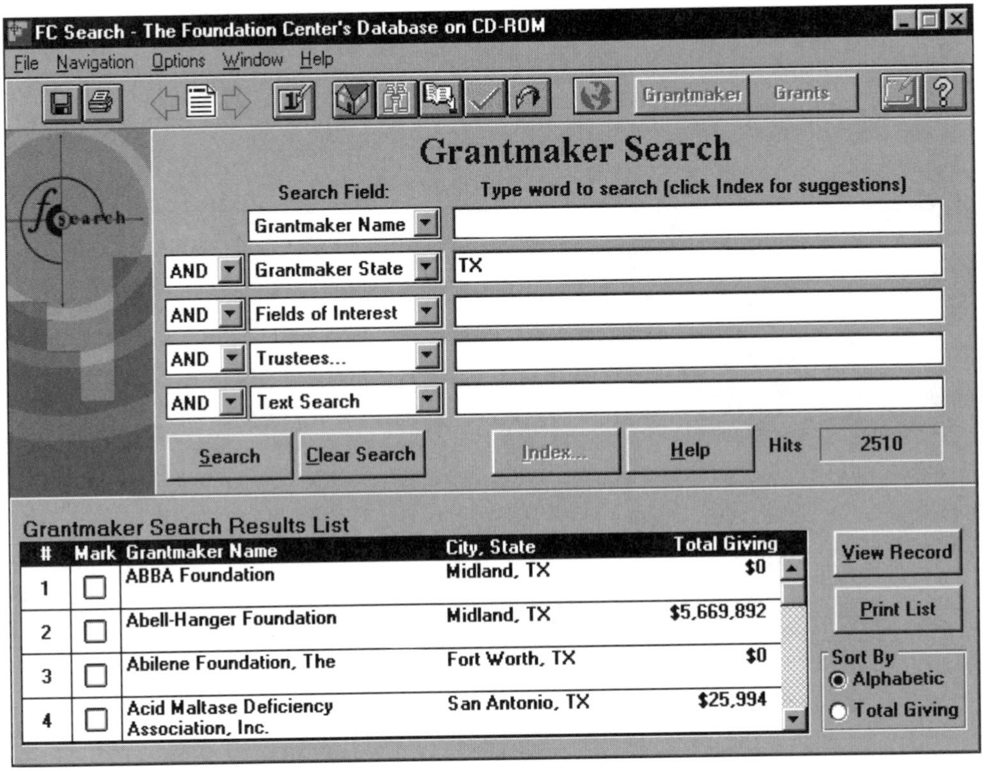

the foundation's annual IRS information return (Form 990-PF), generally the best and sometimes the only source of information about the giving programs of foundations too small to be included in *The Foundation Directory* or *The Foundation Directory Part 2*. More details about the contents of Form 990-PF appear in Chapter 5.

The *Guide to U.S. Foundations* also includes all currently active community foundations, which can be valuable resources for funding local projects. In addition to financial support, many community foundations provide technical assistance to nonprofit organizations in areas such as budgeting, public relations, fundraising strategies, and management.

Figure 39. Advanced Grantmaker/Geographic Focus Search from *FC Search: The Foundation Center's Database on CD-ROM*

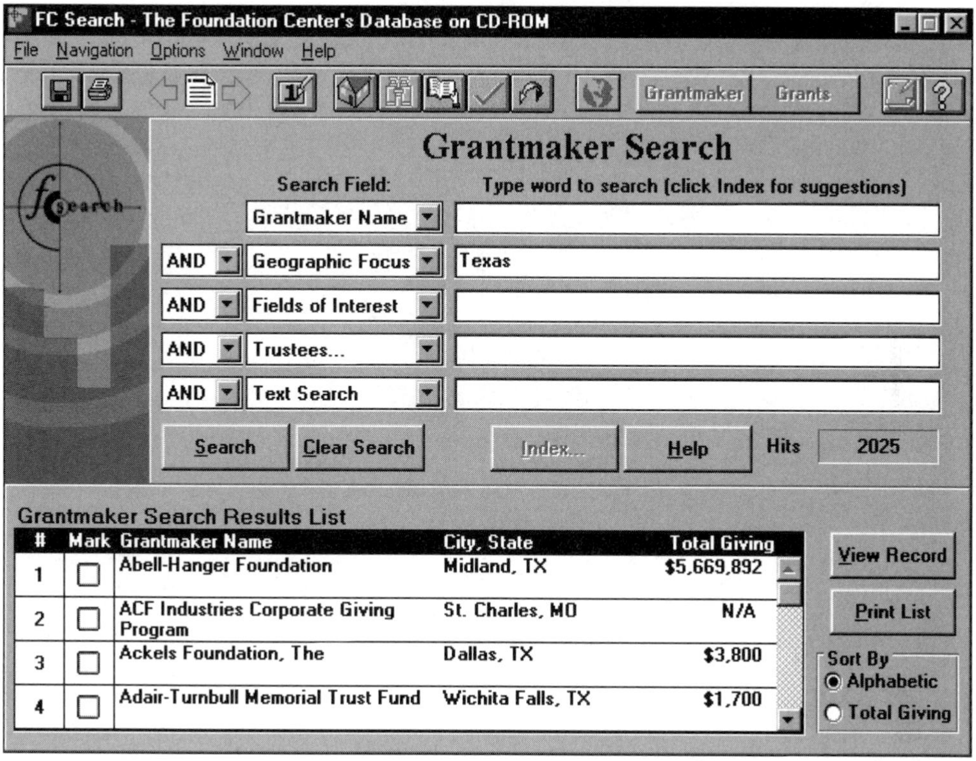

GRANTS APPROACH

By this point, you have probably uncovered a large number of foundation prospects through your geographic search. Before you complete this phase of your research, you should check the various indexes of foundation grants to identify foundations (including those that may not be based in your locale) that have actually awarded grants to organizations in your area.

The Grants file on *FC Search: The Foundation Center's Database on CD-ROM* can be searched quickly to determine which foundations have actually awarded grants in your area. In the Recipient State field, enter your state (see Figure 41). One of the advantages of searching *FC Search* is that you can also enter your subject and search for both geographic limitations and subjects of interest simultaneously.

Figure 40. Subject Index from *The Foundation Directory*

10366, Schoenleber 10367, Schroeder 10368, Seramur 10371, **786 10372**, Shattuck 10373, Shattuck 10375, Siebert 10376, Smith 10378, Straz 10382, Tallman 10387, Taylor 10388, Universal 10393, Vilter 10394, Wagner 10396, **Wagner 10397**, Wausau 10400, Wausau 10401, Wauwatosa 10402, **Weyenberg 10407**, WICOR 10408, **Wildwood 10409**, Windhover 10410, Wisconsin 10411, Wisconsin 10412, Wisconsin 10413, Wood 10414, Ziegler 10417, Ziemann 10418
Wyoming: Goodstein 10423, Hirschfield 10424, Johnson 10425, Lightner 10428, Sargent 10433, **Seeley 10436**, Storer 10439, Surrena 10440, Tonkin 10441, True 10442, Weiss 10443

Human services, emergency aid

California: Forest 463
District of Columbia: Spring 1733
Florida: Conn 1830
Maryland: **O'Neil 3763**
Minnesota: Deluxe 4694
Missouri: Trio 5111
North Carolina: Coffey 7483
Pennsylvania: Plankenhorn 8727

Human services, fund raising

New Jersey: **Eternity 5400**

Human services, mind/body enrichment

Massachusetts: Roehr 4188
Michigan: Cook 4346

Human services, personal services

Alabama: Larkins 48

Human services, reform

California: Rosenberg 934

Human services, self-help groups

Missouri: Fox 4962

Human services, special populations

California: Byers 311, Rivkin 922, Segal 975, Shaklee 982
Connecticut: DeDominicis 1366, Pfriem 1481
Delaware: Robson 1610, Shandle 1613
District of Columbia: Willard 1745
Florida: Bishop 1788, **Pucci 2059**
Georgia: Jackson 2312
Illinois: Berner 2536, Coleman 2609, Foglia 2676, Petersen 2921
Indiana: Magee 3212, McMillen 3217
Massachusetts: Doyle 3941, Ham 3996, Memorial 4104
Minnesota: Deluxe 4694, Minnesota 4770, O'Brien 4785
Nebraska: Hirschfeld 5179
New York: Bodman 5812, Bulova 5839, **Culpeper 5971, Eisner 6070**, Schweitzer 7090
Pennsylvania: Briggs 8399, Plankenhorn 8727
Rhode Island: Hodges 8935
South Carolina: Gibbs 8998
Texas: Butcher 9257, **Cornerstone 9301**, SBC 9623
Virginia: **Alburger 9828**
Washington: Allen 10010, Norclife 10101
Wisconsin: Demmer 10236, LUX 10302

Human services, victim aid

Michigan: Dart 4356
New York: **Schnurmacher 7076**

Humanities

Alabama: **Vulcan 75**
California: Ahmanson 180, Community 356, Foundation 466, Haas 559, **Lewis 719**, Norman 828, Osher 850, Sacramento 941, San Francisco 947, Skaggs 1004, Sonoma 1021, Times 1074, van Loben Sels 1107, **Wilbur 1142**
Colorado: Bonfils 1189, El Pomar 1225, Gates 1232
Connecticut: Griffis 1402, Waterbury 1536
District of Columbia: Meyer 1716
Florida: NationsBank 2031, Wahlstrom 2147
Georgia: Beehive 2198
Hawaii: Atherton 2423, Cooke 2435, Watumull 2464
Illinois: Community 2613, Haffner 2728, Kaplan 2796, Peoria 2918, Replogle 2947, **Rice 2951**, Siragusa 2998
Indiana: Ball 3102, **Liberty 3206**
Kansas: Wichita 3446
Kentucky: Bank 3453, Blue 3454, Community 3461, Sutherland 3507
Maryland: Brown 3645, Cohen 3658, Knott 3723
Massachusetts: Adams 3823, **Cabot 3877**, Community 3901, Harcourt 3998, High 4014, Ratshesky 4173, Stevens 4231, Worcester 4283
Michigan: Berrien 4313, Capital 4331, Community 4339, Ervin 4388, Grand Rapids 4420, Jackson 4449, JSJ 4455, **Kresge 4473**, Midland 4510, Shapero 4562, Young 4634
Minnesota: Andersen 4646, Bigelow 4666, Bush 4672, Butler 4673, General 4712, Minnesota 4767, Saint Paul 4818
Missouri: Hallmark 4980
Nebraska: Cooper 5158, Woods 5230
New Hampshire: New Hampshire 5310, Trust 5318
New Jersey: Dodge 5388, Hyde 5440, Kirby 5466, **Newcombe 5525, Union 5617**
New Mexico: Chamiza 5643, Santa Fe 5660, **Wurlitzer 5665**
New York: Babbitt 5735, Birkelund 5797, Central 5876, **Delmas 6006**, Glickenhaus 6209, Greenwall 6266, **Guggenheim 6281**, Hoyt 6380, Kaplan 6461, Littauer 6606, **Luce 6625, Mellon 6698**, Nicolais 6786, Seevak 7093, Steele 7191, **Whiting 7376, Wiener 7380**
North Carolina: Blumenthal 7454, Bryan 7462, CP&L 7493, Cumberland 7495, Kenan 7556, Triangle 7648, Wachovia 7651
Ohio: Columbus 7745, Dayton 7767, Deuble 7772, El-An 7781, Hoover 7868, Nordson 7994
Oklahoma: Bernsen 8182
Oregon: Jackson 8299, Johnson 8302, Meyer 8314
Pennsylvania: Barra 8367, Cameron 8414, Chastain 8428, Dolfinger 8462, Heinz 8556, Millstein 8683, **Pew 8721**
South Carolina: Community 8993, Spartanburg 9032
Tennessee: Benwood 9071, Community 9092
Texas: Constantin 9297, Dishman 9326, Hobby 9438, Kempner 9469, Meadows 9530, Moss 9543, Permian 9573, **Rapoport 9595**, Rockwell 9609, Ward 9711, Zachry 9744
Utah: Eccles 9773
Virginia: **American 9829**, Charlottesville 9849
Washington: Blue 10023, Wenatchee 10148
West Virginia: Kanawha 10177, McDonough 10181
Wisconsin: Bradley 10212, Hedberg 10263

Immigrants/refugees

California: Allen 183, California 316, Grove 550, Haynes 582, **Koulaieff 686**, San Francisco 947, **Shaler 983**, Stern 1039, van Loben Sels 1107, **Wong 1156**
Connecticut: **Xerox 1547**
District of Columbia: Cafritz 1645, Fowler 1666, **German 1673**, Meyer 1716, **Public 1727**, Szekely 1737
Florida: Thoresen 2137
Hawaii: Ching 2432
Illinois: Fel-Pro 2666, McKay 2864, Washington 3059
Maryland: Meyerhoff 3752
Massachusetts: Boston 3860, Hyams 4035, Stevens 4231, Stevens 4232, Swensrud 4245

Michigan: Grand Rapids 4420, India 4447
Minnesota: Bell 4660, Bremer 4671, Bush 4672, Grotto 4722, Minneapolis 4766, Phillips 4797, U.S. Bancorp 4843
Nevada: **Discount 5245**
New Jersey: Victoria 5621
New Mexico: Santa Fe 5660
New York: **Abelard 5667, Carnegie 5860**, de Hirsch 5994, **Ford 6135, LeBrun 6564**, New York 6773, **Norman 6791, Phillips 6878**, Springate 7178, Warner 7330
Ohio: Akron 7677
Pennsylvania: Chester 8429, **Pew 8721**
Rhode Island: Rhode Island 8958
Texas: Fikes 9366, Trull 9689
Vermont: **Ben 9812**
Virginia: Gannett 9879
Washington: **Kongsgaard 10078**
Wisconsin: Cudahy 10234

Immunology

New York: **Shulsky 7113**

Internal medicine research

Massachusetts: **Gerrity 3983**

International affairs

Arizona: RORD 123
California: Bandai 233, **Cow 372, Friedland 477**, Guess 554, Rocca 929, Sassoon 954, **Stans 1031**, Von der Ahe 1113
Connecticut: Bannow 1330, **GE 1392, Main 1449, Richardson 1487, Rubin 1495**, Shenandoah 1504, **Xerox 1547**
District of Columbia: Delmar 1653, **Winston 1747**
Florida: Catlin 1808, Hovnanian 1946, Schecter 2091
Georgia: McCamish 2339, **Singletary 2387**
Hawaii: Honda 2445, Scott 2457
Illinois: Beidler 2532, Davies 2634, **MacArthur 2839**, Montgomery 2884, Takiff 3028
Maryland: Weiss 3813
Massachusetts: Flatley 3969, **Friendship 3978, Henderson 4007**
Missouri: Kemper 5007
New Hampshire: **Institute 5301**
New Jersey: Hamilton 5429, Johnson 5455, Obernauer 5528
New York: American 5702, **AT&T 5721, Baker 5748**, Birkelund 5797, Bristol 5824, **Bydale 5850, Carnegie 5860, Twentieth 5877**, Delavan 6005, **Donner 6030, Ford 6135**, Gerschel 6191, Gordon 6246, **Guggenheim 6280, Harriman 6311**, Hurford 6394, Janklow 6424, Koppelman 6527, Linder 6595, Mitsui 6727, Morgan 6734, Normandie 6792, Overbrook 6828, PepsiCo 6866, **Phillips 6879**, Reynolds 6950, **Riklis 6968, Rockefeller 6985, Rubin 7025**, Stern 7209, **Tinker 7263, United 7296**, Wallach 7326, Whitehead 7375
North Carolina: **Brady 7457**
Ohio: Nordson 7994, **Taj 8119**
Pennsylvania: Bell 8373, **Carthage 8421**, Ryan 8770, **Scaife 8778**, Sidewater 8779
Texas: Kempner 9469
Virginia: Parker 9952, **Potomac 9962**
Washington: See 10123
Wisconsin: Bradley 10212

International affairs, alliance

Pennsylvania: **Botstiber 8397**

International affairs, formal/general education

District of Columbia: Cafritz 1644

Figure 41. Advanced Grants/Recipient State Search from *FC Search: The Foundation Center's Database on CD-ROM*

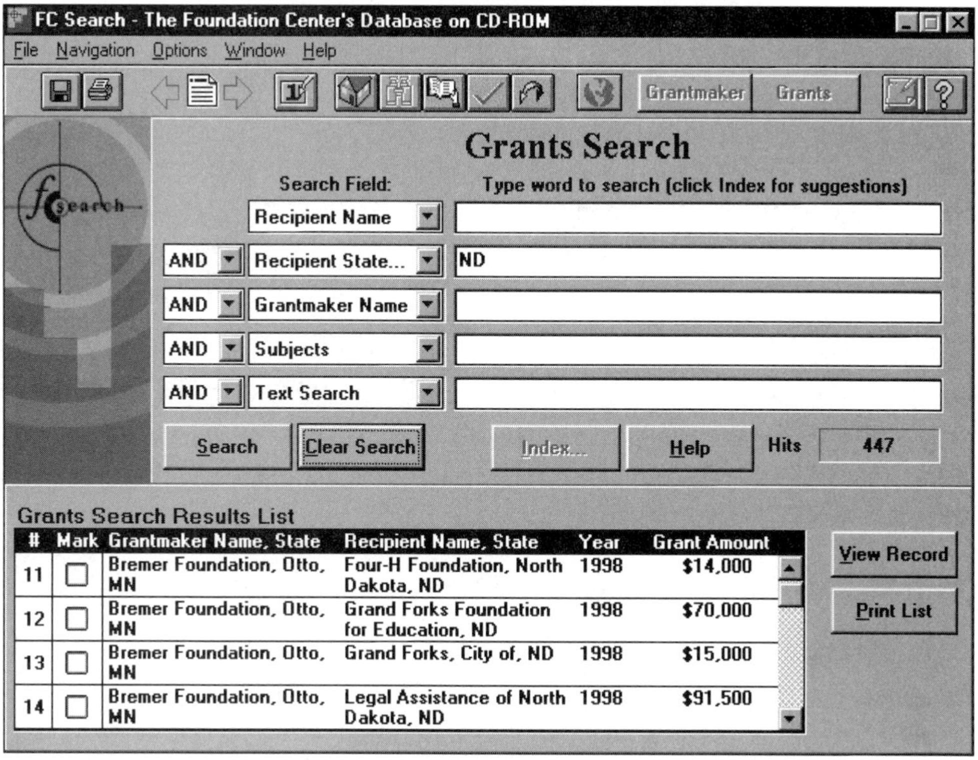

The next stop is *The Foundation Grants Index,* which is arranged alphabetically by state and includes a Type of Support/Geographic Index (see Figure 42) that helps you identify grants to organizations in your state. It also has a Recipient Category Index (see Figure 43) that helps you identify grants to comparable organizations (e.g., hospitals, museums, youth development centers, etc.).

As you scan the listings in *The Foundation Grants Index,* look for patterns and for inconsistencies. Try to eliminate foundations that appear to have awarded grants to organizations in your state solely on the basis of their subject focus or because of an affiliation with a specific institution. For instance, suppose you are looking for a foundation to contribute to a medical research program in central Florida. You might uncover two grants to Florida hospitals among the twenty grants made by the XYZ Foundation, located in Massachusetts, during the last couple of years, the other

Figure 42. Type of Support/Geographic Index from *The Foundation Grants Index*

TYPE OF SUPPORT/GEOGRAPHIC INDEX—FELLOWSHIPS

Michigan 68427, 82242, 82243, 83100, 83499, 83500
Minnesota 82860
Missouri 82344, 83536, 83537
New Jersey 30763, 82049, 82454, 83104
New York 7525, 8374, 8375, 9376, 9434, 27009, 27010, 32493, 69716, 72287, 81897, 81992, 82179, 82209, 82339, 82434, 82756, 82758, 83010, 83052, 83074, 83470, 83507
North Carolina 82253, 82254, 83324
Ohio 82343, 83495
Oklahoma 13174
Pennsylvania 8204, 13663, 31288, 82256, 82258, 82372, 82997, 83097
Rhode Island 68551
Russia 82685
Texas 68100, 82261, 83030, 83107, 83123, 83511
Utah 83133
Vermont 10141, 69037, 69680
Virginia 82053, 82315, 82316, 83474-83476, 83533-83535
Wisconsin 82267, 82268

Youth development

New York 85240
Virginia 29153, 75253

FILM/VIDEO/RADIO

Animals/wildlife

Florida 617
Illinois 460
Massachusetts 770
Missouri 387
Washington 14065

Arts/culture

Alaska 9453, 81120
Arizona 80594, 80595, 81331
Bosnia-Herzegovina 82395
Bulgaria 9105, 9152
California 995, 996, 1042, 1186, 1445, 1640, 2058, 2060, 2068, 2189, 2976, 7249, 7271, 7536, 7562, 9055, 9880, 10892, 12040, 13414, 13641, 14060, 14062, 14665, 14746, 16842, 17290, 18248, 18383, 19052, 19913, 19914, 19971, 35764, 36661, 38272, 39428, 39443, 39454, 39512, 40490, 41614, 42637, 42640, 42981, 45227, 47406, 53578, 57527, 58369, 60887, 63695, 68566, 68592, 69230, 69251, 71233, 73283, 73306, 73372, 73762, 74321, 74827, 74924, 77790, 78302, 78305, 79701, 79933, 81126, 81873, 81874, 82472, 83146, 83156, 83856, 84236
Canada 9082, 40553
Colorado 2399, 12830, 73407, 79958
Connecticut 7632, 11885, 14014, 57557
Croatia 9108
District of Columbia 3320, 13419, 13420, 19232, 36482, 39610, 41086, 41211, 41476, 42644-42647, 44870, 54061, 56005, 67701, 67829, 67846, 69659, 71989, 73218, 73541, 73707, 73738, 74311, 74670, 74821, 75348, 75349, 75365, 81283, 81838, 83158
England 40535, 42171
Estonia 9068, 9137
Florida 617, 2957, 67581, 76982
Hawaii 3337, 13600, 14691, 38202, 40329, 73655, 82080
Hungary 74889
Illinois 3719, 3858, 4230, 36183, 73698, 73703, 73792
Indiana 4344, 4365, 43612
Kansas 5868, 41149, 62554
Kentucky 9072, 43168
Kenya 7568, 68623
Louisiana 79058
Maryland 15065, 15176, 15615, 20830, 21258, 45031, 49954, 52960, 68809
Massachusetts 2979-2982, 4802, 4814, 6275, 6337, 7545, 8350, 9119, 10155, 23296, 36679, 39650,

41687, 42810, 43152, 44907, 52965, 58976, 67913, 74256, 74944, 80911, 81150, 82301
Mexico 3829, 13413, 54203
Michigan 4942, 5084, 5128, 5271, 21948, 40993, 42482, 80520, 84239
Minnesota 5338, 5695, 10196, 10733, 16157, 67648, 68173, 68401, 69721, 74134, 74169, 74170, 74195, 74197, 74318, 80570, 80583, 81097, 82417
Missouri 22391
Montana 39939
Namibia 9121
Nebraska 36640, 43740
Netherlands 9173, 9181, 36944
Nevada 6177, 6186, 10215
New Hampshire 5918
New Jersey 6281, 47542, 62940, 62990, 74253, 74257, 74346, 76950, 82442
New Mexico 3092, 45079, 74938
New York 910, 933, 1307, 3864, 6467-6469, 7094, 7203, 7463, 7605, 7868, 7872, 8056, 8170, 8574, 8885, 9057, 9070, 9149, 9157, 9182, 9284, 9544, 9578, 9603, 9614, 10053, 10328, 11880, 13355, 13789, 13975, 14007, 14308, 18605, 18849, 20820, 21439, 21650, 22726, 23275, 24804, 43141, 44841, 45060, 47708, 48123, 48510, 48552, 52537, 52941, 63388, 67435, 67881, 68372, 68642, 68789, 73837, 74097, 74300, 74323, 74451, 74791, 75359, 77729, 78298, 78507, 80134, 80904, 80905, 81928, 81929, 82101, 82592, 82707, 83261
Nicaragua 15390
Nigeria 46144
North Carolina 10407, 83328
North Dakota 82408
Ohio 10551, 10587, 10608, 10707, 10742, 10778, 10971, 17476, 24209, 37348, 48474, 64929, 65008, 75019, 81275
Oregon 16883, 18745
Pennsylvania 2054, 2249, 11909, 11915, 11955, 12035, 34045, 35917, 58756, 75165, 81826, 83372
Russia 9096, 9148, 9167, 68816, 69258, 74846, 82628
South Carolina 1304, 9205, 18850, 42167, 43695, 74492, 74820, 74883, 77802, 78475, 80132
Switzerland 9151
Tennessee 12179, 14519, 75226
Texas 2099, 12319, 12470, 12525, 12552, 14504, 42931, 74602, 75250, 78992
Utah 2471, 2473, 6183, 6951, 12813, 12814, 79082, 79084
Vermont 7634, 7635, 36953
Virginia 1643, 3859, 11914, 18928, 28333, 39985, 67620, 73749, 74126, 78909, 81964, 83165, 83446, 84946
Washington 14065, 58111, 60966, 74366
West Virginia 65558, 76123
Wisconsin 67234, 74603, 75164, 75380, 75397, 82456

Civil rights

Alaska 9453
California 13313, 13314, 13414, 13641, 14060, 14062, 14373, 18248, 38272, 68592, 78302
Connecticut 14014
District of Columbia 13419, 13420, 47343
Hawaii 13600
Illinois 13895
Kenya 7568
Massachusetts 6337, 7545
Mexico 13413
Namibia 9121
New Jersey 74257
New York 7605, 13355, 13789, 13975, 14007, 14308, 45060, 48647, 67435, 68642, 68789
Ohio 10778
Oregon 16883
Russia 68816, 82628
Tennessee 14519
Texas 12470, 14504
Virginia 83446
Washington 14065
Wisconsin 74603

Zimbabwe 14307

Community improvement/development

Alaska 9453
Brazil 68548
California 7562, 14665, 14746, 16842, 17290, 73762
Canada 67935
District of Columbia 74880
Hawaii 14691
Maryland 15065, 15176, 15615, 68809
Massachusetts 4814, 40538, 74944, 81150
Minnesota 16157, 82417
Montana 39939
Nebraska 18852
Nevada 18459
New York 48510, 56683
Nicaragua 15390
Ohio 17476
Oregon 16883
South Carolina 43695

Crime/courts/legal services

California 18248, 18383, 19052, 84236
Delaware 18454
District of Columbia 18854, 19232, 82059
Michigan 5271
Nebraska 18852
Nevada 18459
New York 18605, 18849
Oregon 18745
Russia 68816
South Carolina 18850
Texas 79485
Virginia 18928
Wisconsin 67234

Education, elementary/secondary

California 2189, 14373, 19913, 19914, 19971, 37052, 79933
Maryland 20830, 21258
Massachusetts 23296, 52965
Michigan 21948
Minnesota 5695, 80583
Missouri 22391
New Jersey 74346
New York 14308, 20820, 21439, 21650, 22726, 23162, 23275, 23384, 24804, 38773, 78507, 80904, 80905, 81928, 81929
Ohio 24209
Pennsylvania 24470
Tennessee 12179
Texas 12470
Utah 2471
Wisconsin 25518

Education, higher

California 79933
District of Columbia 75348, 83239
Iowa 26578
New Jersey 74346
New York 38773
Pennsylvania 34045
Virginia 28333

Education, other

California 35733, 35764, 36661, 37052
District of Columbia 36482, 47343
Illinois 36183, 73792
Maryland 21258
Massachusetts 36679
Missouri 22391
Nebraska 36640
Netherlands 36944
New York 9603
Ohio 37348
Pennsylvania 35917, 37513, 37521
Russia 37154
Vermont 36953

Figure 43. Recipient Category Index from *The Foundation Grants Index*

ANIMAL/WILDLIFE AGENCIES

Annual campaigns

Texas 42939

Building/renovation

Arizona 7
Arkansas 704
California 10, 12, 30, 68, 116, 126, 128, 58437, 58497, 79728, 79857
Colorado 105, 140, 143, 5027
Delaware 160, 161, 162
Georgia 179, 180, 185, 186, 227
Hawaii 229, 230
Illinois 287, 303
Indiana 40917
Iowa 326, 328
Massachusetts 40843, 41720
Michigan 404, 405, 409
Minnesota 416
Missouri 388, 403, 41124
Nebraska 442, 448
Nevada 450, 451
New Jersey 62933
New York 525, 530, 562, 596, 603, 63595
Ohio 402, 678, 683, 684, 691
Oklahoma 701, 703, 705, 707
Oregon 709, 712
Pennsylvania 406, 720, 725, 734, 741, 742, 748, 759, 773, 42572, 58915
Texas 799, 814, 820, 824, 828, 42909, 66654, 70083
Virginia 850, 851

Capital campaigns

Alabama 1
California 86, 87
Connecticut 153
Illinois 286, 316
Iowa 327, 331
Kentucky 334
Louisiana 284
Massachusetts 40824
Michigan 379
Minnesota 417
Nebraska 441
New Jersey 171
New York 506
North Carolina 10427, 10428
Ohio 676, 677, 692
Oklahoma 699
Pennsylvania 736, 749, 772
South Carolina 663
Tennessee 790
Texas 802, 805, 809, 811, 42878
Virginia 844

Collections management/preservation

Illinois 304

Computer systems/equipment

Alaska 4
District of Columbia 483
Illinois 469
Ohio 671
Washington 163

Conferences/seminars

California 628
Colorado 58065
Connecticut 470
District of Columbia 164
Massachusetts 101, 81110
New York 58
Pennsylvania 42589
Tennessee 456

Curriculum development

California 39682

Colorado 649
Connecticut 39453
Illinois 80249, 80252
North Carolina 607, 608
Texas 40054

Debt reduction

Georgia 59427

Endowments

Illinois 296
Maryland 638
Massachusetts 40709
New York 543, 563, 622
Texas 76667

Equipment

California 121, 18191
Colorado 75637
Connecticut 61443
Delaware 159
Florida 170
Louisiana 648
Massachusetts 366
Nebraska 17
New Jersey 488
New York 529, 530, 63522
Pennsylvania 733
Texas 42916
Utah 842

Exhibitions

California 118-120
Georgia 227
Illinois 285
Indiana 324
Massachusetts 561
Missouri 445
New York 595
North Carolina 609
Ohio 401
Pennsylvania 500, 741
Texas 807, 837
Virginia 851

Faculty/staff development

Colorado 139
District of Columbia 643
Georgia 183
Illinois 274
New York 41236

Film/video/radio

Illinois 460
Massachusetts 770
Missouri 387

General support

Arkansas 836
California 11, 14-16, 29, 44, 47, 60, 61, 73, 114, 137, 449, 497, 567, 612, 1733, 1734, 39431, 39563, 41702, 42591, 58438, 58442, 79857, 79858
Colorado 141, 314, 693
Connecticut 43, 58832
District of Columbia 38, 59, 67, 455, 528, 646, 716, 729, 750, 840, 857, 858, 40564, 42182
Florida 41, 288, 593, 740, 39264, 59286
Georgia 46, 181
Idaho 727, 798
Illinois 267, 268, 271, 275-277, 301, 302, 533-537
Indiana 318, 322
Kentucky 774
Maryland 341, 568
Massachusetts 538, 635, 40844
Michigan 377, 382, 395, 410, 412
Minnesota 418, 41703, 62374
Missouri 430, 61717
Montana 49
New Jersey 454, 63026

New Mexico 39
New York 40, 45, 176, 501, 502, 529, 560, 571, 579, 591, 592, 614, 615, 636, 641, 41933, 64300, 65897
North Carolina 604, 665, 9221, 64319, 64320
Ohio 42, 555, 672, 675, 681, 694, 695, 731, 61705, 61706, 64983
Pennsylvania 444, 447, 540, 735, 753, 775
Rhode Island 356
South Carolina 606
Texas 92, 801, 838, 66654
Wisconsin 279, 861

Income development

California 58199
District of Columbia 98
Maryland 90
New York 503

Land acquisition

Michigan 397, 404
New Jersey 489
Texas 831

Management development

California 33, 82
Illinois 469
Maryland 90
Michigan 398, 399
Ohio 674, 682
Pennsylvania 755

Matching or challenge grants

California 131
District of Columbia 769
Indiana 321, 40917
Michigan 404, 405
Minnesota 417
Missouri 403
New Jersey 489
New Mexico 42769
Ohio 401, 402
Pennsylvania 406, 772
Tennessee 40645

Other

Alaska 18
Arizona 280, 433
California 19, 21, 24-26, 28, 36, 37, 54, 70-72, 74, 75, 76, 77, 78, 79, 83, 85, 89, 111, 112, 122, 124, 127, 129, 133-135, 166, 191, 210, 240, 249, 251, 253, 294, 498, 519, 565, 726, 847, 1080, 1359, 1645, 1701, 1884, 2083, 2166, 39194, 39222, 39223, 39492, 39802, 40172, 40193, 57844, 57903, 58007, 58254, 62628
Colorado 142, 144, 145, 195, 281, 40167, 41948, 58610, 63256
Connecticut 53, 149, 154, 155, 245
Delaware 849
District of Columbia 35, 55, 165, 167, 168, 187, 197, 204-206, 215, 235, 349, 367, 376, 392, 516, 517, 544, 548, 551, 589, 590, 689, 860, 866, 870, 40134, 40176, 42673
Florida 8, 151, 172-174, 177, 289, 290, 319, 335, 601, 40126, 40228
France 531, 532
Georgia 175, 178, 184, 189, 199, 209, 224, 226, 666, 59441
Hawaii 61186
Idaho 20, 84, 202, 292, 436, 545, 640
Illinois 22, 23, 231, 242-244, 255, 258, 259, 270, 272, 273, 283, 305, 308-310, 420, 524, 50991
Indiana 320, 424, 60712
Iowa 269
Kansas 60814
Kentucky 225, 389
Louisiana 337, 338, 339, 833
Maine 572
Maryland 188, 222, 239, 342, 343, 344, 345, 346, 511, 40587

eighteen grants having been given to organizations in Massachusetts or in other New England states. Further research might indicate that the foundation's two grants were to the hospital in West Palm where the donor's mother once received medical attention. That is, these grants were unique, one-time events and not an indication of an interest in Florida recipients *per se*. Note the types of organizations receiving grants, the subject focus of the grant recipients, and the amount and type of support offered by particular foundations. You are looking for repeat patterns of giving. Invariably, you'll find that some foundations limit their giving to specific subject areas or types of institutions. If a foundation's giving pattern does not match your funding needs, it does not belong on your prospect list.

Step Two: Refining Your List

You should now have a lengthy list of foundations that might possibly be interested in funding your project or program. Now is the time to refine the list to a reasonable number of grantmakers who would probably look favorably on your program. You should review your geographic prospect list to eliminate those foundations that are not interested in your subject and that do not award the type of support your organization needs. If you used *FC Search* to construct your list, you probably used multiple search criteria, thereby completing this step already. Completing the prospect worksheet (see Figure 11) for each potential funder enables you to quickly eliminate those least likely to fund your project.

Now that you have determined that the funders on your list have demonstrated a real commitment to funding in your geographic area, providing the type of support your organization needs, and funding in your subject field, you are ready to scrutinize your list further to determine those potential funders who are most likely to be interested in your organization or program or project. You'll want to do as much research on all aspects pertaining to these grantmakers as time and resources permit. Posing the questions raised in Chapter 4 is a good place to start:

- Does the funder accept applications?
- Does the amount of money you are requesting fit within the funder's typical grant range?
- Does the funder put limits on the length of time it is willing to support a project?
- What type of organizations does the funder tend to support?

- Does the funder have application deadlines, or does it review proposals continuously?

- Do you or does anyone on your board know someone connected with a potential funder?

Most of these questions can be answered by referring to any one of several resources. *FC Search: The Foundation Center's Database on CD-ROM* will answer many of them. Directories such as *The Foundation Directory* or *The Foundation 1000* or some of the state and local directories will also provide many of the answers you need. For application deadlines and the names of trustees, officers, or donors, Center directories and databases are excellent sources.

On occasion you will need to refer to primary sources such as the IRS Form 990-PF, annual reports, or application guidelines. For instance, suppose your research has identified a prospect that seems a perfect match based on subject, type of support, size of grants, etc., but this foundation's geographic focus does not overlap with the geographic area served by your organization. In this case, it would be in your organization's best interests to investigate a more complete listing of grants awarded than you will find in directories. If the grantmaker publishes an annual report, secure a copy and study the grants list. If not, look at the foundation's 990-PF at the foundation's office, from the IRS, or at the Foundation Center library nearest you. Have any grants been awarded to organizations in your area? Have any grants been awarded to organizations located outside the stated geographic limits? An examination of a complete grants list can be highly revealing concerning foundation priorities.

On other occasions, secondary sources such as articles in newspapers and journals will provide the answers you need. *Philanthropy News Digest (PND)*, the Foundation Center's weekly online summary of the news of the world of philanthropy, is a searchable database that allows you to seek recent information about foundations and their philanthropic efforts. *PND* summaries will also inform you of changes in leadership, very recent major grants, and other such information. You may wish to employ *PND's* search engine to enter the name of a particular foundation and see what, if anything, has been reported about this funder's recent gifts. Another source for information on recently awarded grants is the *Chronicle of Philanthropy's* "Guide to Grants" database on the Web (www.philanthropy.com/grants/), which indexes the grants lists previously printed in the *Chronicle of Philanthropy.*

A review of the resources described in Chapter 5 will help you to decide which directory, annual report, IRS return, application guidelines, etc. will best assist you in answering the specific questions necessary to refine your list to the most likely prospects. When you have answered these questions about the funders on your broad prospect list, you will have narrowed your list to the few that you should approach.

Summary

A grantmaker's geographic focus is most likely to be in the city, county, state, or region in which the foundation is located. On the other hand, there are a significant number of foundations that give nationally and internationally. There are a variety of materials available to the grantseeker to develop a broad prospect list based on where a grantmaker gives its grants. Once a list of potential funders based on giving area is developed, it is very important to find out if those funders are interested in your subject and if they provide the types and amount of support your organization needs. The previous chapter explored the subject approach, and the next chapter discusses the types of support approach. When you have thoroughly utilized these three approaches, you are ready to move on to Chapter 10 for guidelines on presenting your ideas to a funder.

Chapter 8

Finding the Right Funder: The Types of Support Approach

As your research progresses you'll notice that grants from foundations usually fall into fairly distinct categories. These may include cash assistance for capital support, operating funds, or seed money, and noncash support such as donations of equipment or supplies, technical assistance, use of facilities, and management advice. We call these distinct categories "types of support." The types of support approach helps you identify grantmakers that have expressed an interest in providing the specific types of support your organization needs.

In fact, when considering the types of support your organization needs, it is especially important to investigate avenues other then the traditional dollar grant, or what funders call "in-kind" gifts. For example, a nonprofit that needs a photocopier or computer might look for a local company willing to donate the equipment instead of seeking a grant to buy such equipment. Many grantmakers, especially corporate givers, willingly donate office space, computer time, and facilities; some even lend out executive talent. Securing outright cash donations from these same corporations, on the other hand, can be much more difficult. (For more information about corporate giving, see Chapter 9.) You'll find that many foundations tend to limit their giving to one or, at most, a few types of support. Therefore, in the planning stages that precede a search for funding sources, you should clarify the specific types of support your organization needs and include only those grantmakers on your prospect list that favor those types of support.

COMMON SUPPORT TYPES

The following are some common support types:

1. *Capital campaigns:* campaigns, usually extending over a period of years, to raise substantial funds for enduring purposes, such as a physical plant or endowment.

2. *Conferences and seminars:* grants to cover the expenses of holding a conference.

3. *Emergency funds:* one-time grants to cover immediate short-term funding needs on an urgent basis.

4. *General/Operating support:* grants to cover the day-to-day personnel, administrative, and miscellaneous expenses of a project or organization; also referred to as unrestricted support.

5. *In-kind gifts:* contributions of equipment, supplies, or other property, technical or other services, as distinguished from a monetary grant. Some funders may donate space or staff time as in-kind support.

6. *Seed money:* grants or contributions used to begin a new project or organization. Seed grants may cover salaries and other operating expenses for a new project. Also referred to as start-up funds.

7. *Program development:* grants to support specific projects or programs as opposed to a general purpose grant; also called special project grants.

For definitions of the thirty-two types of support used in Center directories, see Appendix D.

Step One: Developing a Broad Types of Support Prospect List

Once you have determined the type of support your organization needs, you can begin researching foundations that provide that type of support. You will want to review descriptions of grants that have been awarded to organizations similar to your own for the type of support you need. You will also want to use the Types of Support Index in various grantmaker directories that are organized by location, subject, and/or population served.

GRANTS APPROACH

Begin by looking at the types of support foundations have provided nonprofits in the past. Although a foundation's guidelines may indicate funding for specific types of support, the type of grants a funder actually provides is a much better indicator of where the real commitment lies. *FC Search* is a good starting point for a search by grants. The Grants file can be searched in multiple ways, including by types of support. The pop-up index will help you decide on the appropriate terms that describe the types of support your nonprofit needs. A distinct advantage of using *FC Search* is the fact that you can search for types of support simultaneously with subject and location (Grantmaker State or Recipient State). This approach can significantly speed your research efforts.

If you don't have access to *FC Search*, your first stop should be the print directory, *The Foundation Grants Index*. As we noted earlier, the *Grants Index* offers concise descriptions of grants of $10,000 or more reported to the Foundation Center during the previous year by about 1,300 major U.S. foundations. Turn to the Recipient Category Index of the *Grants Index* (see Figure 44), which provides a breakdown of grants by specific types of support. You can use this index to identify grants of the type in which you are interested that have been made to organizations similar to your own. The index shows grants awarded to thirty-six different types of organizations (e.g., churches/temples, human service agencies, libraries, performing arts groups, schools, and so on) arranged by any of the thirty-two specific types of support that have been awarded to those institutions.

To speed your research, the grant records are then subdivided by the states in which the grant recipients are located. Note the sequence numbers. Each number leads you back to a grant description in the main text of the volume, rather than to a page number. In addition, each grant record includes the names of the grantmaking foundation and recipient organization, along with details—amount, purpose, and so on—about the grant itself. Remember to consider individual grant records as evidence of a

Figure 44. Recipient Category Index from *The Foundation Grants Index*

73737, 73895, 74066, 74106, 74107, 74118, 74444, 74467, 74567, 74679, 74792, 82554
North Carolina 31504, 74986
Ohio 16127
Oregon 45016
Pennsylvania 24800, 50094, 56280, 65713
Russia 40442, 40930, 42995, 68672
South Africa 44890
Texas 50546, 60899, 70087, 74809, 74816, 75241, 75383
Vermont 74322
Virginia 22109, 25391, 25523, 54710, 67554, 67555, 67560, 70031, 82035
Washington 35243, 75362
West Bank/Gaza 68577, 83196
Wisconsin 21224, 21234

Scholarships

Florida 73210

Seed money

California 16902
Colorado 21219
District of Columbia 17003, 41441, 42625, 73765, 73886
Indiana 18703
New Hampshire 22549
New York 19204, 67918
Oregon 40428, 42436
Pennsylvania 24533

Technical aid

California 44558
District of Columbia 36310, 40929, 47389-47391, 47724, 52686, 52963, 53044, 60909, 68713, 73879, 74440, 84445
Indiana 73842
Iowa 63475, 73881
New Jersey 46511
New York 22340, 47570
Vermont 73943
Virginia 48279

PUBLIC/GENERAL HEALTH ORGANIZATIONS

Awards/prizes/competitions

Colorado 45416, 45421
Illinois 46034
Maryland 49214, 50129
Massachusetts 49209
Virginia 27545

Building/renovation

Alabama 44180, 44183
Arizona 44205, 44211-44214, 45759, 50499
Brazil 49831, 49839
California 44241, 44726, 45113, 45330, 45340, 53896, 70010
Colorado 45367, 53991, 58635
Delaware 45560
England 46357
Florida 45762
Georgia 45885, 45886, 45894, 45897, 54155, 59597, 69841
Haiti 45812
Hawaii 59623
Illinois 79246
Iowa 46430
Kansas 45808, 49758
Maryland 46492, 46557
Massachusetts 65590
Michigan 46845, 46872, 46880, 54418, 68193
Missouri 49755
New Jersey 47333, 47371, 47373, 54558, 55251
New York 47022, 47334, 47370, 48319, 48320, 48323, 48388, 48389, 48655, 49830, 51277
North Carolina 49511, 49517, 49561, 49562, 55141
North Dakota 47074, 47083

Ohio 36483, 49568, 49723, 65245
Oklahoma 55217, 55226
Oregon 49799, 49809, 55228, 78810
Pennsylvania 45760, 49861
Tennessee 46363, 50189, 50191, 50202
Texas 4783, 50240, 50293, 50332, 50361, 55342, 55405, 55427, 66374, 66527, 66562, 66704, 66896, 66897, 76628
Utah 50465
Washington 50525, 50536
Wisconsin 50576, 50591

Capital campaigns

Arizona 44229
California 44962, 45940, 47323, 53875
Colorado 45433, 45450
Delaware 45555, 45564
District of Columbia 61081
Florida 45807, 48030, 49860
Georgia 45851, 49769, 59600
Hawaii 45942
Illinois 46243, 46254
Maryland 46501
Massachusetts 46395, 46759, 50027
New Jersey 47981, 54015
New York 44236, 48879, 48891, 48893, 48897, 48969, 49830, 57273
North Carolina 48028, 49474
Ohio 46848, 49596-49598, 49669, 49670, 49701, 49743, 55188, 65253
Oklahoma 49791
Pennsylvania 45558, 49848
Rhode Island 50181
Texas 49833, 50228, 50446
Wisconsin 50590

Collections acquisition

Switzerland 45095

Collections management/preservation

California 2206

Computer systems/equipment

Botswana 46949
California 44412, 44792, 45142, 58507
Colorado 45439
Connecticut 45533
Georgia 47614
Indiana 60752
Kansas 46439, 46456
Massachusetts 46645, 49905
Mexico 22062
Minnesota 47066, 47120
New Jersey 47376
New York 47370, 48125, 48321, 48946
North Carolina 49493
North Dakota 48551
Ohio 49625
Pennsylvania 46265, 49901, 49931, 50034, 50038, 50136, 51815
Texas 50387
Virginia 47717
West Virginia 49877, 49886

Conferences/seminars

California 465, 44380, 44455, 44459, 44462, 44469, 44502, 44503, 44544, 44546, 44694, 44774, 44999, 45093, 47409, 47441, 47497, 47961, 52245, 53724, 53737, 53764, 58475
District of Columbia 44831, 45463, 46509, 46959, 47392, 47593, 47727, 48253, 48254, 49038, 49213, 50564, 70217
England 48491
Florida 50523
Georgia 49034, 49056, 67906, 68295
Illinois 47606, 52533, 52904, 54583
Kansas 52650
Kenya 48494, 49025, 49054
Louisiana 51581
Maine 44859
Maryland 34293, 48287, 52905, 81458

Mexico 46174, 48501
New York 38856, 45459, 47839, 48297, 53273, 54767
Nigeria 48523
Pennsylvania 49021
South Africa 46964
Switzerland 45096, 49073
Tanzania 49055, 68810
Texas 50333
Virginia 44850, 47768
Washington 48514
Zimbabwe 49029

Curriculum development

Connecticut 47495
Indiana 52642
Maryland 34293, 47672
Massachusetts 44854
New York 38856, 53834
Ohio 47754
South Dakota 47827
Virginia 49634

Debt reduction

Connecticut 45533
Texas 50301

Emergency funds

Texas 50367

Endowments

Arizona 48345
California 2206, 50653
District of Columbia 44530, 61060
Florida 49688
Illinois 46335
Minnesota 47164
New York 48048, 48643
Ohio 10900, 49600, 49690, 49697
Oregon 51477
Pennsylvania 50030
Texas 12377, 50301, 51923, 55435
Wyoming 47302

Equipment

Arizona 44208, 44209, 45759, 54456
California 44241, 44250, 44254, 44255, 44405, 45322, 53701, 53704, 53708, 53943, 53953, 60611, 75559
Canada 46349, 46356
Colorado 45363, 45367, 45439
Connecticut 45465, 45532
Florida 44227, 45762, 45814
Haiti 45812
Hawaii 45944
Illinois 46353, 54252
Indiana 46404
Israel 55503
Massachusetts 46763, 54371
Michigan 68193
Minnesota 47081
New Hampshire 48673
New Jersey 30498, 47346, 47347, 47350, 47352, 47353, 52890, 54569, 54571, 54572, 54598
New York 47374, 48316, 51277
North Carolina 49503, 49529, 49532, 49902, 53324
North Dakota 47072, 47073
Ohio 49658, 64875
Oklahoma 49770, 49772
Oregon 47426, 49798, 49802, 49805, 49808
Pennsylvania 45562, 49935, 65550
South Carolina 46328, 46774
Tennessee 50205
Texas 47301, 50217, 50329, 50336, 50338, 50340, 50342, 50364, 50366, 50367, 50443, 55360, 55419, 55441, 66562, 66694
Utah 47292, 54518
Virginia 55476
Washington 50528

foundation's giving interests. Look for grant records that describe funding for projects or organizations that appear to be similar in several respects to your own.

The Type of Support/Geographic Index (see Figure 45) is another helpful way to access pertinent grant records. This index allows you to cross-reference support type within twenty-eight broadly defined subject categories against the state location of the grant recipient.

When working with either index, be sure to note on your prospect worksheet (see Figure 11) the name of the foundation awarding the grant, its location, and any limitations on its giving program. Then scan the full listing of grants reported by that foundation in the Index to Grants by Foundation section to determine its general subject focus, the types of organizations it awards grants to, and the typical size of its grants.

Next you may wish to refer to the Center's *Grant Guides*. Remember, the *Grant Guide* series duplicates the information contained in *The Foundation Grants Index* and repackages it in particular focus areas for your convenience. Among the *Grant Guide* series, four titles provide ready access to grants that have been awarded for specific types of support. They are:

- "Matching and Challenge Support"

- "Program Evaluation Grants"

- "Scholarships, Student Aid and Loans"

- "Technical Assistance/Management Support"

Each *Grant Guide* is arranged alphabetically by state and, within each state, by foundation name, followed by the actual grant records (see Figure 46). At the back of each *Guide* is an alphabetically arranged list of foundations covered in that volume. For each foundation, the address and a brief statement of geographic and subject restrictions on its giving are included. This feature is especially useful when referring to a *Grant Guide* that focuses on a particular type of support, since it allows you to quickly exclude foundations that are inappropriate in terms of stated geographic or subject limitations, leaving you with a list of foundations that match your requirements in all three categories.

GRANTMAKER DATABASES AND DIRECTORIES

To adopt the grantmaker approach, once again you should begin with *FC Search*. In the Grantmaker file, Types of Support is a searchable field only in the Advanced Search mode. There is a pop-up index to help you select the appropriate terminology to

Figure 45. Type of Support/Geographic Index from *The Foundation Grants Index*

ANNUAL CAMPAIGNS

Animals/wildlife

Texas 42939

Arts/culture

Arizona 923
California 1451, 1456, 6180
Connecticut 11632
District of Columbia 6238, 12253
Georgia 2893, 3230, 10441
Illinois 3645
Massachusetts 4740, 4742, 4744
Michigan 5206
Minnesota 5581
New Mexico 12316
New York 8180, 9923, 12231, 12232, 12297
North Carolina 22648
Ohio 10539, 10542, 10753, 10975, 10996, 33602
Pennsylvania 11276, 11631, 11655, 12142
Texas 12302, 12376, 12415
Vermont 4429
Wisconsin 13143, 13232

Civil rights

District of Columbia 59035

Community improvement/development

District of Columbia 15108

Education, elementary/secondary

Arizona 19821
California 19817, 19822, 43280
Connecticut 22973, 24336, 24342
Georgia 20935, 22650
Iowa 28390
Maryland 22653
Massachusetts 19916, 24331
Minnesota 22281
New Jersey 22649, 22651, 22657, 24330
North Carolina 22648
Oklahoma 24387
Pennsylvania 24339, 24706, 24761
Rhode Island 25001, 25002
Texas 25101, 25329
Virginia 25369

Education, higher

California 26375, 31146
District of Columbia 26958
Illinois 28038
Iowa 28390, 28393
Lebanon 31387
Maryland 31102
Massachusetts 34058
Michigan 29510, 29512, 29518
New Hampshire 26354
New York 28348, 32554
North Carolina 34446
Ohio 31114, 33317, 33455, 33456, 33602, 33695
Oregon 26378, 26380
Pennsylvania 33987
Rhode Island 33345
Virginia 29666, 32955, 33238, 33446, 35212

Education, other

New Jersey 24330
New York 36786

Environment

New York 41717, 42885
Texas 42939
Wyoming 42893

Food/nutrition/agriculture

California 43280

Health—general/rehabilitative

Connecticut 45475
Delaware 45563
Michigan 46869
New Jersey 22657

Health—specific diseases

Pennsylvania 55286

Human services—multipurpose

California 58083
District of Columbia 59035
Minnesota 62391, 62393
Ohio 64880
Pennsylvania 65604

Philanthropy/voluntarism

Arizona 70443-70446
California 70207, 70211
Colorado 70421, 70434, 70436, 70440
Connecticut 70458, 71945
Delaware 70529, 70532
District of Columbia 70852
Georgia 70664, 72412
Hawaii 70695, 70700-70702
Illinois 70786, 70787, 70792, 70837, 70850
Indiana 70567, 70884, 70920
Iowa 70925
Louisiana 72404, 72405
Michigan 71065-71068, 71108, 71109, 71112-71116, 71129, 71226, 71231, 71274, 71287, 71347, 71350, 71351
Minnesota 70416, 71376, 71438, 71459
Missouri 71531, 71605
Nebraska 71627
New Jersey 71707, 71708, 71720-71722
New York 71943, 71944, 71967, 71970, 72026
North Carolina 72498
Ohio 72416, 72429, 72430, 72452, 72495, 72550-72553
Oregon 70424, 70425, 70427, 72497
Pennsylvania 70531, 70533, 72657, 72680, 72722, 72725, 72743, 72759, 72760, 73110
Tennessee 70864
Texas 72882, 72952, 72953
Utah 70426
Virginia 73038
Washington 70420, 70423, 70433
Wisconsin 70793, 73145, 73159

Public affairs/government

District of Columbia 75233

Religion

California 76867
Maryland 77775
Minnesota 78153
Tennessee 77778

Youth development

Illinois 84228
Louisiana 85539

AWARDS/PRIZES/COMPETITIONS

Animals/wildlife

New York 51669
Pennsylvania 51731

Arts/culture

California 1343, 1346, 1347, 1349, 1909, 2103, 2888, 6291, 11911, 12043, 30934, 58426
Colorado 2406, 2417
District of Columbia 4512
Florida 20948
Hawaii 1342, 1345
Illinois 54399

Kansas 35050
Maryland 7282, 35063
Massachusetts 37853, 49209
Michigan 10547
Minnesota 5478
New York 5860, 5876, 6606, 6694, 7294, 9607, 10003, 12913, 13502, 14304, 41774
Ohio 10763
Oregon 11146
Pennsylvania 11724
Poland 2837
Russia 9065, 9076
Texas 12584, 12604, 37852
Vermont 6336
Virginia 11410, 12904, 54400

Civil rights

California 13435
Colorado 13482
District of Columbia 13505, 71277
Illinois 13656
Michigan 82458
New York 13502, 13946, 14304
Rhode Island 78959

Community improvement/development

California 15080
Colorado 14947
Florida 17675
New York 16673, 16682, 16693, 16695, 16736, 16738, 16740, 16743, 17658, 74410
Ohio 16386, 19338
Pennsylvania 11724

Crime/courts/legal services

California 13435, 18357
Florida 18826
Illinois 18681
North Carolina 19311
Ohio 19338
Texas 19584

Education, elementary/secondary

Arizona 20435
California 1909, 2103, 6291, 30934
Colorado 58627, 79967
England 24839
Florida 20948
Idaho 20436
Illinois 21316
Iowa 79965
Maryland 82290
Massachusetts 79799
Michigan 22099
Minnesota 20441, 22268
Montana 20428
New Jersey 22585, 73532, 73533
New Mexico 20439, 81336
New York 6694, 9607, 10003, 31406
North Carolina 22565
North Dakota 20445
Ohio 10763, 25416
South Dakota 20426
Tennessee 25039, 53508
Texas 25143
Utah 25349, 79962
Vermont 6336
Washington 79966
Wisconsin 79964
Wyoming 20429

Education, higher

Arkansas 54824
Brazil 31472, 82550
California 25940, 26049, 26505, 26520, 30934, 54822
Colorado 79967
Connecticut 26753, 54829
Georgia 27335
Indiana 28182
Kansas 35050

Figure 46. Sample Page from a *Grant Guide*

4266. W N I T-TV, Channel 34, Elkhart, IN. $12,360, 1996. For program season.

IOWA

Roy J. Carver Charitable Trust

Limitations: Giving primarily in IA. No support for religious activities or political organizations. No grants to individuals, or for fundraising benefits, program advertising, annual operating support, or endowments.

4267. Dubuque Museum of Art, Dubuque, IA. $15,967, 1997. For at-risk youth photography pilot program.
4268. Mississippi Valley Regional Blood Center, Davenport, IA. $10,000, 1997. To create permanent exhibit at Family Museum of Arts and Science on biology of blood.

Gardner and Florence Call Cowles Foundation, Inc.

Limitations: Giving limited to IA, with emphasis on Des Moines. No grants to individuals, or for scholarships or fellowships; no loans.

4269. Civic Center of Greater Des Moines, Des Moines, IA. $20,000, 1996. For operating support.
4270. Civic Center of Greater Des Moines, Des Moines, IA. $20,000, 1996. For operating support.
4271. Des Moines Art Center, Des Moines, IA. $100,000, 1996. For endowment funds.
4272. Des Moines Art Center, Des Moines, IA. $17,000, 1996. For conservation project.
4273. Des Moines Community Playhouse, Des Moines, IA. $16,500, 1996. For building expansion.
4274. Des Moines Community Playhouse, Des Moines, IA. $11,480, 1996. For education outreach programs.
4275. Des Moines Community Playhouse, Des Moines, IA. $11,480, 1996. For educational outreach.
4276. Des Moines Metro Opera, Indianola, IA. $30,000, 1996. For operating support.
4277. Des Moines Metro Opera, Indianola, IA. $30,000, 1996. For operating support.
4278. Des Moines Symphony Association, Des Moines, IA. $120,000, 1996. For educational outreach and guest artist.
4279. Des Moines Symphony Association, Des Moines, IA. $40,000, 1996. For operating support.
4280. Science Center of Iowa, Des Moines, IA. $105,000, 1996. For upgrading planetarium equipment.
4281. Science Center of Iowa, Des Moines, IA. $50,000, 1996. For upgrading planetarium.

E & M Charities

Limitations: No support for private foundations. No grants to individuals, or for research.

4282. American Family Association, Tupelo, MS. $10,000, 1996.

Maytag Corporation Foundation

Limitations: Giving limited to areas of company operations, particularly Newton, IA, Galesburg and Herrin, IL, Jefferson City, MO, Bow, NH, North Canton, OH, Williston, SC, Cleveland and Jackson, TN and Burlington, VT. No support for health agencies, churches, religious causes, fraternal organizations, or international relations. No grants to individuals (except for employee-related scholarships), or for benefit dinners, complimentary advertising, or sponsorship of charity events.

4283. Civic Center of Greater Des Moines, Des Moines, IA. $10,000, 1997.
4284. Des Moines Art Center, Des Moines, IA. $20,000, 1997. For building improvements.
4285. Des Moines Metro Opera, Indianola, IA. $25,000, 1997.
4286. Des Moines Symphony Association, Des Moines, IA. $35,000, 1997. For Newton Performance.
4287. Iowa Public Television, Johnston, IA. $10,000, 1997. For Ready to Learn.
4288. Living History Farms, Urbandale, IA. $20,000, 1997.
4289. University of Iowa Foundation, Iowa City, IA. $50,000, 1997. For continued support for Fellowship Fund for Writers' Workshop.

R. J. McElroy Trust

Limitations: Giving primarily in the KWWL viewing area in northeast IA. No grants to individuals (except for fellowship program).

4290. Americas Agricultural-Industrial Heritage Landscape, Waterloo, IA. $55,000, 1996. For Silos and Smokestacks Program.
4291. Cedar Arts Forum, Waterloo, IA. $12,000, 1996. For educational programs.
4292. Four Mounds Foundation, Dubuque, IA. $30,000, 1996. For Y.E.S. Project.
4293. Grout Museum of History and Science, Waterloo, IA. $25,000, 1996. For educational and intern programs.
4294. K W W L-TV, Waterloo, IA. $33,255, 1996. For broadcast journalism internships.
4295. Old Creamery Theater Company, Amana, IA. $14,000, 1996. For Young People's Touring Company program.
4296. University of Northern Iowa, Performing Arts Center, Cedar Falls, IA. $100,000, 1996.
4297. Waterloo Community Playhouse, Black Hawk Children's Theater, Waterloo, IA. $15,000, 1996.
4298. Waterloo Community Playhouse, Education Center, Waterloo, IA. $80,000, 1996.
4299. Waterloo Community School District, Waterloo, IA. $10,000, 1996. For Cultural Literacy Program.
4300. Waterloo-Cedar Falls Symphony Orchestra, Waterloo, IA. $18,000, 1996. For educational programs.

The Principal Financial Group Foundation, Inc.

Limitations: Giving primarily in Des Moines and areas of company operations in Mason City and Waterloo, IA, Grand Island, NE, and Spokane, WA. No support for athletic, fraternal, sectarian, religious, denominational or social organizations, organizations redistributing funds, private foundations, trade, industrial or professional associations, libraries, individual K-12 schools, organizations outside U.S. whose activities are mainly international, or veterans' groups. No grants to individuals, or for conference or seminar attendance, goodwill ads, endowments, festival participation, or hospital or health care capital fund drives.

4301. Civic Center of Greater Des Moines, Des Moines, IA. $40,000, 1997. For general support.
4302. Civic Center of Greater Des Moines, Des Moines, IA. $13,500, 1997. For bridge funding and general operating support.
4303. Civic Center of Greater Des Moines, Des Moines, IA. $10,000, 1997. For computers.
4304. Des Moines Art Center, Des Moines, IA. $35,000, 1997. For general support.
4305. Des Moines Art Center, Des Moines, IA. $20,000, 1997. For bridge funding and general operating support.
4306. Des Moines Metro Opera, Indianola, IA. $35,000, 1997. Toward production of Merry Widow.
4307. Des Moines Metro Opera, Indianola, IA. $12,000, 1997. For bridge funding and 25th anniversary season.
4308. Des Moines Symphony, Des Moines, IA. $48,667, 1997.
4309. Living History Farms, Urbandale, IA. $75,000, 1997. For capital campaign.
4310. Living History Farms, Urbandale, IA. $25,000, 1997. For education programs.
4311. Salisbury House, Des Moines, IA. $100,000, 1997. For capital campaign.
4312. Science Center of Iowa, Des Moines, IA. $20,000, 1997. For daily programs of informal science education.

KANSAS

Dane G. Hansen Foundation

Limitations: Giving primarily in Logan, Phillips County, and northwestern KS; scholarships limited to residents of 26 northwestern KS counties.

4313. K A N Z FM Radio-Kanza Society, Garden City, KS. $10,000, 1996.
4314. Kansas State University Foundation, Huck Boyd Media Center, Manhattan, KS. $25,000, 1996.
4315. Smoky Hill Public Television Corporation - K O O D 9, Bunker Hill, KS. $16,000, 1996.

GRANTS FOR ARTS, CULTURE & THE HUMANITIES   73

describe the types of support your organization needs. You can also search for subject and geographic limitations, as well as a number of other fields, while you search for types of support, thereby streamlining your research efforts.

If *FC Search* is not available, you might begin with *The Foundation 1000* and its Types of Support Index, particularly if you have a program or project that may be of interest to some of the country's largest foundations. This index identifies the top 1,000 foundations by the types of support they typically provide. Notice that the arrangement is alphabetical by type of support, then by state. You will also notice that certain foundation names are in boldface (see Figure 47). Boldface indicates a foundation with a national or broad regional focus. Foundations listed in regular type generally limit their giving to the city or state in which they are located. This distinction can speed your research by allowing you to zero in on those foundations whose geographic focus matches that of your organization at the same time that you are identifying those foundations which provide the type of support your organization needs.

To further expand your prospect list, turn to the Types of Support indexes provided in *The Foundation Directory* and *The Foundation Directory Part 2.* Keep in mind that, as with *The Foundation 1000,* these indexes list the types of support funders say they are interested in, rather than the types of support represented by the actual grants they have awarded. While this may seem like a trivial distinction, it can be a significant one for the grantseeker.

While a history of grants actually awarded is generally considered to be a better indication of a foundation's willingness to provide a particular type of support than a mere statement to that effect, you should not take such indications too literally. In other words, just because a prospective funder has failed to offer a particular type of support in the past does not mean it will refuse to do so in the future. Funders that specifically restrict the types of support they provide (e.g., "no grants for endowment"), on the other hand, should probably be taken at their word and eliminated from your prospect list.

SPECIALIZED FUNDING GUIDES

There are a number of specialized guides and handbooks that cover funding geared to a specific type of support. For example, if you were trying to find funds to purchase equipment for a science laboratory in a private secondary school, the *Directory of Building and Equipment Grants* by Richard M. Eckstein would be an appropriate resource for you. If you are trying to fund a research project, Oryx Press' annual *Directory of Research Grants* may be helpful. Refer to Appendix A for a select listing of these and other

Figure 47. Types of Support Index from *The Foundation 1000*

INDEX OF TYPES OF SUPPORT

Illinois: **Abbott 1**
Michigan: **Earhart 277,** Hudson 460, **Kellogg 509**
Minnesota: Jerome 481
Nebraska: **Buffett 116**
New York: **Central 152,** Clark 171, **Delmas 243, Ford 324,** Lauder 545, **Rockefeller 805,** Wallace 949, **Wenner 943**
Ohio: **Scripps 840**
Utah: Ashton 39
Virginia: **Freedom 336,** Mustard 672

In-kind gifts
Alabama: Sonat 868, **Vulcan 944**
California: Gap 347, McConnell 600
Connecticut: GTE 394
District of Columbia: **MCI 614**
Florida: Beveridge 80
Georgia: Callaway 132
Illinois: **Amoco 26,** Dillon 253
Iowa: Maytag **594,** Principal 762
Maine: UNUM 933
Massachusetts: BankBoston 57
Michigan: **Chrysler 165,** Gerber 362
Minnesota: **Minnesota 646**
Missouri: Ameren 23, **Hallmark 408, McDonnell 607, Monsanto 650,** Ralston 771
New Jersey: **Union 928**
New York: **Metropolitan 637,** Morgan 660, **Open 713**
Ohio: Eaton 278, GenCorp 356
Oklahoma: Schusterman 839
Pennsylvania: Bayer 64, **Consolidated 202, Rockwell 808**
Texas: **Cooper 204, RGK 793**
Utah: Swanson 898
Virginia: Norfolk 689
Washington: Boeing 89

Internships
California: **Getty 367, Packard 720,** Parsons 727, Peninsula 732
Connecticut: **Olin 708**
District of Columbia: **German 364**
Florida: **Davis 236**
Georgia: **Coca-Cola 178, UPS 934**
Illinois: Comer 185, Fry 343
Iowa: McElroy 609
Massachusetts: **Kendall 516,** Stoddard 886
Minnesota: Bremer 101, **Minnesota 646**
New Jersey: Schering 833, **Union 928**
New York: Bodman 88, Emerson 293, **Ford 324, Kress 537,** Lang 542, **List 560, Luce 568,** New York 680, Noble 683, **Open 713, Pforzheimer 739,** Revson 787, **Rockefeller 804,** Rubinstein 818
North Carolina: Duke 272, Morehead 657
Ohio: Gund 398, **Scripps 840**
Oklahoma: Schusterman 839
Pennsylvania: Fels 309, Heinz 427, McKenna 617, **Pew 737**
Tennessee: Frist 341
Texas: Cain 127, Meadows 624
Wisconsin: Bradley 99, Northwestern 693

Land acquisition
Arizona: Morris 662
California: Ahmanson 8, ARCO 37, **Compton 198,** Copley 206, Cowell 210, Goldman 376, Haas 402, Hedco 426, Hewlett 438, Irwin 477, Marin 582, McBean 596, **Packard 720,** San Diego 823, Santa Barbara 826
Colorado: Boettcher 90, El Pomar 289, Gates 350, Johnson 486
Connecticut: Hartford 417, **Olin 708**
Delaware: Crystal 217, Laffey 539, Longwood 565
District of Columbia: **Wallace 947**
Florida: Beveridge 80, Bush 122, **Chatlos 157,** Dade 224, **Davis 236,** Selby 845
Georgia: Callaway 132, Campbell 135, Community 188, Evans 300, Whitehead 979, Woodruff 993

Hawaii: Castle 150
Illinois: Chicago 160, Dillon 253
Indiana: Indianapolis 472, **Lilly 554,** Lincoln 555
Iowa: Hall 407, Principal 762
Kentucky: Brown 108
Maryland: Abell 4, Meyerhoff 640
Massachusetts: Davis 232, State 877, Stoddard 886
Michigan: Dalton 225, Gerstacker 365, Gilmore 371, Grand Rapids 386, **Kresge 536,** Steelcase 879
Minnesota: Carolyn 141
Nebraska: Kiewit 519
New Jersey: Grassmann 388, Hyde 470, Turrell 925, **Union 928,** Victoria 943
New Mexico: McCune 603
New York: Barker 59, Cary 146, Freeman 337, Hayden 422, Lang 542, McCann 598, O'Connor 697, Ohrstrom 706, **Weeden 961**
North Carolina: Bryan 110
Ohio: Columbus 184, Dana 227, GAR 348, Gund 398, Kulas 538, Procter 764, Schmidlapp 836, Star 874, Stranahan 888, **Timken 910**
Oklahoma: Helmerich 432, McMahon 621
Oregon: Oregon 714
Pennsylvania: Hillman 444, Laurel 546, McKenna 617, Mellon 630, Penn 733, Trexler 920
Rhode Island: Champlin 154, Rhode Island 794
Tennessee: Plough 749
Texas: Amarillo 21, Carter 143, Cockrell 179, Communities 187, Cullen 219, Fikes 313, Halsell 409, Hillcrest 442, Hoblitzelle 449, Houston 457, Johnson 487, Kimberly 520, McDermott 606, Meadows 624, Moody 655, Richardson 796, Rockwell 807
Virginia: Norfolk 688
Washington: **Weyerhaeuser 972**
Wisconsin: Alexander 13

Matching funds
Alabama: Alabama 9, **Vulcan 944**
Arizona: Morris 662
Arkansas: **Frueauff 342,** Rockefeller 806, Wal-Mart 946
California: Ahmanson 8, Amateur 22, ARCO 37, **BankAmerica 56, Banyan 58,** California 130, Clorox 176, Compton **198, Confidence 200, Cowell 210,** Crail 212, Drown 270, Forest 327, Getty 366, **Getty 367,** Haas 401, Haas 402, Haas 403, Harden 412, Hedco 426, Hewlett 438, Hofmann 454, Irvine 476, Jones 495, Marin 582, McBean 596, McConnell 600, Norris 690, **Packard 720,** Parsons 727, Peninsula 732, Powell 754, Riordan 798, San Diego 823, Santa Barbara 826, **Seaver 841,** Sierra 853, Smith 862, Sonoma 869, Stauffer 878, Taper 899, Transamerica 915, Valley 938, Valley 939, Weingart 964, WWW 996
Colorado: Boettcher 90, Buell 115, Denver 247, Gates 350, Johnson 486, **U S WEST 926**
Connecticut: **Aetna 7,** Community 189, **Educational 285,** Hartford 417, **Olin 708,** Tremaine 919
Delaware: Laffey 539, **Raskob 775,** Welfare 966
District of Columbia: **Bauman 62,** Cafritz 126, **Fannie 304,** Graham 384, **Hitachi 447, McGowan 612,** Meyer 638, **Moriah 661, Public 768, Wallace 947**
Florida: Beveridge 80, Bush 122, **Chatlos 157,** Community 190, Dade 224, **Davis 236, DeMoss 246,** duPont 275, **Knight 529,** Selby 845, Winn-Dixie 984
Georgia: Callaway 132, Callaway 135, Campbell 135, **Coca-Cola 178,** Community 188, **Turner 924, UPS 934**
Hawaii: Alexander 12, Atherton 42, McInerny 615
Illinois: Chicago 160, Coleman 180, **Crowell 215,** Crown 216, Dillon 253, Fel-Pro 307, Fry 343, **MacArthur 574, McCormick 602,** Northern 691, Retirement 784
Indiana: Ball 53, Ball 54, **Cummins 223,** Dekko 241, Indianapolis 472, Lilly 553, **Lilly 554,** Lincoln 555, Ogle 705
Iowa: Hall 407, **Maytag 594,** McElroy 609
Kentucky: Brown 108, Community 196
Maine: UNUM 933

Maryland: Abell 4, Goldseker 378, Meyerhoff 640, **Weinberg 963**
Massachusetts: Balfour 52, BankBoston 57, Boston 94, **Fleet 316,** High 441, Hyams 469, Peabody 730, State 877, Stoddard 886
Michigan: Dalton 225, DeVos 249, Dow 267, **Ford 326,** General 358, **Gerber 362,** Gerstacker 365, Gilmore 371, Grand Rapids 386, **Herrick 435,** Hudson 460, Kalamazoo 501, **Kresge 536, Mott 666,** Steelcase 879, Towsley 914, **Whirlpool 973,** Wickes 980
Minnesota: Bigelow 81, Blandin 84, Bremer 101, Bush 123, **Lutheran 570,** Mardag 581, McKnight 620, **Minnesota 646,** Saint Paul 821
Missouri: Ameren 23, **Anheuser 31, Hallmark 408,** Kansas City 502, **Kauffman 506,** Monsanto 650
Nebraska: ConAgra 199, Kiewit 519, Omaha 712, **Union 930**
Nevada: Cord 208
New Hampshire: Foundation 330, Lindsay 557
New Jersey: Campbell 136, Dodge 257, Fund 345, Hyde 470, **Johnson 488, KPMG 534,** MCJ 616, Prudential 766, Rippel 799, **Schumann 838,** Turrell 925, **Union 928,** Victoria 943, Warner 953
New Mexico: Maddox 577, McCune 603
New York: **AT&T 41, Avon 47, Baker 51,** Bodman 88, Booth 93, Cary 146, Claiborne 170, Cummings 222, **Dana 228, Dodge 256, Donner 263,** Emerson 293, **Engelhard 295, Ford 324,** Gebbie 353, Goldsmith 379, Guttman 399, **Harriman 413, Hasbro 419,** Hayden 422, Heckscher 425, **Humanitas 463,** International 475, **Johnson 485,** List 560, Littauer 561, **Luce 568, Mellon 629,** Morgan 658, Noble 683, O'Connor 697, Ohrstrom 706, Park 724, **Pforzheimer 739,** Pinkerton 747, Prospect 765, **Ramapo 772, Rockefeller 804,** Ross 816, Samuels 822, Scherman 834, Steele 881, **Teagle 900, Tinker 911, United 932,** van Ameringen 940, van Ameringen 941
North Carolina: Blumenthal 86, Cannon 137, Duke 272, Foundation 331, **Kenan 514,** Reynolds 788, Reynolds 791, Wachovia 945, Winston-Salem 988
Ohio: Bruening 109, Cincinnati 167, Cleveland 175, Columbus 184, Community 194, Corbett 207, 1525 311, First 314, GAR 348, Gund 398, Hoover 456, Jennings 480, Kulas 538, Mathile 591, Mead 623, Montgomery 653, Murphy 669, Nationwide 675, Nord 686, Prentiss 756, Reinberger 781, Second 843, **Timken 910,** TRW 922
Oklahoma: Chapman 155, Kirkpatrick 524, McMahon 621, **Noble 684,** Reynolds 789, Sarkeys 828, Schusterman 839
Oregon: Collins 181, Meyer 639, Oregon 714
Pennsylvania: Alcoa 10, Barra 60, Benedum 74, **Consolidated 202,** Fels 309, Heinz 428, Heinz 429, Hillman 444, Huston 468, Jewish 483, Laurel 546, Mellon 630, Penn 733, **Pew 737,** Philadelphia 740, **Rockwell 808, Scaife 832,** Smith 863, **Templeton 903,** Trexler 920, Westinghouse 969
Rhode Island: **Ford 325,** Rhode Island 794
South Carolina: Self 846
Tennessee: Assisi 40, Benwood 75, **Bridgestone 102,** Chattanooga 158, Christy 164, Davis 233, Frist 341, **Lyndhurst 571, Maclellan 575,** Plough 749
Texas: Abell 5, Amarillo 21, Anderson 29, Brown 107, Cain 127, Carter 143, CH 153, Cockrell 179, Communities 187, **Cooper 204,** Cullen 219, Dunn 274, Fikes 313, George 360, Harrington 414, Hillcrest 442, Hoblitzelle 449, Johnson 487, **Kleberg 525,** McDermott 606, McGovern 610, McGovern 611, Meadows 624, Moody 655, **Rapoport 774, RGK 793,** Richardson 796, Rockwell 807, SBC 829, Shell 850, Strake 887, Sturgis 895, Temple 901, Wortham 995
Utah: Eccles 281, Swanson 898
Virginia: Gannett 346, **Jones 496**
Washington: Boeing 89, Bullitt 118, Kreielsheimer 535, McCaw 599, Murdock 667, **Stewardship 884**
Wisconsin: Alexander 13, Bradley 99, Cudahy 218, **Johnson 484,** Milwaukee 644, Northwestern 693, Siebert 852, Wisconsin 989

specialized guides; and be sure to check with your local library for new titles of publications developed specifically for your geographic area. Of particular interest to the grantseeker adopting a types of support approach might be guidebooks on capital campaigns as well as those dealing with "bricks and mortar" and equipment grants.

Step Two: Refining Your List

You should now have a lengthy list of foundations that might possibly be interested in funding your project or program. Now is the time to refine the list to a reasonable number of grantmakers who probably would look favorably on your program. You should review your types of support prospect list to eliminate those foundations that are not interested in your subject and/or that do not award grants in your geographic area. If you used *FC Search* to construct your list, you probably used multiple search criteria, thereby completing this step already. It is also relatively simple to do it while developing your list from print sources. Completing the prospect worksheet for each potential funder enables you to quickly eliminate those less appropriate candidates.

Now that you have determined that the funders on your list have demonstrated a real commitment to providing the type of support your organization needs, funding in your subject field, and funding in your geographic area, you are ready to scrutinize your list further to determine those potential funders who are most likely to be interested in your organization or program or project. You'll want to do as much research on all aspects pertaining to these grantmakers as time and resources permit. Posing the questions raised in Chapter 4 is a good place to start:

- Does the funder accept applications?

- Does the amount of money you are requesting fit within the funder's typical grant range?

- Does the funder put limits on the length of time it is willing to support a project?

- What type of organizations does the funder tend to support?

- Does the funder have application deadlines, or does it review proposals continuously?

- Do you or does anyone on your board know someone connected with a potential funder?

Most of these questions can be answered by referring to any one of several sources. *FC Search: The Foundation Center's Database on CD-ROM* will answer many of them. Directories such as *The Foundation Directory* or *The Foundation 1000* or some of the state and local directories will also provide the answers you need. For application deadlines, board meeting dates, and the names of trustees, officers, or donors, Center directories and databases are excellent sources.

Sometimes you will need to refer to original sources such as the IRS Form 990-PF, annual report or application guidelines. For instance, suppose you are trying to identify funders who would be interested in providing money for staff development to help teachers incorporate math skills in middle school classes. You have identified a funder that gives in your geographic area with an interest in elementary and secondary education. However, there is no indication in any of the directories, neither through grants lists nor in grantmaker statements about types of support, that this funder will provide money for staff development. On the other hand, there is no statement explicitly saying that the grantmaker will *not* give for this purpose. At this point, you should do some further investigation using primary sources. If the grantmaker publishes an annual report, secure a copy and study the grants list. If not, look at the foundation's 990-PF at the foundation's office, from the IRS, or at the Foundation Center library nearest you. Are there any grants that appear to be for staff development? Do any of the grants relate to improving teaching skills? An examination of a complete grants list can be very revealing about foundation priorities.

On other occasions, secondary sources such as articles in newspapers and journals will provide the answers you need. *Philanthropy News Digest (PND)*, the Foundation Center's weekly online summary of the news of the world of philanthropy, is a searchable database that will allow you to seek recent information about foundations and their philanthropic efforts. *PND* summaries will also inform you of changes in leadership, very recent major grants, and other such information. Using the example above, you may wish to enter the name of the foundation in question and see what kinds of grants it has awarded recently. Another source for information on recently awarded grants is the *Chronicle of Philanthropy*'s "Guide to Grants" database on the Web (www.philanthropy.com/grants/), which indexes the grants lists previously printed in the *Chronicle of Philanthropy*.

A review of the resources detailed in Chapter 5 will help you to decide which directory, annual report, IRS return, application guidelines, etc. will assist you in answering the detailed questions necessary to refine your list to the most likely candidates. When you have answered these questions about the funders on your broad prospect list, you will have narrowed your list to the few that you should approach.

Summary

Grantmakers offer a wide variety of support for nonprofit organizations, from in-kind gifts from corporate donors to multi-million dollar grants for building construction from some of the large private foundations. A nonprofit seeking funds must first determine the types of support the organization needs. The grantseeker must then investigate the types of support each grantmaker provides. A grantmaker's type(s) of support is one of the three cornerstones of funding research, the other two being subject (field of interest) and geographic focus. You can find out which types of support a specific grantmaker provides in several different ways, including referring to electronic databases, directories, informational tax returns, annual reports, and newspaper articles. For guidelines to identify foundations with an interest in your subject field, see Chapter 6; for information on pinpointing the geographic parameters of grantmakers, see Chapter 7. Having followed the recommended procedures for these three funding research approaches, you should have a well-honed prospect list. Now you may be ready to move on to Chapter 10, which will lay the groundwork for presenting your project to a funder. But first, Chapter 9 describes effective utilization of funding resources on a specific type of funder—the corporate giver.

Chapter 9

Resources for Corporate Funding Research

According to *Giving USA*, published by the AAFRC Trust for Philanthropy, U.S. business contributions to nonprofits (including both corporate foundation giving and direct giving by corporations) came to $8.2 billion in 1997, or 5.2 percent of total charitable giving (see Figure 5). Nonmonetary support for nonprofits, often called noncash support or "in-kind gifts," is frequently considered an operating expenditure rather than a charitable contribution by the company that incurred the expense, and, hence, is often omitted from corporate contribution statistics. The Conference Board estimates that donations of noncash resources, at tax-valuation rates, constitutes about 25 percent of corporate giving. Therefore, at fair market value, noncash contributions would approach 33 percent of all corporate contributions.[1] Although corporate grants are typically smaller than grants from independent foundations, nonprofits would be wise

---

1. "Corporate Contributions in 1996." Report Number 1202-98-RR (New York: The Conference Board, 1998), pp. 4 and 18.

to consider corporations as part of their overall funding strategies. As discussed in Chapter 1, the Foundation Center tracks corporate direct giving (when possible), in addition to giving by corporate foundations, because this can be a significant potential source of support for nonprofits.

Unlike foundations and other charitable agencies, corporations clearly do not exist to give money away. Their allegiance, instead, is to their customers, shareholders, employees, and—most of all—to the bottom line. There is no simple answer as to why corporations support nonprofit organizations and their causes. Many, if not most, contribute out of a combination of altruism and self-interest, and it is nearly impossible to determine where one leaves off and the other begins. It is fair to assume, however, that corporate givers will seek some benefit from their charitable activities. Regardless of the motivation behind corporate giving, the attitudes of top management more than any other factor impact the giving philosophies of corporations. Chief executive officers often play a primary role in company giving, with contributions officers usually reporting directly to the CEO or to the chief financial officer.

Corporate Foundations and Corporate Direct Giving

Corporations may provide support to nonprofit organizations in a variety of ways. Some companies give only through direct giving programs; others choose to channel the majority of their charitable activities through a private foundation; still others use both vehicles to support nonprofit organizations in their communities. Regardless of which method of charitable support the company chooses, it is important for the grantseeker to understand the differences between a corporate foundation and a corporate direct giving program administered within a company.

CORPORATE FOUNDATIONS

Corporate foundations obtain their funds from profit-making companies or corporations, but are legally independent entities whose purpose is to make grants, usually on a broad basis, although not without regard for the business interests of the corporation. In practice, corporate foundations generally maintain close ties with the parent company, and their giving is usually in fields related to corporate activities or in communities where the parent company operates. The governing board of a corporate foundation is frequently composed of officers of the parent company.

Some corporate foundations have substantial endowments from which they make grants. Others maintain small endowments and rely on regular annual contributions ("gifts received") from the parent company to support their giving programs. These annual contributions are most often "pass-through" gifts. They do not increase the corporate foundation's endowment. Rather, they pass through the foundation to the intended beneficiaries in the nonprofit sector. Corporate foundations may be less subject to the ups and downs of the profit cycle or the vagaries of the stock market than corporate direct giving programs. In years of heavy profits, corporations may use their foundations to set aside funds that can be called upon to sustain their charitable giving in years when corporate earnings are lower.

Since corporate foundations must adhere to the same rules and regulations that other private foundations follow, including filing a yearly Form 990-PF with the IRS, it is usually much easier for the grantseeker to obtain information about a corporate foundation than it is about a corporate direct giving program. In fact, when approaching corporations, the lack of information about corporate direct giving may be one of the biggest obstacles the grantseeker faces.

CORPORATE DIRECT GIVING PROGRAMS

Corporate direct giving—all non-foundation company giving—is based solely on corporate resources and tends to rise and fall with corporate profits. For federal tax purposes companies can deduct up to 10 percent of their pretax income for charitable contributions. Corporate direct giving is less regulated and less public than that of company-sponsored foundations. Corporations are not required to publicize direct giving programs or to sustain prescribed levels of funding. They can also make various other types of contributions, sometimes treated as business expenses, which are not necessarily included in giving statistics.

Managers of corporate direct giving programs today increasingly seem to favor nonmonetary, or in-kind, support along with, or in lieu of, cash grants. Such support includes products, supplies, and equipment; facilities and support services (e.g., meeting space, mailing, computer services); and public relations (e.g., printing and duplicating, graphic arts, advertising). As part of noncash support, corporations may also provide employee expertise in areas such as legal assistance and tax advice, market research, and strategic planning. In addition, many companies encourage and reward employee voluntarism, and some even permit their employees to take time off with pay to perform volunteer work. Corporations tend to support organizations where their employees are involved as volunteers, and some companies donate funds to these organizations exclusively.

Newer forms of corporate activity, including event sponsorship and cause-related marketing—neither of which meet the definition of pure "giving"—have been on the rise in recent years. With event sponsorship, a company provides the money and/or volunteers necessary to promote the nonprofit's program or event to a wide audience. In exchange the company receives favorable publicity for "doing good" in the community. Both the business and the nonprofit increase their incomes and communicate with large numbers of customers and donors by means of corporate sponsorship of a nonprofit's event or program. Cause-related marketing, currently experiencing a resurgence, is a joint venture between a business and a nonprofit group to market products or services through a public association. Although some critics feel that a charitable contribution should not provide the donor with a profit, cause-related marketing has proven effective for a variety of causes, including some non-traditional charities such as those supporting people with AIDS or battered women. Companies find that such marketing-related donations increase sales or help target new markets.

Although corporate foundations and corporate direct giving programs are legally separate entities and are subject to different regulations and reporting requirements, grantseekers often confuse the two giving sources. The confusion is easily understood when you consider that the corporate foundation's grantmaking program and the corporation's direct giving program are often coordinated under the same general policy and may even be administered by the very same staff.

Resources

As we have noted, it is far easier for the grantseeker to locate information about corporate foundations than about corporate direct giving programs. Because corporate foundations are private foundations, as defined in the Tax Reform Act of 1969 and its subsequent amendments, the public has access to their Forms 990-PF. Because there are no public disclosure laws about a company's direct charitable giving program, the public knows only those activities about which the company chooses to release information. However, with patience and creativity, the grantseeker can locate pertinent information about corporate direct giving programs as well.

FC SEARCH

FC Search: The Foundation Center's Database on CD-ROM is a good place to begin your quest to identify potential corporate funders that may be interested in your program or organization. *FC Search* contains a comprehensive database with information on more than 2,000 company-sponsored foundations and on more than 1,000 corporate direct giving programs. Because direct giving program records are not public information, the Center sends questionnaires to corporations soliciting information about their giving programs. If company personnel complete and return the questionnaire, the information appears in *FC Search* and certain Center print publications. If there is no response to the questionnaire, the Center has no reliable way to gather the information. Therefore, while there are a significant number of corporate direct giving programs in *FC Search*, the list should not be considered comprehensive.

To concentrate solely on corporate donors, enter the Advanced Grantmaker database in *FC Search* and use the Grantmaker Type field as one of your criteria. Then select either company-sponsored foundations or corporate direct giving programs or both from a list of five types of grantmakers (see Figure 48). The Corporate Name field lets

Figure 48. Advanced Grantmaker/Grantmaker Type Index from *FC Search: The Foundation Center's Database on CD-ROM*

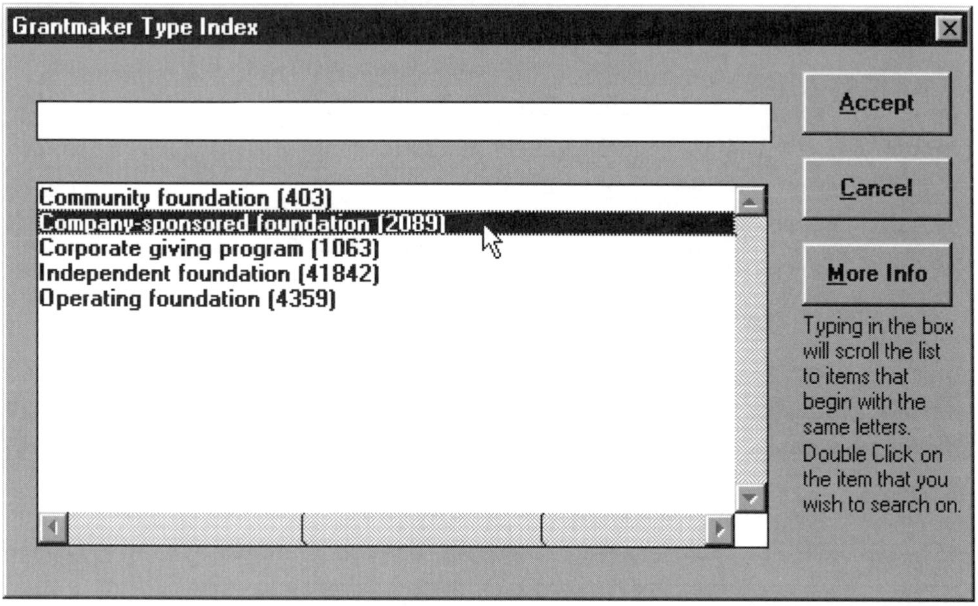

you select a grantmaker, either a company-sponsored foundation or a direct giving program, by specific company affiliation. The Corporate Location field allows you to search for grantmakers with company affiliations in particular cities (see Figure 49). Because it accesses plant and subsidiary locations, not just corporate headquarters, the Corporate Location field is useful in identifying local corporate funding in a specific geographic area. If the corporate direct giving program or the company-sponsored foundation has a presence on the World Wide Web, *FC Search* will indicate that by providing the grantmaker's URL (Web page address), and you can connect directly to that grantmaker's Web site (see Figure 50).

THE WORLD WIDE WEB AS AN INFORMATION SOURCE

The World Wide Web is an important source of information about corporate community involvement and grantmaking activities. Most of the corporate giving information

Figure 49. Advanced Grantmaker/Corporate Location Search from *FC Search: The Foundation Center's Database on CD-ROM*

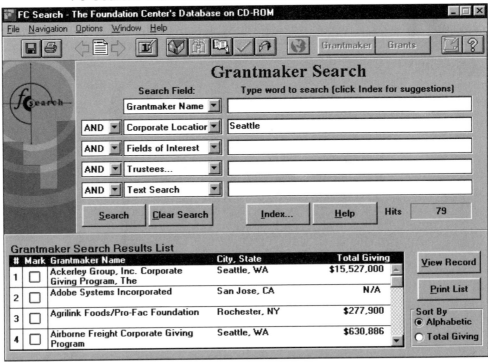

Figure 50. Sample Corporate Foundation Entry from *FC Search: The Foundation Center's Database on CD-ROM*

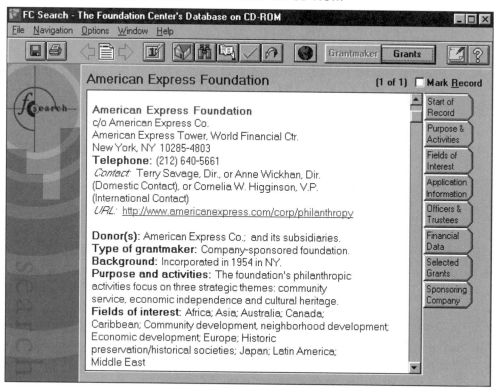

available on the Web today is about corporate foundations, including specific information concerning grantmaking activities, application procedures, contact person, geographic limitations, fields of interest, types of support, and so forth. Referring to a "portal" or "gateway" site, a comprehensive site offering several services around a specific topic, is probably the easiest way to research corporate grantmaking on the Web. The Foundation Center's Web site at www.fdncenter.org contains hyperlinks (direct connections with a click of the mouse) to corporate foundations and corporate direct giving programs with a presence on the Web (see Figure 51). Another resource to help you get started is the Council on Foundations' Web site at www.cof.org, which provides links to Web sites of Council members that are corporate foundations and corporate direct giving programs.

Figure 51. Corporate Grantmakers on the Internet from the Foundation Center's Web Site

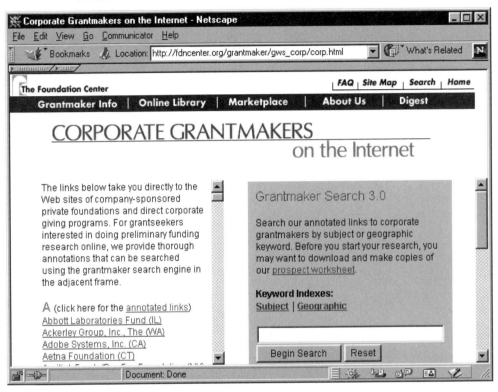

Other Web pages useful as sources of corporate giving information include Internet Prospector's Corporate Giving Page (w3.uwyo.edu/~prospect), which contains links and descriptions of several corporate direct giving programs and corporate foundations, and *Philanthropy Journal*, whose Web site (www.pj.org/) contains links to a corporate giving newsletter, a hypertext directory of corporate foundations and corporate direct giving programs, and a hypertext list of other prospect research pages. The Northern California Community Foundation's home page (www.foundations.org/index.html) contains a hypertext directory of foundations and corporate grantmakers.

As another way to uncover information on corporate giving on the Web, try some of the search engines mentioned in Chapter 5, such as Google (www.google.com), Infoseek (www.infoseek.com), or Yahoo! (www.yahoo.com). The key to finding sites that enable you to focus in on precisely what you want while eliminating thousands of irrelevant Web sites is choosing the proper wording and knowing the rules pertaining to the specific search engine you are using. Each site works differently, in terms of search procedures and information covered.

The specific keywords or subject descriptors you choose can greatly improve the search results you receive. Try searching initially using phrases like "corporate giving," "community relations," and "corporate contributions." Once you have a sense of what kind of information is available on the Web, you may be able to further narrow your searches by adding words more specific to your own needs (e.g. "arts corporate giving"). You may also want to try the same search using different search engines to see how your results vary. Other keywords to try are "in-kind gift" if you are looking for product donations, or "community reinvestment act" for those seeking loans.

In the event that you are interested in researching the corporate giving policies of a specific company at the company's Web site, you may be disappointed. Although a corporate Web site may mention the corporation's direct giving program, it usually does not go into great detail about the company's charitable endeavors. Frequently, the corporate giving information is contained on a "page within a page" at a company's Web site. In other words, you have to read through many different sections to get to the information you want. The best way to save time is to find the site map for that company's site (see Figure 52). A site map is a listing of all of the pages contained within a particular Web site. These listings are often more reliable than the more tedious process of reading through each section of a specific Web site. Look for terms in the site map or on the menu list such as "About Us," "History," "Community," "Corporate Relations," and even "News Releases." These subjects are the ones most likely to contain information about a company's direct giving program. Even if you are unable to locate specific information about a company's charitable activities, studying the company's Web site, as with reading the print version of a company's annual report, can provide you with important clues to its "personality" and interests.

For more details on corporate giving sites, see *The Foundation Center's Guide to Grantseeking on the Web*. This guide has a chapter devoted to corporate giving information on the Web, listing many useful sites and suggesting specific search strategies.

DIRECTORIES

Several print directories can help you locate information about corporate foundations and corporate direct giving. Appendix A lists a number of important resources. The *National Directory of Corporate Giving,* published by the Foundation Center, indexes companies by their trustees, officers, and donors; location; type of business; subject

Figure 52. Sample Site Map

areas of giving; and types of support provided. Entries include plant and subsidiary locations, *Forbes* or *Fortune* rankings, descriptions of business activities, financial data, contact persons, giving interests, application guidelines, and types of support awarded (see Figure 53). All entries are sent first to the corporations for verification, and the information becomes part of the Foundation Center's database, where it is continually updated.

Corporate Foundation Profiles, another print directory from the Foundation Center, provides in-depth information on the largest corporate foundations. The 10th edition (1998) contains detailed analytical profiles (see Figure 54) of 195 corporate foundations, plus basic financial data on another 1,200 corporate foundations with annual giving in excess of $50,000. The profiles, arranged alphabetically by company name, are compiled from a variety of sources, including direct information from the foundations, published foundation annual reports, news releases, newspaper and

Figure 53. Sample Entry from *National Directory of Corporate Giving*

1250
INTERNATIONAL PAPER
COMPANY
Purchase, NY

Business activities: Manufactures paper, wood products, and packaging products
Financial profile for 1996: Number of employees, 84,300; assets, $28,252,000,000; sales volume, $20,143,000,000
Fortune 500 ranking: 1996—44th in revenues, 241st in profits, and 93rd in assets
Forbes ranking: 1996—42nd in sales, 245th in net profits, and 81st in assets
Corporate officers: John T. Dillon, Chair., Pres., and C.E.O.; James P. Melican, Exec. V.P., Legal and Corp. Affairs; Marianne M. Parrs, Sr. V.P. and C.F.O.; Robert M. Byrnes, Sr. V.P., Human Resources; E. William Boehmler, V.P. and Treas.; James Guedry, V.P. and Secy.; Andrew R. Lessin, Cont.
Subsidiaries: Anchor/Lith-Kem-Ko, Inc., Orange Park, FL; Arizona Chemical Co., Panama City, FL; Dixon Paper Co., Denver, CO; Federal Paper Board, Montvale, NJ; GCO Minerals Co., Houston, TX; Hammermill Paper Co., Memphis, TN; Ilford, Inc., Paramus, NJ; International Paper Realty Corp., Park Ridge, NJ; international Paper Sales Co., New York, NY; Masonite Corp., Chicago, IL; Shumate Business Forms Co., Lebanon, IN; Veratec, Inc., Walpole, MA
Plant(s): Mobile, Selma, AL; Camden, Gurdon, AR; Carson, Los Angeles, Modesto, San Jose, Stockton, CA; Aurora, Colorado Springs, Pueblo, CO; Miami, Orlando, Tampa, FL; Chicago, Itasca, St. Charles, IL; Elkhart, Indianapolis, Lebanon, IN; Kansas City, Overland Park, Wichita, KS; Louisville, Monticello, KY; Bastrop, Mansfield, Pineville, LA; Winchester, MA; Moss Point, MS; Statesville, NC; Erie, PA
Giving statement: Giving through a corporate giving program and a foundation.

International Paper Company Charitable Giving Program
2 Manhattanville Rd.
Purchase, NY 10577 (914) 397-1581

Contact: Sandra C. Wilson, V.P.
Financial data (yr. ended 12/31/93): $3,516,660 for 2,768 grants (high: $291,056; low: $50).
Purpose and activities: The corporate giving program is decentralized and more industry-related than the International Paper Company Foundation, with each division responding to local community needs. Support for general charitable concerns, including economic development.
Fields of interest: General charitable giving.
Types of support: Annual campaigns; capital campaigns; building/renovation; endowment funds; conferences/seminars; fellowships; scholarship funds; sponsorships; donated equipment; donated land; donated products.
Geographic limitations: Giving primarily in communities where company facilities are located; areas where employee population is large; giving is done by major foreign subsidiaries in their own countries.
Support limitations: No grants to individuals.
Publications: Corporate report.

Application information: Application form not required.
Initial approach: Send requests to nearest company facility
Deadline(s): None
Final notification: 2 to 3 weeks

International Paper Company Foundation
2 Manhattanville Rd.
Purchase, NY 10577 (914) 397-1503
FAX: (914) 397-1505

Establishment information: Incorporated in 1952 in NY.
Donor(s): International Paper Co.
Contact: Kenneth Reeves, V.P.
Financial data (yr. ended 12/31/95): Assets, $46,205,000 (M); expenditures, $3,025,256; qualifying distributions, $2,921,256, including $2,370,157 for 343 grants (high: $15,000; low: $700), $490,099 for employee matching gifts and $61,000 for foundation-administered programs.
Purpose and activities: Grants are primarily for model projects in company communities with focus on pre-college levels of education, programs for minorities and women in the sciences, health and welfare services for children, and community and cultural affairs. Operates EDCORE (Education and Community Resource Program) Program in selected International Paper communities for public schools by invitation only.
Fields of interest: Arts/cultural programs; early childhood education; elementary school/education; secondary school/education; vocational education; engineering school/education; adult/continuing education; adult education—literacy & basic skills; libraries/library science; reading; education; environment; health care; substance abuse, services; human services; children & youth, services; youth, services; rural development; engineering; minorities; economically disadvantaged.
Program(s):
Civic Affairs: The foundation continues to support local initiatives, particularly the National 4-H Forestry Invitational.
Culture and the Arts: Fine and performing arts groups are supported. Typical projects receiving support are those that sponsor plays, music, and dance performances at schools and integrate the arts into the curriculum.
Economic Education: In 1976, the foundation began sponsoring the National Awards for Excellence in Teaching Economics administered by the National Council on Economic Education. The foundation also supports minorities in engineering education and helped establish NACME (National Action Council for Minorities in Engineering).
Education and Community Resources Program (EDCORE): Established in 1956, this by invitation only program emphasizes community involvement and an active foundation role in program supervision and technical assistance for participating school districts. EDCORE also encourages the participation of local International Paper Company management and staff in school activities. Teacher training and staff

development are carried out through John Hinman Fellowships. School wide redesign grants are awarded for curriculum development and other school or district-wide efforts. The foundation does not accept unsolicited applications for this program.
Employee Matching Gift: The foundation matches up to a total of $200 per employee, per year on a two-to-one basis; after $200, gifts are matched one-for-one (up to $6,000). Gifts from all full-time employees and directors to secondary schools, junior and community colleges, four-year colleges, graduate schools, and seminaries and theological schools are eligible.
Fellowships: To promote advanced study in science, technology, and engineering, the foundation awards a number of fellowships each year, through sponsoring institutions, not individuals.
Types of support: General/operating support; continuing support; program development; seed money; curriculum development; employee-related scholarships; matching funds.
Geographic limitations: Giving primarily in communities where there are company plants and mills, and in Memphis, TN.
Support limitations: No support for athletic organizations or religious groups. No grants to individuals, or for endowment funds or capital expenses; no loans.
Publications: Annual report, occasional report, informational brochure (including application guidelines), grants list, application guidelines.
Application information: Address requests from organizations in company communities to the local company contact person; no applications accepted for EDCORE (Education and Community Resource Program) or for fellowships. Application form required. Applicants should submit the following:
1) brief history of organization and description of its mission
2) detailed description of project and amount of funding requested
3) copy of IRS Determination Letter
4) listing of board of directors, trustees, officers and other key people and their affiliations
5) copy of most recent annual report/audited financial statement/990
6) listing of additional sources and amount of support
Initial approach: Letter, telephone, or proposal with application to local facility
Copies of proposal: 1
Board meeting date(s): June
Deadline(s): Mar. 1 for current year funding
Final notification: July
Officers and Directors:* Philip Giaramita,* Pres.; Kenneth Reeves, V.P.; Carol Berardi, Secy.; John Jepson,* Treas.; John T. Dillon, James P. Melican, Jr.
Trustee: State Street Bank & Trust Co.
Number of staff: 1 full-time professional; 2 part-time support.
EIN: 136155080
Selected grants: The following grants were reported in 1993.
$95,000 to National Council on Economic Education, NYC, NY.
$50,500 to United Negro College Fund, NYC, NY.
$25,000 to Southeastern Consortium for Minorities in Engineering, Atlanta, GA.

Figure 54. Sample Entry from *Corporate Foundation Profiles*

151—Revlon

151
REVLON GROUP FOUNDATION
c/o McAndrews & Forbes Holdings, Inc.
38 E. 63rd St.
New York, NY 10021

Purpose: Giving primarily to an organization supporting Israel.

Limitation(s): Giving primarily in New York, NY, and Philadelphia, PA. No grants to individuals.

Support area(s): Types of support not specified.

Financial data (yr. ended 4/30/96):
Assets: $45,504 (M)
Gifts received: $2,666,500
Expenditures: $2,795,043
Grants paid: $2,794,993 for 56 grants (high: $579,500; low: $100; general range: $1,000–$150,000)

Officers: Patricia M. Duff, Pres.; Richard E. Halperin, Exec. V.P.; Laurence Winoker, V.P. and Cont.; Glenn P. Dickes, V.P.

Directors: Howard Gittis, Ronald O. Perelman, Bruce Slovin.

Sponsoring company: Revlon Group Incorporated
Business: Operates holding company; manufactures and distributes cosmetics, fragrances, and pharmaceuticals.
Employees: 7,000
Sales volume: $1,780,000,000
Corporate locations: New York, NY (headquarters); subsidiaries in New York, NY.

Background: A company-sponsored foundation; incorporated in 1952 in PA. Funds donated by Food Fair Stores, Inc., Pantry Pride, Inc., Revlon Group, Inc.

Policies and application guidelines: Applications not accepted. Contributes only to pre-selected organizations.

GRANTS ANALYSIS

Although the foundation provided financial information for 1996, the following grants analysis reflects grants paid in 1995. Contributions paid in 1995 totaled $2,885,970. This figure represents a 9 percent increase over giving in 1994.

Subject Analysis:

Subject Area Distribution of Grant Numbers and Grant Dollars Paid in 1995

Subject area	No. of grants	Dollar value	Pct.	General range of grants
Religion				
Jewish programs	20	$2,412,590	84	
Grants under $10,000	3	11,980	<1	
SUBTOTAL:	23	2,424,570	84	$20,000–150,000
Education				
Elementary & secondary	1	150,000	5	
Other	3	95,000	3	
Grants under $10,000	7	19,300	1	
SUBTOTAL:	11	264,300	9	1,000–25,000
Environmental protection	1	150,000	5	
Other	20	47,100	2	
TOTAL:	55	$2,885,970	100%	

High award of the year: $415,000, Machne Israel, Brooklyn, NY.

High single recipient: Machne Israel, Brooklyn, NY (16 awards, totaling $2,278,590).

Top subject area by dollars: Religion (also, largest by grant numbers)
Largest award in field: $415,000, Machne Israel.
Second largest award: $329,500, Machne Israel, Brooklyn, NY.
Largest single recipient: Machne Israel, Brooklyn, NY (16 awards, totaling $2,278,590).

Second largest subject area by dollars: Education
Largest award in field: $150,000, Manhattan High School for Girls, NYC, NY.

Second largest award: $50,000, University of California at Los Angeles Foundation, Los Angeles, CA.

Third largest subject area by dollars: Environmental protection
Largest award in field: $150,000, New York City Outward Bound Center, NYC, NY.

Recipient Type Analysis:

Analysis of Grants of $10,000 or More Awarded in 1995*

Recipient type	Dollar value	No. of grants
Churches/temples	$2,412,590	20
Schools	150,000	1
Environmental agencies	150,000	1
Educational support agencies	75,000	2
Technical assistance centers	50,000	1
Colleges & universities	20,000	1
Disease-specific health associations	10,000	1
Human service agencies	10,000	1
Youth development organizations	10,000	1

*Awards may support multiple recipient types, i.e., a university library, and would thereby be counted twice.

Top recipient type by dollars: Churches/temples (also, largest by grant numbers)
Largest award in field: $415,000, Machne Israel.
Second largest award: $329,500, Machne Israel, Brooklyn, NY.
Largest single recipient: Machne Israel, Brooklyn, NY (16 awards, totaling $2,278,590).

Second largest recipient type by dollars: Schools
Largest award in field: $150,000, Manhattan High School for Girls, NYC, NY.

Third largest recipient type by dollars: Environmental agencies
Largest award in field: $150,000, New York City Outward Bound Center, NYC, NY.

Type of Support Analysis:

Continuing support: 21 grants, totaling $2,524,590

Population Group Analysis:

Analysis of Grants Over $10,000 Designated for Special Populations*

Group	Dollar value	No. of grants
Children & youth	$170,000	3
Women & girls	160,000	2
Blind & vision impaired	10,000	1
Single parents	10,000	1

*Grants which support no specific population are not included; awards may support multiple populations, i.e., an award for minority youth, and would thereby be counted twice.

Top population group by dollars: Children & youth (also, largest by grant numbers)
Largest award in field: $150,000, Manhattan High School for Girls, NYC, NY.
Second largest award: $10,000, Gladney Fund, Fort Worth, TX; $10,000, Youth Renewal Fund, NYC, NY.

Second largest population group by dollars: Women & girls
Largest award in field: $150,000, Manhattan High School for Girls (See above).
Second largest award: $10,000, Gladney Fund (See above).

Third largest population group by dollars: Blind & vision impaired
Largest award in field: $10,000, Retinitis Pigmentosa (RP) Foundation Fighting Blindness, NYC, NY.

Geographic Analysis:

The geographic distribution of institutional awards of $10,000 or more is as follows. (Grants to individuals and with unknown locations are excluded.)

U.S. regional breakdown: Middle Atlantic, $2,723,590 (24 awards); South Atlantic, $54,000 (2 awards); Pacific, $50,000 (1 award); West South Central, $10,000 (1 award).

GRANTS: The following is a partial list of grants paid by the foundation in the fiscal year ended 4/30/95.

periodicals articles, and IRS Forms 990-PF. *Corporate Foundation Profiles* is indexed by subject, types of support, geographic location, international giving, and names of trustees, officers, and donors.

Standard reference works about companies, such as *Standard and Poor's Register of Corporations,* the *Dun and Bradstreet Reference Book of Corporate Management,* National Register Publishing's *Directory of Corporate Affiliations,* and Chamber of Commerce directories, are typically available in the business reference department of your local public library. Although some of these directories mention company charitable giving in passing, none provides extensive information on this topic. However, you can obtain valuable information about the locations of subsidiaries and the activities and interests of a company by referring to these more general resources. Corporate annual reports, the business section of local newspapers, the *Wall Street Journal,* and business journals, such as *Crain's* (with editions for Cleveland, Detroit, New York, and elsewhere) or *American Cities Business Journals* (with editions for Atlanta, Denver, Philadelphia, and elsewhere), are also good sources of information about businesses, their "personalities," financial health, and other topics of interest to grantseekers.

PRIMARY SOURCES

As required of all private foundations, corporate foundations must file Form 990-PF with the IRS annually. As with all private foundation information returns, the 990-PF for a specific corporate foundation may be obtained at the foundation's own office, from the IRS (see Chapter 5), through the attorney general and/or charities registration office in the state in which the foundation is chartered (see Appendix B), or at Foundation Center libraries and Cooperating Collections. As noted previously, Cooperating Collections usually limit their IRS forms to the states in which they are located (see Appendix F).

A company's direct contributions to charitable causes are reported to the IRS on the company's corporate income tax form. This information is private and not available for public scrutiny.

Some corporate foundations and a few corporate direct giving programs issue annual reports, grants lists, or application guidelines. If the company in which you have an interest issues such a document, you will want to examine a copy. Foundation Center libraries collect these grantmaker publications and make them available to the public. Some Cooperating Collections obtain such reports on companies in their local area. Entries in the *National Directory of Corporate Giving* indicate if a corporate foundation or corporate direct giving program issues annual reports or brochures or guidelines. Some companies issue press releases when they make a significant contribution or participate in a prominent community activity. The Web site *PR Newswire* (www.prnewswire.com) is a good source for such announcements, as is *Philanthropy News Digest* at the Center's Web site (www.fdncenter.org/pnd/current/index.html).

Local businesses information

Because corporate giving, whether direct or via a foundation, tends to be concentrated in communities where the company operates, geography is a significant factor in fundraising from corporations. For this reason, grantseekers are encouraged to seek support from local businesses and not just from the more well-known multinational corporations. However, ferreting out information about these smaller, often intensely private, companies can be time-consuming and challenging.

Researching by Subject, Geographic Focus, and Types of Support

When looking for corporate funders, grantseekers should employ the same strategies as they do with other potential donors. Ask yourself the following questions: (1) Is the corporate funder interested in the same subject as my organization or project? (2) Does the funder give in the geographic area served by my organization or project? (3) Does the company provide the types of support needed by my organization or project? Detailed descriptions of three approaches—subject, geographic focus, types of support—are described in Chapters 6, 7, and 8. The subject approach and the geographic approach are significant in the corporate giving arena, since, whether by means of a corporate foundation or by direct giving, corporate contributions tend to be concentrated in fields related to corporate interests, or in communities where the company operates. The types of support approach permits the grantseeker to expand the search for in-kind and other noncash gifts.

You can develop a broad prospect list of corporations by employing the three basic research approaches simultaneously using *FC Search: The Foundation Center's Database on CD-ROM*, or sequentially using a variety of print resources. If you have access to *FC Search,* we suggest you begin your research there, since you can search using all three approaches simultaneously. You will need to use the Advanced Search feature of the Grantmaker file. First, choose Grantmaker Type as one of your search fields and select either company-sponsored foundations or corporate direct giving programs, or both.

Your other search fields should include Fields of Interest, Types of Support, and an appropriate field to designate geographic giving preferences (see Figures 55 and 56).

SUBJECT APPROACH

To make the best use of the subject approach, consider how a grant or in-kind gift to your nonprofit would actually benefit the company making the contribution. For instance, could a partnership between your organization and a specific company help that company sell more products, reach new customers, and/or improve its image in the community? Does your nonprofit organization offer programs or services that could be used by or benefit the company or its employees?

A good place to start is either with the Fields of Interest field on *FC Search* or the Subject and Types of Business indexes in the *National Directory of Corporate Giving*,

Figure 55. Advanced Grantmaker/Grantmaker Type Search from *FC Search: The Foundation Center's Database on CD-ROM*

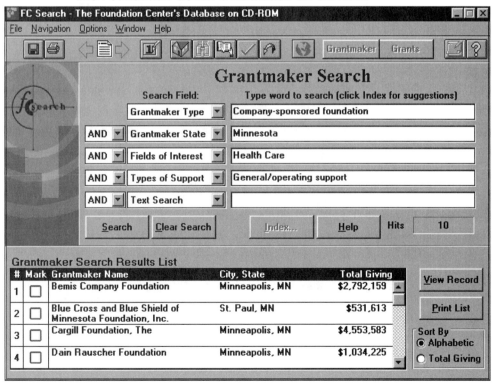

Figure 56. Advanced Grantmaker/Grantmaker City vs. Corporate
Location Search from *FC Search: The Foundation
Center's Database on CD-ROM*

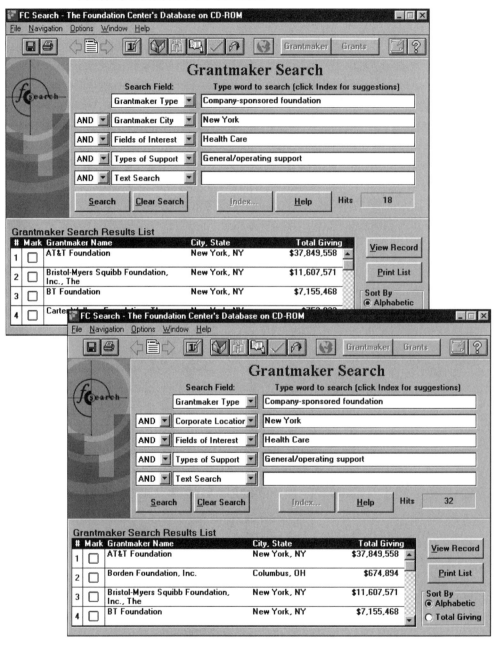

which refer back to the main entries in the alphabetically arranged text. The Types of Business index (see Figure 57) is unique to the *National Directory of Corporate Giving* and can be particularly helpful in discovering a common bond between a nonprofit organization and corporate interests and activities. Some shared nonprofit/corporate interests will be rather obvious. A sporting goods manufacturer might subsidize an athletic program for disadvantaged youth; a manufacturer of musical instruments may support a school's music appreciation program; a pharmaceutical company or alcoholic beverage distributor would be a likely candidate to fund a drug-education program. Other common fields of interest may be less obvious. For instance, textile manufacturers predominately employ women, and child care is frequently an issue for working women. Therefore, an after-school day care center may be able to secure a gift from a local clothing manufacturer whose employees utilize the day care center's services for their children.

GEOGRAPHIC APPROACH

The grantseeker should also pay particular attention to the geographic location of potential corporate donors, and not just the company's headquarters. Find out where plants, field offices, and subsidiary operations are located, since companies tend to spread charitable dollars in these locations as well. You may be able to obtain the names of businesses and corporations in your area simply by consulting the local yellow pages. Company executives can be convinced to support a program because it provides direct service to employees and other community residents, because it brings public recognition and/or prestige to a company and its management, and/or because it will improve customer relations and help build a future customer base in an important market.

If using *FC Search*, you will find that in the Advanced Search mode, you have several fields from which to choose when designating geographic limitations: (1) Grantmaker State, (2) Grantmaker City, (3) Corporate Location, or (4) Geographic Focus. Using Grantmaker City as your search field will yield a different result than a search by Corporate Location (see Figure 56). A Grantmaker State or Grantmaker City search will yield hits for only those states or cities where the company-sponsored foundation or corporate direct giving program is headquartered. When concentrating on a city, it is wise to use both state and city, since a city's name may appear in more than one state. For example, there is Portland, Maine, and Portland, Oregon, and you would want to clearly indicate which city you have in mind. A Corporate Location search will include not only the headquarters city of the foundation or direct giving program, but also any cities where the company has plants, offices, or subsidiaries. The results of a

Figure 57. Types of Business Index from *National Directory of Corporate Giving*

TYPES OF BUSINESS INDEX

This index is an alphabetical listing, in bold face type, of products, services, or types of businesses provided by the corporations in this *Directory*. Corporations are identified by abbreviated versions of their names and referenced by the sequence numbers assigned in the Descriptive Directory.

Abrasive, asbestos, and nonmetallic mineral products, ABB 4, American Optical 92, Armstrong 151, CertainTeed 478, Cincinnati 515, Erie 819, Fibreboard 861, Johns 1289, Kennecott 1340, Martin 1498, Norton 1743, Owens-Corning 1804, SGL 2104, Transco 2324, USG 2392, Walter 2438

Accounting, auditing, and bookkeeping services, Altschuler 64, Andersen 117, Cohn 551, Deloitte 713, Ernst 820, Grant 1051, KPMG 1377, Levy 1424, Novogradac 1748, Price 1913, Stauffer 2218

Administration/environmental quality program, Bristol 370, Burns 408

Advertising, Burnett 407, Catalina 452, Dun 767, Foote 931, Gannett 981, Haan 1083, Hill 1149, Lefton 1414, Media 1537, Ogilvy 1765, Playboy 1879, Servco 2099, Thompson 2291, Tulsa 2336, Young 2525

Agricultural services—crop, Harvest 1123, Scoular 2079

Agricultural services—management, Arbor 137

Agricultural services—soil, Freeport-McMoRan 956

Aircraft and parts, AlliedSignal 58, AMETEK 106, Barnes 239, Boeing 341, Boston Sand 356, Brunswick 388, Cessna 479, Coltec 564, Curtiss-Wright 673, Deutsch 724, Fokker 926, General Electric 999, General Motors 1001, Gleason 1022, Goodrich 1034, Grimes 1063, Guardian 1074, Hughes 1198, Interlake 1242, Johnson 1290, Kaman 1315, Learjet 1408, Lockheed 1447, McDonnell 1526, Monitor 1607, New Piper 1691, Olin 1776, Parker 1820, Raytheon 1965, Raytheon 1966, Remmele 1993, Rockwell 2027, Sequa 2097, SIFCO 2124, Sundstrand 2242, Talley 2258, Teleflex 2268, Textron 2285, TRW 2335, United Technologies 2377, Vesper 2412, Woodward 2500

Airports, DynCorp 773, Kimberly 1357, Ryder 2046

Ammunition, ordinance, and accessories, Browning 385, Duchossois 765, FMC 924, Olin 1776, Oregon 1789, Pentair 1841

Amusement and recreation services/miscellaneous, Anheuser 121, Baltimore 201, Blackman 321, Colorado 562, Disney 738, GTECH 1071, Harrah's 1108, Jacksonville 1269, Kansas 1319, Mirage 1589, New Jersey 1688, New York 1692, New York 1693, New York 1694, Portland 1893, Ralcorp 1950, Six 2136, Turf 2337

Animal services, except veterinary, Charles 485

Apparel and accessories/miscellaneous, Justin 1308, Kimberly 1357

Apparel and accessory stores/miscellaneous, Cheyenne 496, Fall 839, Hartmarx 1118, Recreational 1975

Apparel—girls' and children's outerwear, Kahn 1310, Kleinert's 1366, Mamiye 1481, Oshkosh 1796, Oxford 1806, Wrangler 2509

Apparel—men's and boys' coats and suits, Belleville 272, Genesco 1004, Wrangler 2509

Apparel—men's and boys' outerwear, Adidas 18, Delta 715, Descente 721, Hartmarx 1118, Hudson 1195, Jantzen 1274, Jockey 1287, Kahn 1310, Kendall 1338, Klein 1363, Levi 1422, National Service 1662, New Balance 1682, NIKE 1708, Oshkosh 1796, Oxford 1806, Phillips-Van 1862, Reebok 1981, VF 2413, Wrangler 2509

Apparel—women's outerwear, Ballet 196, Claiborne 528, Descente 721, Genesco 1004, Hartmarx 1118, Jantzen 1274, Kahn 1310, Kellwood 1333, Kenar 1337, Klein 1363, Levi 1422, NIKE 1708, Oxford 1806, Reebok 1981, Tanner 2261, United Togs 2378, VF 2413, Wrangler 2509

Apparel—women's, girls', and children's undergarments, Jockey 1287, Kleinert's 1366, Levi 1422, Sara 2062

Apparel, piece goods, and notions—wholesale, Adidas 18, Baker 188, Brown 384, Claiborne 528, Descente 721, Dollar 743, Genesco 1004, Hanes 1097, Heritage 1139, Jockey 1287, Myers 1635, NIKE 1708, Nomura 1718, Parthenon 1822, Patagonia 1823, Phillips-Van 1862, Reebok 1981, Stride 2233, Wolff 2498

Appliance stores/household, Circuit 517, Greeley 1060, Heilig 1131, Lowe's 1459, Smulekoff 2149, Toshiba 2311

Appliances/household, Bemis 277, Black 319, Coleman 554, Dollar 743, Eliason 801, Gillette 1017, Matsushita 1508, Maytag 1515, National Presto 1661, Philips 1859, Raytheon 1966, Sara 2062, Scott 2078, Smith 2145, State 2214, Tomkins 2309, Toshiba 2311, Whirlpool 2473

Asphalt and roofing materials, Bird 315, Georgia-Pacific 1008, Goodyear 1036, Harsco 1114, Massachusetts 1501, Monarch 1604, Russell 2043

Audio and video equipment/household, Atlantic 170, BOSE 351, Crown 659, Ikegami 1216, Joslyn 1302, Kaman 1315, Koss 1375, MCA 1518, Peavey 1826, Philips 1859, Reader's 1969, Sony 2164, Sparrow 2186, Western 2462

Auto and home supplies—retail, Fairmount 838, Harco 1102, Sears 2089, Trak 2320

Bakeries, Publix 1932

Bakery products, Barbara's 234, Campbell 427, CPC 638, Fleming 913, Fleming 914, Frito-Lay 965, General Mills 1000, Heinz 1133, Keebler 1326, Kellogg 1331, Lance 1393, Nabisco 1636, Rich 2007, RJR 2020, Schnuck 2072, Sunshine 2245, Tasty 2263, White 2474

Bands, orchestras, and entertainers, Solo 2158, Ticketmaster 2297

Banks/commercial, Abbotsford 6, AMCORE 69, American National 90, American Savings 95,

American State 98, AmSouth 113, Apple 128, Associated 160, Audubon 175, Bailey 185, Banc 202, Bancorp 203, Bangor 207, Bank IV 208, Bank Leumi 209, Bank of America 210, Bank of America 211, Bank of America 212, Bank of Boston 213, Bank of Granite 214, Bank of Hawaii 215, Bank of Louisville 216, Bank of New York 217, Bank of Tokyo 218, Bank of Utica 219, Bank One 220, Bank One 221, Bank One 222, Bank One 223, Bank One 224, Bank One 225, Bank Plus 226, Bank United 227, BankAmerica 228, BankBoston 229, Bankers 230, Barclays 235, Barnett 240, Beneficial 279, Beverly 301, Boatmen's 337, Boatmen's 338, Brown 383, California 422, CCB 456, Central Fidelity 462, Central National 465, Centura 474, Chase 487, Citibank 520, Citizens 521, Citizens 523, Citizens 524, Citizens 525, City 526, City 527, Colonial 557, Columbus 567, Columbus 569, Comerica 571, Commerce 572, Commerce 573, Commercial 575, Compass 582, CoreStates 617, County 628, Crestar 653, Cullen/Frost 667, Dai-Ichi 679, Dauphin 695, DCB 701, Dean 704, Deposit 719, European 823, Exchange 826, Exchange 827, Fairfax 836, Farmers 844, Farmers 846, Fifth 865, First American 870, First Bank 872, First Citizens 873, First Citizens 874, First Commercial 875, First Empire 876, First Hawaiian 878, First Interstate 881, First Interstate 882, First Interstate 883, First Maryland 884, First Merchants 885, First Mid 886, First National 888, First National 889, First National 890, First National 891, First National 892, First of America 894, First Security 895, First Security 897, 1st Source 898, First 899, First 900, Firstar 901, FirsTier 902, Fleet 908, Fort 940, Frost 968, Fuji 970, Fulton 975, GAB 978, Gardiner 983, Glendale 1023, Goldome 1030, Guaranty 1073, Hamilton 1091, Harris 1110, Hawaii 1125, Heritage 1140, Holland 1161, Home Saving 1169, Home State 1170, Hopkins 1180, Huntington 1203, Huntington 1204, Imperial 1223, Industrial 1231, INTRUST 1255, Iowa 1257, Israel 1262, Key 1343, Key 1344, Key 1345, Key 1346, KeyCorp 1348, La Salle 1385, Lakeside 1390, Liberty 1430, LTCB 1460, Manufacturers 1485, Marshall 1497, Mascoma 1500, MBNA 1517, Mellon 1540, Mercantile 1546, Merchants 1548, Midway 1572, Milwaukee 1582, Minnesota 1587, Morgan 1617, National Bank 1645, National Bank 1646, National City 1649, National City 1650, National City 1651, National City 1652, NationsBank 1667, NBD 1672, NBD 1673, Newmil 1702, North 1727, Northern Trust 1734, Northern Trust 1735, Norwest 1745, Old 1773, Old 1774, Old 1775, One 1782, Park 1817, Park 1818, Peoples 1843, Perry 1849, Pioneer 1869, PNC 1884, PNC 1885, Premier

Figure 58. Geographic Index from *National Directory of Corporate Giving*

Omaha 1778, Physicians 1865, Scoular 2079
Subsidiaries: Amoco 108, Browning 386, Deposit 719, Enron 809, First Bank 872, Guarantee 1072, Harvest 1123, Hy-Vee 1205, Lee 1412, Owen 1803, Pulitzer 1935, Scrivner 2081, Tenet 2271, Union Pacific 2361, US 2390
Division(s): Ahern 27, ServiceMaster 2101
Office(s): Andersen 117, Coastal 547, Dain 682, Grant 1051, PaineWebber 1815, Piper 1870
Plant(s): ASARCO 157, Bausch 251, Bemis 276, Campbell 427, Comdisco 570, Deloitte 713, Kellogg 1331, Sequent 2098, Tenneco 2274, Weyerhaeuser 2469, Williams 2482

Scottsbluff
Subsidiaries: Stauffer 2219

South Sioux City
Corporate Giving Program(s): Great 1056
Corporate Headquarters: Great 1056

Tecumseh
Plant(s): Campbell 427

Valley
Foundation(s): Valmont 2399
Corporate Headquarters: Valmont 2399
Plant(s): 3M 2295, Valmont 2399

Weeping Water
Plant(s): Martin 1498

West Point
Plant(s): Valmont 2399

York
Subsidiaries: Stauffer 2219

NEVADA

Battle Mountain
Plant(s): Coastal 547

Carson City
Plant(s): Southwest 2176, Wyman 2514

Elko
Plant(s): International Game 1247

Ely
Foundation(s): Mount 1628
Corporate Headquarters: Mount 1628

Fallon
Plant(s): Kennametal 1339

Henderson
Subsidiaries: Meredith 1552
Plant(s): Kerr 1342, Levi 1422, Sara 2062

Las Vegas
Corporate Giving Program(s): Southwest 2176
Foundation(s): Mirage 1589, Primerit 1915, Southwest 2176
Corporate Headquarters: Mirage 1589, Primerit 1915, Southwest 2176
Subsidiaries: Bally's 197, EG&G 794, First Security 897, Household 1185, Ikon 1217, Landmark 1394, Lawyers 1404, Lewis 1426, M.D.C. 1469, Meredith 1552, Mirage 1589, Southwest 2176, Sprint 2190, Viad 2415
Division(s): Hilton 1153
Office(s): Andersen 117, Dain 682, PaineWebber 1815, 360 2296
Plant(s): ABM 8, Deloitte 713, GATX 986, Humana 1200, International Game 1247, Portland 1891, Pulte 1936, Southwest 2176, TRW 2335, Weyerhaeuser 2469

Laughlin
Subsidiaries: Mirage 1589
Plant(s): International Game 1247

Nellis
Plant(s): Bemis 276

North Las Vegas
Subsidiaries: Tenet 2271

Reno
Corporate Giving Program(s): International Game 1247, Porsche 1888
Foundation(s): Dermody 720, Porsche 1888, Sierra 2123
Corporate Headquarters: Dermody 720, International Game 1247, Porsche 1888, Sierra 2123
Subsidiaries: Armstrong 151, Deere 709, FMC 924, Gannett 981, Lockheed 1447, May 1514, Pacific 1811, Phillips 1860, U.S. Bancorp 2345
Division(s): Lawson 1403
Office(s): Grant 1051, PaineWebber 1815, Willis 2484
Plant(s): ABM 8, Alexander 45, Deloitte 713, Donnelley 748, FMC 924, Hexcel 1145, Longs 1453, Portland 1891, Sherwin 2116

Silver Peak
Plant(s): Cyprus 675

Sparks
Subsidiaries: Cyprus 675, Diebold 732
Plant(s): Ralston 1953, Westvaco 2468

Stateline
Plant(s): International Game 1247

NEW HAMPSHIRE

Amherst
Plant(s): Bassett 246, Sequa 2097

Bedford
Subsidiaries: Ikon 1217

Bennington
Corporate Headquarters: Monadnock 1603

Berlin
Plant(s): James 1273

Canaan
Office(s): Mascoma 1500

Concord
Corporate Giving Program(s): Chubb 508
Corporate Headquarters: Chubb 508
Subsidiaries: Jefferson-Pilot 1281, New England 1685, Providian 1926
Office(s): PaineWebber 1815
Plant(s): Fuller 973

Derry
Subsidiaries: Columbia/HCA 566
Office(s): Hannaford 1099

Durham
Office(s): Hannaford 1099

Enfield
Office(s): Mascoma 1500

Exeter
Foundation(s): Mueller 1632
Office(s): Hannaford 1099

Franklin
Office(s): Hannaford 1099

Gilford
Office(s): Hannaford 1099

Greenland
Office(s): NIKE 1708

Groveton
Subsidiaries: Wausau 2449

Hampton
Corporate Headquarters: Wheelabrator 2471
Subsidiaries: Waste 2447

Hanover
Office(s): Mascoma 1500
Plant(s): Houghton 1184

Hillsboro
Plant(s): Norton 1743

Hooksett
Subsidiaries: CIGNA 511

Hudson
Subsidiaries: Lockheed 1447
Plant(s): Raytheon 1966

Jaffrey
Foundation(s): Bean 258
Corporate Headquarters: Bean 258
Subsidiaries: Bean 258, Teleflex 2268
Plant(s): Millipore 1581

Keene
Corporate Giving Program(s): Netherlands 1680
Foundation(s): Kingsbury 1358, MPB 1629, National Grange 1655
Corporate Headquarters: Kingsbury 1358, MPB 1629, National Grange 1655, Netherlands 1680
Subsidiaries: Timken 2302
Plant(s): Timken 2302

Laconia
Plant(s): New Hampshire 1687

Lebanon
Foundation(s): Mascoma 1500
Corporate Headquarters: Mascoma 1500
Subsidiaries: New England 1685
Office(s): Mascoma 1500
Plant(s): Timken 2302

Littleton
Plant(s): Norton 1743

Londonderry
Corporate Giving Program(s): Blue Seal 335
Corporate Headquarters: Blue Seal 335
Subsidiaries: Cummins 669
Plant(s): Dexter 728

Manchester
Subsidiaries: Northeast 1728
Office(s): Andersen 117, Hannaford 1099
Plant(s): Deloitte 713, Lawyers 1404, State 2217

Merrimack
Corporate Giving Program(s): Kollsman 1374, Unitrode 2380
Corporate Headquarters: Kollsman 1374, Unitrode 2380
Subsidiaries: Sequa 2097
Division(s): Sanders 2059
Plant(s): Anheuser 121, M/A-COM 1471, Unitrode 2380

Milford
Division(s): Dataproducts 693
Plant(s): Norton 1743

Nashua
Corporate Giving Program(s): Sanders 2059
Foundation(s): Concord 586, Worthen 2506
Corporate Headquarters: Concord 586, Sanders 2059, Worthen 2506
Subsidiaries: Anheuser 121, BankBoston 229, Fleet 912, Lockheed 1447, Sanders 2059
Division(s): Sanders 2059
Plant(s): New England 1684

North Charleston
Subsidiaries: Teleflex 2268

North Conway
Office(s): Hannaford 1099

North Hampton
Office(s): Hannaford 1099

Peterborough
Foundation(s): New Hampshire 1687
Corporate Headquarters: New Hampshire 1687

Geographic Focus search will indicate whether the corporate funder gives nationally or internationally or in particular states. Since many foundations and companies do not indicate their geographic focus, it is wise to conduct at least two geographic searches: (1) one search using the Grantmaker State field to indicate your geographic criteria, and (2) another search substituting Geographic Focus for Grantmaker State as the field for geographic criteria.

Another good starting point is the Geographic Index in the *National Directory of Corporate Giving* (see Figure 58), which refers back to the main entries.

TYPES OF SUPPORT APPROACH

Companies provide many types of support, including funds for operating budgets, employee matching gifts, and program development, as well as noncash contributions such as in-house printing, loaned executives, and donations of company products. Again, the *National Directory of Corporate Giving* will be a valuable print source for types of support information. Use the Types of Support Index, which has definitions at the beginning of the index (see Appendix D). There is also a Types of Support field in the Advanced Search mode on *FC Search*.

Refining Your List

As with all prospective funders, you will want to learn all you can about a corporate giver before submitting a request. Find out whether the corporate giver issues an annual report or printed guidelines. If not, ask for an annual business report. While corporate annual reports usually do not contain actual information on charitable activities, they can aid you in shaping an appeal. Business reports often present a company's philosophy and its plans for the future, which in turn may prove helpful when it comes to linking a funding request to the corporation's interests. You should also stay abreast of economic conditions and the local business news. A company that is laying off employees or running a deficit may not be the best one to ask for a donation.

If the company you are researching is a public company, that is, one whose stock is publicly traded, the Securities and Exchange Commission's (SEC) database (www.sec.gov/edgarhp.htm) is a good place to locate information. Called EDGAR, this text-only database contains an archive of all the financial documents filed with the SEC over the past three years. There are many different types of material about the company and its operation. The primary challenge is digging through a lot of irrelevant information to locate what you need. The 10-K report is the company's annual report and will probably be one of the most useful documents for you.

Some companies prefer to receive a preliminary letter of inquiry; others have application forms, and still others require multiple copies of formal proposals. If at all possible, find out the preferred means of approach in advance of submitting a proposal. If you are applying to a corporate foundation, the application information will most likely appear in *FC Search* and in print directories, such as the *National Directory of Corporate Giving.*

For direct giving programs of privately held companies, you will probably need to telephone the company itself to ask for application information. If you are unable to identify the correct person to call, ask to be connected to the department of "community affairs" or "public affairs" or "public relations" or "communications," or some other term that connotes a relationship to the larger community. In large cities, the correct contact might be in the department of "urban affairs." If corporate giving is not operated out of that office, the person you talk with will probably be able to put you in touch with the correct individual. If the company is large enough to appear in the standard business directories, such as *Standard & Poor's* or *Directory of Corporate Affiliations*, you may want to refer to one of those books at your local public library to identify a vice president or director responsible for corporate giving.

Once you have developed a list of possible corporate prospects, you should review it to eliminate those that are not interested in your subject area, that do not give in your geographic area, and/or that do not award the type of support your organization needs. If you used *FC Search* to construct your list, you probably used multiple search criteria, thereby completing this step already. Completing the prospect worksheet (see Figure 11) for each potential funder enables you to quickly eliminate those least likely to fund your project.

You are now ready to scrutinize your list still further to determine those potential corporate funders who are most likely to be interested in your organization or project. You'll want to do as much research on all aspects pertaining to these corporate grantmakers as time and resources permit. Posing the questions raised in Chapter 4 is a good place to start:

- Does the funder accept applications?

- Does the amount of money you are requesting fit within the funder's typical grant range?

- Does the funder put limits on the length of time it is willing to support a project?

- What type of organizations does the funder tend to support?

- Does the funder have application deadlines, or does it review proposals continuously?

- Do you or does anyone on your board know someone connected with the funder?

Most of these questions can be answered by referring to any one of several resources already covered. *FC Search: The Foundation Center's Database on CD-ROM* will answer many of them. Two print directories, *National Directory of Corporate Giving* and *Corporate Foundation Profiles,* will also provide many of the answers you need. For instance, note that in each entry for a company-sponsored foundation in the *National Directory,* you will find an indication of the largest grant paid (high) and the smallest grant paid (low) during the most recent fiscal year. In addition, up to ten grants reported during a given fiscal year will be listed for those foundations with annual giving of at least $50,000. *Corporate Foundation Profiles* is an excellent source for information about the size of grants by type of support. However, keep in mind that only the very largest company-sponsored foundations are covered in detail in *Profiles.* Other print sources on corporate giving will be found in Appendix A. For application deadlines and the names of trustees, officers, or donors and other such information about corporate foundations, Center directories and databases are excellent sources.

During the course of your research you may need to consult primary sources, such as the IRS Form 990-PF, and annual reports or application guidelines. Keep in mind that 990-PFs are not available for corporate direct givers, only for corporate foundations. The *National Guide to Corporate Giving* will indicate whether or not a corporate foundation or corporate direct giving program issues an annual report or informational brochure.

Secondary sources such as articles in newspapers and journals may also prove informative. *Philanthropy News Digest (PND)*, the Foundation Center's weekly online summary of the news of the world of philanthropy, is a searchable database that allows you to seek recent information about companies and their philanthropic efforts. *PND* summaries will also inform you of recent major grants, funding initiatives, and other such information. Here you will also find requests for proposals issued by corporate givers. You may wish to use *PND's* search engine to enter the name of a foundation or company and see what, if anything, has been reported about this funder's recent gifts. Another source of information on recently awarded grants is *PR Newswire* on the

Web (www.prnewswire.com). *PR Newswire* provides access to news releases from corporations.

Personal Contacts

In fundraising, personal contacts help—if for no other reason than to get information—but their impact varies. It makes sense that corporate foundations and corporate direct giving programs with separate staff and explicit guidelines or formal procedures are unlikely to require personal contacts, while companies with informal giving programs and no specific guidelines are more likely to be amenable to personal contacts. The grantseeker who "knows someone" will want to utilize that relationship, but should do so judiciously. Grantseekers without personal contacts may want to develop them in order to facilitate receipt of corporate gifts. Establishing a rapport with a corporate funder can be difficult. Such cultivation requires long-term effort.

Summary

Companies make charitable donations of money, products, services, and staff time in the communities in which they do business. These gifts make the community a better place to live and do business, and they enhance the companies' standing among customers and workers. Companies may make their gifts through a private foundation or a direct giving program or both. Finding information about a corporate foundation is relatively easy because of the public disclosure laws related to private foundations. Finding information about corporate direct giving programs is more difficult, since the only public information about such programs is that which the company chooses to release. Although company donations, whether from a corporate foundation or from a corporate direct giving program, are usually smaller than contributions by independent foundations to similar causes, corporate funding is a significant part of a strategic fundraising plan for many nonprofits.

Remember not to limit your thinking about corporations to asking only for money or in-kind support. Look to local businesses as sources for board members and volunteer support. Keep in mind as well that a good relationship with one company may pave the way to good relationships with others.

The next chapter is devoted to putting together a proposal that will present your organization and cause in the best light to a prospective funder, be it a corporation or a private foundation.

Chapter 10

Presenting Your
Idea to a Funder

By now you should have a short list of grantmakers that seem likely to fund your project on the basis of your nonprofit organization's subject focus, the geographic area and population groups you serve, and the type and amount of support you require for your project. And, you have thoroughly researched each funder on your list to uncover as much current information as possible about these grantmakers. It is time to present your idea to those funders on your list and convince them to support it.

While many foundations are quite flexible about the format and timing of grant applications, others have developed specific procedures to facilitate the decision-making process. In an effort to save time for the grantmaker and the grantseeker, some regional groups of grantmakers have adopted a common grant application format so that grant applicants can produce a standard proposal for participating grantmakers. Common grant application forms can be downloaded from the Foundation Center's Web site (www.fdncenter.org/onlib/cga/index.html). Before applying to a funder that accepts a common grant application form, you should still find out whether your project matches the funder's stated interests, ascertain whether the funder would prefer a letter of inquiry in advance of receiving a proposal, determine the funder's deadline for proposals, and find out how many copies of the proposal are required.

Whether the grantmaker uses a common grant application form or has its own individual format, follow the stated procedures to the letter. You'll want to review the notes you have made about a potential funder during the course of your research and obtain the most recent copy of annual reports, application guidelines, or informational brochures issued by that funder. Knowing whom to contact and how to submit your application can be critical in ensuring that your request receives serious consideration.

If no guidelines are provided, use the format described in this chapter. The Proposal Writing Short Course at the Foundation Center's Web site provides a useful framework as well. *The Foundation Center's Guide to Proposal Writing* and other such books, noted in Appendix A, are available at Center libraries and many Cooperating Collections.

Timing and Deadlines

Timing is an essential element of the grant-application process. Grant decisions are often tied to board meetings, which can be held as infrequently as once or twice a year. Many foundations need to receive grant applications at least two to three months in advance of board meetings to allow time for review and investigation, and some require an even longer lead time. If the foundation you have targeted has no specified application deadline, try to determine when its board meets and submit your request as far in advance of its next board meeting as possible. Then be prepared to wait three to six months, or even longer, for the proposal-review process to run its course.

Initial Inquiries

Many foundations, both large and small, prefer to have grant applicants send a letter of inquiry before, or even in place of, a formal proposal. Some grantmakers may be willing to offer advice and/or assistance in preparing the final proposal for applicants whose ideas seem particularly relevant to their funding programs. If the foundation cannot provide funding because of prior commitments or a change in its program focus, this can also save you a lot of time in preparing a full proposal application. Some grantmakers will actually make their funding decisions based solely on a letter of inquiry.

Unless the funder specifies otherwise, your letter of inquiry should be brief, no more than two pages. It should describe in clear, concise prose both the purpose of your organization and the parameters of the project for which you are seeking funds. You should be specific about the scope of your project, how it fits into the grantmaker's own program, the type and amount of support you are seeking, and the other funders, if any, being approached. Your opening paragraph should summarize the essential ingredients of your request, including the amount of money and type of support you are seeking. All too often grant applicants bury these important facts in long descriptions of their organization or project. Most grantmakers will also want to see a copy of the IRS letter determining your organization's tax-exempt status. Depending on what you have learned about the funder, offer to send a full proposal for their consideration or ask about the possibility of a meeting with foundation staff or officials to discuss your project.

You may need to be somewhat assertive in your approach to foundations. Give the funder adequate time to respond to your inquiry, but don't be afraid to follow up with a phone call three to four weeks after you've sent your letter to confirm that it was received, and if not, to offer to send a copy. The call also provides the opportunity to ask whether you can supply additional information and to inquire about the timing of the review process. Remember, there's a fine line between behaving in a proactive manner and being perceived as "pushy" by prospective funders. Take care not to cross that line.

The Proposal

The full grant proposal may be your only opportunity to convince a grantmaker that your program is worthy of its support. Depending on what you've uncovered about a funder's application procedures, it will either be your first direct contact with the funder or will follow an initial exchange of letters or conversations with staff and/or trustees. In either case, the proposal should make a clear and concise case for your organization and its programs. Grantmakers receive and review hundreds, sometimes thousands, of proposals every year. In reviewing your proposal, they need to be able to identify quickly and efficiently how you want to put the requested grant funds to work to benefit the community or to further the causes in which the grantmaker has an interest.

At this stage your board may feel it's time to turn to outside help and hire a consultant to develop a proposal. Although bringing in a professional proposal writer can bolster your confidence, it is rarely necessary and may even prove inadvisable, since no one knows your project better than you do. Grantmakers aren't impressed by slick prose and fancy packaging. They want the facts, presented clearly and concisely, and they want to get a feeling for the organization and the people who run it.

There are a number of excellent books on the proposal-writing process, and you may find it useful to review several of them before you get started. Many of these titles, listed in Appendix A, can be found at Foundation Center libraries or Cooperating Collections. Some may be found in your local public library. *The Foundation Center's Guide to Proposal Writing* takes you step-by-step through the proposal-writing process, supplementing advice from the authors, who are experienced fundraisers, with excerpts from actual proposals, and offering helpful hints from grantmakers interviewed in the preparation of the *Guide*. The *Guide* serves as the basis of the Center's proposal writing seminars, held each spring and fall throughout the country. Announcements of upcoming seminars appear on the Center's Web site at www.fdncenter.org and in newsletters issued by Center libraries. Also at the Center's Web site, you may wish to consult the Center's Proposal Writing Short Course, an abbreviated version of the aforementioned proposal writing guide.

While application criteria and proposal formats vary, most funders expect to see the following components in a grant proposal:

TABLE OF CONTENTS

If your proposal is quite lengthy, you may wish to include a table of contents at the beginning. The table of contents makes it easier for the prospective funder to find specific components of the proposal. While your proposal should be brief (most funders recommend limiting it to ten pages or less), a table of contents helps you organize your presentation and outline the information therein.

EXECUTIVE SUMMARY

The summary briefly describes the problem or need your project hopes to address; your plan of action, including how and where the program will operate, its duration, and how it will be staffed; a brief statement about the budget for the project, including the specific amount requested from the funder and your plans for long-term funding; and the anticipated results. The summary should be presented as the first section of your proposal and can be as short as one or two paragraphs; it should never be longer than a page.

Even though the executive summary is the first item in the proposal, it should be the last thing you actually write. By that point you will have thought through and thoroughly documented the need you plan to address, your plan of action, and the projected outcomes of your project, making it easier to pull out the most important facts for the summary.

STATEMENT OF NEED

State as simply and clearly as possible the problem, need, or opportunity your project will address. Be sure to narrow the issue to a definable problem or opportunity that is solvable or reachable within the scope of your project. A broad picture of the many problems that exist within your community will only detract from your presentation. You want to paint a compelling picture of a pressing need, which might inspire a funder to support you, but you should avoid describing a problem that is overwhelming in its size and/or complexity, which might make it seem hopeless to the prospective funder.

Be sure to document your description of the problem with citations from recent studies and current statistics, statements by public officials and/or professionals, and previous studies by your agency and/or other agencies. Your object is to convince the funder that the problem or need is real and that your approach builds upon the lessons others have learned. Show the funder that you have researched the problem carefully and that you have a new or unique contribution to offer toward its resolution. And remember, no matter how well you document a specific need, you are unlikely to convert a grantmaker who has no interest in your specific subject area.

PROJECT DESCRIPTION

Now that you've presented the problem, you need to clarify exactly what it is you hope to accomplish. You need to state the goals and objectives of this project, the methods you plan to use to implement these objectives, a time frame in which this will take place, and how you will determine the success or effectiveness of your project or program.

Goals and Objectives

Goals are abstract and subject to conditions. As such, they are not always entirely attainable. Objectives, on the other hand, are based on realistic expectations and therefore are more specific. Since clearly stated objectives also provide the basis for evaluating your program, be sure to make them measurable and time-limited. The realization of each stated objective will be a step toward achieving your goal. For example, if the problem you've identified is high unemployment among teenagers in your area, your objective might be to provide 100 new jobs for teenagers over the next two years. The goal of the project would be a significant reduction in or even the elimination of teenage unemployment in your community.

Don't confuse the objective of a program with the means to be used in achieving that end. You might achieve your objective of providing 100 new jobs for teenagers through a variety of methods, including working with local businesses to create jobs, running a job placement or employment information center, or providing jobs within a program operated by your agency. But your measurable objective remains the same: to provide 100 new jobs for teenagers over the next two years.

Implementation Methods and Schedule

The methods section of your proposal should describe the plan of action for achieving your goals and objectives, as well as how long it will take. Why have you chosen this particular approach? Who will actually implement the plan? If you're involving staff or volunteers already active in your program or consultants from outside your organization, note their qualifications and include abbreviated versions of their resumes in the appendix to your proposal. If you'll need to hire new staff, include job descriptions and describe your plans for recruitment and training. You should also provide a timetable for the project, making sure to indicate the projected starting and completion dates for each phase of the program. Be sure to allow ample time for each stage, bearing in mind the possibility of delays while you await funding.

Evaluation Criteria and Procedures

Evaluation criteria provide a measure for determining how effective your project has been in achieving its stated objectives. If your objectives are specific and measurable, it will be easier to evaluate your success. Although evaluating the outcome and end results of a project is a primary concern, don't overlook the need to evaluate the process or procedures as well. A good evaluation plan will enable you and others to learn from your efforts.

The evaluation component of a proposal often presents a major stumbling block to the inexperienced grantseeker. Try to remember that evaluation is nothing more than an objective means by which both you and the funder determine whether or not you have accomplished what you set out to do. It is an important part of your proposal because, among other things, it demonstrates that you are aware of the responsibility implicit in receiving a grant. Evaluation should *not* be an after-thought. It should be built into the design of your procedures as a continuous monitoring system.

The following are some examples of evaluation tools: observation by a disinterested person or specialist, interviews and/or questionnaires completed by those benefiting from your project, rating scales, standardized tests, checklists, attendance records, surveys, and longitudinal studies. The list will vary according to your needs and ingenuity. From the point of view of the funder, however, it is your own good faith and the funder's appraisal of your probable success that are at issue rather than which evaluation procedure you select. Having said this, an effective evaluation procedure will attempt to answer the following questions:

- Did you operate as intended, following the methods outlined in your procedures section?

- What beneficial changes have been brought about that are directly attributable to your project?

- Is your project the only variable responsible for these changes?

- What conclusions may be drawn from this evaluation?

- What future directions may be projected for your field as a result of your accomplishments under this grant?

BUDGET

Developing a budget requires both candor and common sense. For example, if your proposal involves hiring staff, don't forget that Social Security payments, worker's compensation, and benefits have to be included. Try to anticipate your full expenses in advance. It's unrealistic to expect additional funding at a later date to cover needs overlooked in your initial request.

Remember, too, that foundation and corporate donors are experienced in evaluating costs. Don't pad your budget, but don't underestimate the amount you need, either. If other funders have contributed to your project, be sure to say so. The fact that others have confidence in your organization is a plus. If you expect to receive in-kind donations of equipment, office space, or volunteer time, be sure to mention these as well. Many funders want your budget (or your budget narrative) to reflect the amount of any staff time, resources, or overhead costs your organization will contribute to the cost of the project.

When seeking funds for a specific project, be sure to supply both the budget for your project and, in the appendix, the overall operating budget of your organization. Typically, the budget for a nonprofit organization includes two sections: personnel and nonpersonnel costs (see Figure 59). When in doubt, seek professional assistance from an accountant or someone with financial expertise in compiling a budget.

In addition to lists of current funders, most funders will want to know your future funding plans, how you plan to support your project after their grant money has run out. Even with requests for one-time support (e.g., the purchase of equipment), you should describe how you'll handle related expenditures such as ongoing maintenance. Vague references to alternative funding sources are not enough. Grant decision makers want *specifics*. Do you plan to solicit additional support from the public or other grantmakers? Do you expect the program ultimately to become self-supporting through client fees or sales of products or services? Is there a local institution or government agency that will support your program once it has demonstrated its value? Show the funder that you have thought through the question of future funding and outline potential funding sources (government grants and private grantmakers) and income-producing activities (direct mail, fees for services, sale of products).

BACKGROUND ON YOUR ORGANIZATION

Even if your organization is large and relatively well known, you shouldn't assume that the grant decision makers reading your proposal will be familiar with your programs or accomplishments. In fact, they may not be aware of your existence. Therefore, you need to provide them with enough background information to build confidence in your group and its ability to carry out the program you are proposing. State the mission of your organization and provide a brief history of your activities, stressing relevant accomplishments and awards as well as your present sources of support. You should include a list of your board of directors in the appendix to the proposal (see below), and you may also want to call attention to well-known individuals on your board or staff who have played a major role in your organization. Remember, your purpose is to convince the prospective funder that you are capable of producing the proposed program results and are deserving of support.

You can do the groundwork for this section by keeping a "credibility file" that documents your progress and activities. Save letters of encouragement and praise, newspaper articles, and studies that support your work. Soliciting letters of endorsement from individuals and organizations that have benefited from your work is perfectly acceptable, and you may want to include some in the appendix.

Keep it short and to the point. The background statement should be no longer than a page.

Figure 59. Sample Budget Format for a Nonprofit Organization's Grant Project

Personnel:
    Salaries (may be prorated)
    Benefits
    Consulting fees   Subtotal: _____

Nonpersonnnel:
    Rent
    Utilities
    Equipment (lease or purchase)
    Supplies
    Travel and meetings
    Publicity
    Insurance
    Postage
    Printing
    Other   Subtotal: _____

                                      Total: _____

CONCLUSION

Close your proposal with a few paragraphs that summarize the proposal's main points. Reiterate what your organization seeks to accomplish and why it is important. Since it is your final appeal, at this juncture, you are justified in employing language intended to be persuasive. But remember, a "little" emotion goes a long way.

APPENDIX

The appendix should include all appropriate supporting documents for your request, including a copy of your agency's tax-exempt determination letter from the IRS, a list of your board of directors (with affiliations), your current operating budget and an audited financial statement, a list of recent and current funding sources (both cash and in-kind), resumes of key staff members and consultants, and letters of endorsement and relevant

Presenting Your Ideas to a Corporate Giver

There are a few tips that are particularly applicable to corporate funders. First, make an effort to understand the corporate hierarchy. At some companies, sponsorships and nonmonetary support may be handled by the marketing department, while employee voluntarism may be coordinated in the human resources department. Second, draw up a realistic budget and be prepared to divulge your sources of income. Corporate grant decision-makers are likely to scrutinize the bottom line, and many will ask for evidence of your nonprofit's fiscal responsibility and of efficient management. And, third, and possibly most important, consider what a business stands to gain by giving your organization a grant, now or in the future, directly or indirectly. Then state this clearly in the proposal. If your program is innovative, if it tackles an emerging issue of importance to the company or its customer base, or if it addresses a need that few other agencies are addressing, emphasize that fact, without undue self-promotion and in as non-controversial a fashion as possible.

news clippings. Remember, appendices may not be read that carefully by grant decision makers. If something is essential, include it in the body of the text.

Cover Letter

A cover letter should accompany every proposal. The cover letter, which should be on your organization's letterhead and signed by your board chairman, president, or chief executive officer, highlights the features of your proposal most likely to be of interest to the grantmaker. It should point out how you selected the funder and why you believe that particular grantmaker will be interested in your proposal, thus establishing an immediate link between the two organizations. It should also include the amount of money and type of support you are seeking.

Figure 60. Stylistic Hints for Proposal Writers

1. Use the active rather than the passive voice.

2. Avoid jargon; use acronyms only when absolutely necessary.

3. Stick to simple declarative sentences.

4. Keep your paragraphs short; employ headings and subheadings.

5. Address yourself to a human being: Picture the grant decision maker across the desk from you as you write. Always address your cover letter to an individual. Never begin with "Dear Sir" or "To Whom It May Concern."

6. Write with the needs of the people you hope to help in mind, making sure to demonstrate how your program will be of benefit to them.

7. Unless you have evidence to the contrary, assume that the reader is unfamiliar with your organization.

8. Do not resort to emotional appeals; base your arguments on documented facts.

Writing Style and Format

Make your proposal as readable as possible by using active language and by being specific about what it is you hope to accomplish. Keep your proposal succinct and to the point.

It is a good idea to use the group approach to generate ideas, but let one writer draft the proposal. Writing by committee doesn't work when you need a concise and well-organized final product (see Figure 60). Ask colleagues who have been successful in securing foundation grants to review the proposal. You may also want to have someone unfamiliar with your project read the proposal to be sure its meaning is clear and that it avoids specialized jargon.

Prior to submission, review the application procedures issued by the grantmaker, if any. Have you fulfilled the requirements and addressed any concerns? Do your proposal and cover letter establish strong connections between your project and their interests? Grantseekers often ask whether they should tailor proposals to individual funders. Unfortunately, the answer to this question is "yes and no." While it is generally not a good idea to develop a proposal or make major adjustments in your operations to conform to the interests of a particular funding source, you should let your proposal reflect any connections that exist between you and the grantmaker you have targeted. Establishing links is what fundraising is all about.

What Happens Next?

Submitting your proposal is nowhere near the end of your involvement in the grant-seeking process. A few weeks after you have submitted your proposal, follow up with a phone call to make sure your materials were received if this has not been acknowledged. If the grantmaker seems open to the idea, you may want to arrange a meeting with foundation representatives to discuss your program or project.

Grant review procedures vary widely, and the decision-making process can take anywhere from a few weeks to six months or much longer. During the review process, the funder may ask for professional references or for additional information either directly from you or from outside consultants. This is a difficult time for the grant-seeker. You need to be patient but persistent. Some foundations outline their review procedures in annual reports or application guidelines. If you are unclear about the process or timetable, don't hesitate to ask.

REJECTION IS NOT THE END

Most grantmakers receive many more worthwhile proposals than they can possibly fund in a given year. In an annual report, the M.J. Murdock Charitable Trust described the situation as follows:

> It is seldom that the Trust is faced with having to decline a poor proposal. Rather, it is a matter of having to decide among a great many worthy proposals. A denial, therefore, is hardly ever a rejection on the merits of a proposal, but it is simply the result of a highly competitive system and the limitation of financial resources.

Just because a grantmaker is unable to fund a particular proposal does not mean the door is closed forever. Some funders are willing to discuss with you why your proposal was declined. You can ask whether the funder needed additional information. Would they be interested in considering the proposal at a future date? Could they suggest other sources of support you should pursue? Such follow-up discussions may be particularly helpful if the grantmaker has demonstrated a commitment to funding projects in your geographic area and subject field.

Rejection is not necessarily the end of the process, and it may be worthwhile to cultivate the funder's interest. Put grant decision makers on your mailing list so that they can become further acquainted with your organization. Remember, there's always next year.

WHEN YOU GET THE GRANT

Congratulations! You have received formal notification of your grant award and are ready to implement your program. Before you begin to hire staff or purchase supplies, take a few moments to acknowledge the funder's support with a letter of thanks. You also need to pay careful attention to the wording of the grant letter and determine if the funder has specific forms, procedures, and deadlines for reporting the progress of your project under the grant. Clarifying your responsibilities as a grantee at the outset, particularly with respect to financial reporting, will prevent misunderstandings and more serious problems later. So be sure you understand all the qualifications attached to your grant before you start to spend the money.

While you must respect the wishes of grantmakers that request anonymity, you will find that many others appreciate acknowledgment of their support in press releases, publications, and other products resulting from or concerning grant-related activities. A few of the larger, staffed foundations offer assistance to grantees in developing press releases and other publicity materials. Again, if you are unsure about the grantmaker's expectations, be sure to ask.

Keep detailed records of all grant-related activities, including contacts with and payments from the funder. Prepare a schedule of deadlines for reports and follow-up phone calls. Communicate with funders selectively. Don't inundate them with mail or invitations, but don't forget to keep them "in the loop" regarding important events or developments relating to your project. This is the beginning of what you hope will be a long and fruitful relationship. Treat it with the care and attention it deserves.

Appendix A

Additional Readings

World of Foundations

Edie, John A. *First Steps in Starting a Foundation*. 4th ed. Washington, D.C.: Council on Foundations, 1997.
>   Discusses in non-technical language the various types of organizations that are all generally labeled as foundations by the public, as well as the requirements for establishing, and regulations governing, each type.

Family Foundation Library: Management, Governance, Grantmaking, Family Issues.
4 vols. Washington, D.C.: Council on Foundations, 1997.
>   Four volumes of basic information of interest to family foundations. Each volume includes sample forms and policies.

Foundation Management Series. Washington, D.C.: Council on Foundations, biennial.
>   Now in four separate volumes, presents the results of the Council's survey of foundations on a large variety of topics, including asset

management, administrative expenses, salaries, governance policies, staffing, benefits, and personnel policies.

Freeman, David F. *The Handbook on Private Foundations*. Revised ed. New York: The Foundation Center, 1991.
Provides practical information on most aspects of foundations, including history, reasons for creating a foundation, the grantmaking process, governance and administration, tax regulations and legal issues, and management of assets.

Hopkins, Bruce R. and Jody Blazek. *Private Foundations: Tax Law and Compliance.* New York: John Wiley & Sons, 1997.
Intended as a desk reference for lawyers, accountants, and tax practitioners, covers federal tax laws related to the establishment of private foundations.

Kaplan, Ann, ed. *Giving USA*. New York: AAFRC Trust for Philanthropy, annual.
Statistical analysis of charitable contributions by corporations, foundations, individuals, and through bequests. Also provides data about charitable recipients.

McIlnay, Dennis P. *How Foundations Work*. San Francisco, CA: Jossey-Bass, 1998.
Author postulates that there are six identities of foundations: judges, editors, citizens, activists, entrepreneurs, and partners. Understanding these roles provides a new way to comprehend foundations' complex and sometimes contradictory nature.

Renz, Loren, and Steven A. Lawrence. *Foundation Giving*. New York: The Foundation Center, annual.
Provides comprehensive statistical analysis of foundation growth and giving trends, incorporating a summary of data collected by the Foundation Center since 1975.

Internet resources:

AAFRC Trust for Philanthropy (www.aafrc.org)
  Contains information about philanthropy, including charts on distribution of funds to private nonprofit organizations.

Council on Foundations (www.cof.org)
  This national nonprofit membership organization for grantmakers offers information useful for grantseekers as well, organized into broad subject categories.

Foundation Center's Grantmaker Information on the Internet (www.fdncenter.org/grantmaker)
  Information about private, community, and corporate foundations, corporate giving programs, and grantmaking public charities. Links to hundreds of grantmaker Web sites.

Foundation Center's Funding Trends and Analysis (www.fdncenter.org/grantmaker/trends/)
  Excerpts from recent research reports on foundation giving trends.

Corporate Foundations and Corporate Giving

Corporate Giving Directory. Detroit, MI: The Taft Group, annual.
  Contains profiles of more than 1,000 corporate giving programs making contributions of at least $200,000 annually.

Corporate Foundation Profiles. New York: The Foundation Center, biennial.
  Provides detailed profiles of 195 of the largest corporate foundations in the United States and brief descriptive profiles of some 1,200 smaller corporate foundations.

Humbert, Greg. *Matching Gift Details: The Guidebook to Corporate Matching Gift Programs.* Washington, D.C.: Council for Advancement and Support of Education, annual.
  Lists corporations that match employee gifts to nonprofit institutions.

National Directory of Corporate Giving. New York: The Foundation Center, biennial.
A directory of more than 2,500 corporations that make contributions to nonprofit organizations through corporate foundations or direct giving programs.

Schoenenberger, Lori, ed. *Corporate Giving Yellow Pages.* Detroit, MI: The Taft Group, annual.
Alphabetically arranged corporate entries include both corporate direct giving programs and corporate foundations.

Smith, Craig. *Giving by Industry: A Reference Guide to the New Corporate Philanthropy.* 1999-2000 ed. Gaithersburg, MD: Aspen Publishers, 1999.
Details the primary corporate givers within twenty industry categories and provides examples of the most common types of philanthropy.

Steele, J. Valerie, ed. *National Directory of Corporate Public Affairs.* Washington, D.C.: Columbia Books, annual.
Provides profiles of nearly 1,900 companies identified as having public affairs programs and lists approximately 14,000 corporate officers engaged in the informational, political, and philanthropic aspects of public affairs.

Tillman, Audris D. *Corporate Contributions in 1997.* 32nd ed. New York: Conference Board, 1999.
This survey of major U.S. corporations provides a detailed overview, complete with charts and tables on 1997 contributions practices.

Internet resources:

Charity Aid Foundation's CCInet (www.charitynet.org/CCInet/frames/fpages.html)
Links to hundreds of corporate Web sites focusing on giving and community relations.

Corporate Information (www.corporateinformation.com)
One of the most comprehensive sites for links to corporate information on public and private companies in the U.S. and abroad.

Foundation Center's Corporate Grantmakers on the Internet (www.fdncenter.org/grantmaker/gws_corp/corp.html)
Links to Web sites of corporate grantmakers.

PR Newswire (www.prnewswire.com)
News from corporations worldwide; frequently contains information on major corporate gifts.

Laws Regulating Foundations and Nonprofits

Bromberger, Allen R., ed. *Getting Organized*. 4th ed. New York: Lawyers Alliance for New York, 1993.
Introductory manual for organizations that wish to incorporate and secure recognition of federal and state tax-exempt status.

Colvin, Gregory L. *Fiscal Sponsorship: Six Ways to Do It Right*. San Francisco, CA: Study Center Press, 1993.

Hopkins, Bruce R. *The Law of Tax-Exempt Organizations*. 7th ed. New York: John Wiley & Sons, 1998.
Comprehensive handbook about the laws regulating nonprofit organizations.

Hopkins, Bruce R. *The Legal Answer Book for Nonprofit Organizations*. New York: John Wiley & Sons, 1996, and

Hopkins, Bruce R. *The Second Legal Answer Book for Nonprofit Organizations*. New York: John Wiley & Sons, 1998.
Quick answers to the most common questions concerning the laws regulating nonprofit organizations.

Hopkins, Bruce R. *The Law of Fund-Raising*. 2nd ed. New York: John Wiley & Sons, 1996.
Covers all aspects of state and federal nonprofit fundraising law, including comprehensive summaries of each state's charitable solicitation acts.

Kirschten, Barbara L. *Nonprofit Corporation Forms Handbook.* 1998 ed. Eagan, MN: West Group, 1998.
> Provides model corporate documents to facilitate the incorporation of nonprofit organizations in various jurisdictions, as well as guidance in applying to the IRS for recognition of exemption from federal income tax.

Mancuso, Anthony. *How to Form a Nonprofit Corporation in All 50 States.* 4th ed. Berkeley, CA: Nolo Press, 1997.
> A soup-to-nuts guide to forming and operating a tax-exempt corporation under Section 501(c)(3) of the Internal Revenue Code.

Olenick, Arnold J., and Philip R. Olenick. *A Nonprofit Organization Operating Manual: Planning for Survival and Growth.* New York: The Foundation Center, 1991.
> Leads nonprofits through the maze of tax and legal codes and offers advice on accounting procedures.

Internet resources:

Independent Sector Public Policy Program (www.indepsec.org/programs/ govrelat.html)
> This site is especially useful for keeping up with legislative and legal issues. Some information is available to members only.

Legal and Tax Answers for Nonprofit Organizations (www.exemptlaw.com)
> Answers questions about starting a nonprofit, securing federal tax-exempt status, board composition, etc.; includes downloadable IRS forms and publications.

National Center for Charitable Statistics. Resources on Nonprofits and Philanthropy (nccs.urban.org)
> NCCS, a program of the Center on Nonprofits and Philanthropy at the Urban Institute, is the national repository of data on the nonprofit sector in the U.S.

National Center on Philanthropy and the Law. Nonprofit Legal Bibliography Project (www.law.nyu.edu/ncpl/legalbibliography/nonprofitproject.html)

Nonprofit Resource Center Legal Links (www.not-for-profit.org/legal.htm)
   Includes lists of recommended books related to nonprofit legal issues, and links to numerous federal and state Web resources.

Nonprofit Management and Planning

Angelica, Emil W., and Vincent L. Hyman. *Coping with Cutbacks: The Nonprofit Guide to Success When Times Are Tight.* St. Paul, MN: Amherst H. Wilder Foundation, 1997.
   Strategies for dealing with anticipated and actual government funding cutbacks. Suggests a six-step self-study process to determine the best possible options for an organization.

Barry, Bryan W. *Strategic Planning Workbook for Nonprofit Organizations.* Revised ed. St. Paul, MN: Amherst H. Wilder Foundation, 1997.
   Workbook describing the step-by-step process for developing and effecting a strategic plan. Numerous worksheets and planning tips help both experienced nonprofit executives and volunteer leaders envision the future of their organization and construct the best path to reach that goal.

Bernstein, Philip. *Best Practices of Effective Nonprofit Organizations: A Practitioner's Guide.* New York: The Foundation Center, 1997.
   Identifies and explains the procedures which provide the foundation for social achievement in all nonprofit fields.

Blazek, Jody. *Financial Planning for Nonprofit Organizations.* New York: John Wiley & Sons, 1996.
   Provides a step-by-step process to understand the major areas of financial planning including general administration; the roles and responsibilities of staff, board members, and professional advisors; developing and implementing budgets; asset and resource management; and internal controls to prevent waste and fraud.

Connors, Tracy Daniel. *The Nonprofit Handbook: Management.* 2nd ed. New York: John Wiley & Sons, 1997.

> A comprehensive reference guide to the policies and procedures shared by a great majority of small- and medium-sized nonprofit organizations. Contains drafts of policies and procedures as well as sample plans, forms, records, and reports.

DiLima, Sara Nell, and Lisa T. Johns, eds. *Nonprofit Organization Management Forms, Checklists & Guidelines.* Frederick, MD: Aspen Publishers, 1997.

> Sample forms, checklists, guidelines, policies and procedures for various aspects of nonprofit management, including planning, fundraising, human resources, accounting and finance, board relations, and public relations.

Herman, Robert D. *Jossey-Bass Handbook of Nonprofit Leadership and Management.* San Francisco, CA: Jossey-Bass, 1994.

> Provides descriptions of effective leadership and management practices that apply to nonprofit organizations. Sections discuss the context and institutions within which nonprofit organizations operate; key leadership issues; managing operations and people; and developing and managing financial resources.

Oertel, Patty. *The Nonprofit Answer Book: An Executive Director's Guide to Frequently Asked Questions.* Los Angeles, CA: Center for Nonprofit Management, 1998.

> Written in FAQ format and in non-technical language, answers many common questions about nonprofits.

Olenick, Arnold J., and Philip R. Olenick. *A Nonprofit Organization Operating Manual: Planning for Survival and Growth.* New York: The Foundation Center, 1991.

> This manual addresses the essential financial and legal aspects of managing a nonprofit organization.

Rutter, E. Jane. *The Self-Sustaining Nonprofit: Planning for Success.* Columbia, MO: Grants Link, Inc., 1997.

> Provides practical guidelines and advice to nonprofits that are making the transition from a volunteer organization to a formal structure. Covers

topics of incorporation, developing internal structures, financial and service planning, and growth.

Salamon, Lester M. *America's Nonprofit Sector: A Primer.* 2nd ed. New York: The Foundation Center, 1999.
> Presents the latest research on the changing roles of nonprofits in various sectors of society, including health care, education, social services, arts, culture, recreation, advocacy, and international aid.

Sandler, Martin W., and Deborah A. Hudson. *Beyond the Bottom Line: How to Do More with Less in Nonprofit and Public Organizations.* New York: Oxford University Press, 1998.
> The authors present the winning strategies of the best-managed nonprofit and government agencies: staying focused on their mission, using mission as a recruiting tool, a unifying force, and to set priorities; using change as an ally to revitalize the organization; creating a climate for innovation by taking risks, tolerating mistakes, and sharing power; planning carefully and measuring performance in customers' terms.

Smith, Bucklin & Associates. *The Complete Guide to Nonprofit Management.* New York: John Wiley & Sons, 1994.
> Sections cover mission, governance, fundraising, marketing, educational programs, meetings, public relations, political support, financial management, information systems, personnel, legal requirements, and selecting and using consultants.

Young, Dennis R., et al. *Governing, Leading, and Managing Nonprofit Organizations: New Insights for Research and Practice.* San Francisco, CA: Jossey-Bass, 1993.
> Contributions by various authors are organized into four parts: issues of governance, human resource and financial management, managing for social change, and public policy issues.

Internet resources:

National Center for Nonprofit Boards (www.ncnb.org)
Useful information about recruiting and communicating with board members, resolving board conflicts, and developing board job descriptions.

Nonprofit Manager's Library (www.mapnp.org/library)
A no-frills library of free management courses in topics such as board roles and responsibilities, communications skills, finance and taxes, program development, program evaluation, and consultants.

Nonprofit Resource Center (www.not-for-profit.org)
Designed for managers, board members, and volunteers, this is a one-stop directory for Internet resources of interest to nonprofit organizations, covering such topics as fundraising, finance and accounting, and management.

The Fundraising Process

Foundation Center. *The Foundation Center's Guide to Grantseeking on the Web.* New York: The Foundation Center, 1998.
A comprehensive manual including how to use the Internet to locate information on foundations, public charities, corporate givers and government funders; listings of databases, online journals, and interactive services of interest to grantseekers; and an in-depth tour of the Foundation Center's Web site.

Grace, Kay Sprinkel. *Beyond Fund Raising: New Strategies for Nonprofit Innovation and Investment.* New York: John Wiley & Sons, 1997.
Covers values, changing attitudes, leadership, capitalizing on the community's investment, stewardship, board development, levels of board and staff operation, and planning.

Mixer, Joseph R. *Principles of Professional Fundraising: Useful Foundations for Successful Practice*. San Francisco, CA: Jossey-Bass, 1993.
Applies concepts and theories from psychology, organizational behavior, and management to provide a framework that enhances the effectiveness of professional fundraising.

New, Anne L. *Raise More Money for Your Nonprofit Organization: A Guide to Evaluating and Improving Your Fundraising*. New York: The Foundation Center, 1991.
Workbook of questionnaires to help fundraising officials and nonprofit executives evaluate their organization's present state of fundraising, and show them what directions to take to improve it.

New, Cheryl Carter, and James Aaron Quick. *Grantseeker's Toolkit: A Comprehensive Guide to Finding Funding*. New York: John Wiley & Sons, 1998.
A grantseeking handbook with the stated goal of helping readers achieve competitive applications. Begins with the design of a project to solve a problem, then focuses on the research process for locating potential funders interested in the project.

Weinstein, Stanley. *The Complete Guide to Fund-Raising Management*. New York: John Wiley & Sons, 1998.
A comprehensive treatment of fundraising principles and practices, including information about creating case statements, record keeping, prospect research, cultivating donors, major gifts, grants, direct mail, telemarketing, special events, planned giving, and capital campaigns.

Zukowski, Linda M. *Fistfuls of Dollars: Fact and Fantasy about Corporate Charitable Giving*. Redondo Beach, CA: EarthWrites Publishing, 1998.
Covers the basics of corporate giving solicitation, as well as the elements of proposals and budgets. Also discusses how to respond to a funding decision.

Internet resources:

Foundation Center's Orientation to Grantseeking (www.fdncenter.org/onlib/orient/intro1.html)
  Primer on the funding research process for both individuals and nonprofits seeking grants.

National Society of Fundraising Executives (www.nsfre.org)
  Professional association for fundraisers, offering support and educational programs.

Fundraising—Special Topics

ANNUAL GIVING

Graham, Christine. *Keep the Money Coming: A Step-By-Step Strategic Guide to Annual Fundraising.* Sarasota, FL: Pineapple Press, 1992.
  Basic information on planning an annual fund campaign, with sections on utilizing various fundraising techniques, including direct mail, membership, and events.

Greenfield, James M. *Fund-Raising Fundamentals: A Guide to Annual Giving for Professionals and Volunteers.* New York: John Wiley & Sons, 1994.
  A companion volume to *A Legal Guide to Starting and Managing a Nonprofit Organization,* (John Wiley & Sons, 1993), explains six principal fundraising methods and describes how to manage a comprehensive annual giving program. Illustrated with numerous sample letters, gift reports, and other documents.

Williams, Karla A. *Donor Focused Strategies for Annual Giving.* Frederick, MD: Aspen Publishers, 1997.
  A step-by-step approach to establishing an annual giving program, including guidance on how to create a hospitable environment, build a constituent base, set giving objectives, and design an infrastructure.

CAPITAL CAMPAIGNS AND ENDOWMENTS

Gearhart, G. David. *The Capital Campaign in Higher Education: A Practical Guide for College and University Advancement.* Washington, D.C.: Council for Advancement and Support, 1995.
   Provides a summary of the major elements of planning and conducting capital campaigns for colleges and universities.

Graham, Christine P. *Blueprint for a Capital Campaign: An Introduction for Board Members, Volunteers and Staff.* Shaftsbury, VT: CPG Enterprises, 1997.
   A concise guide on how to plan and implement a capital campaign, together with a recommended reading list.

Kihlstedt, Andrea, and Catherine Schwartz. *Capital Campaigns: Strategies That Work.* Frederick, MD: Aspen Publishers, 1997.
   Written for small- to mid-sized nonprofit organizations that are considering a capital campaign. Covers the entire process from planning the campaign to finishing, evaluating, and reporting on the campaign.

DIRECT MAIL/TELEMARKETING

Fine, Seymour H. *Marketing the Public Sector: Promoting the Causes of Public and Nonprofit Agencies.* New Brunswick, NJ: Transaction Publishers, 1992.
   Provides social sector executives with guidelines on how to implement marketing strategies that can improve service to their constituencies, disseminate ideas, and educate the public.

Harr, David J., and Robert H. Frank. *Service Efforts and Accomplishments of a Telemarketing Campaign: The Experience of the Federation on Child Abuse and Neglect.* Pittsburgh, PA: Reese Brothers, Inc., 1993.
   Case study establishes a clear cost basis for the components of a fundraising campaign, and evaluates the cost, efficiency, and effectiveness of the telemarketing component. Makes several recommendations for achieving results and improving accounting methods.

Huntsinger, Jerald E. *Making Direct Response Fund Raising Pay Off: Outstanding Fund Raising Letters and Tips.* Chicago, IL: Bonus Books, 1992.
Presents ideas and reader response from Huntsinger's column in *Non-Profit Times.*

Lautman, Kay Partney, and Henry Goldstein. *Dear Friend: Mastering the Art of Direct Mail Fund Raising.* 2nd ed. Rockville, MD: Fund Raising Institute, 1991.
Step-by-step guide to direct mail fundraising, written on a track system that provides techniques for the novice as well as for the experienced fundraiser.

Squires, Conrad. *Teach Yourself to Write Irresistible Fund-Raising Letters.* Chicago, IL: Precept Press, 1993.
Step-by-step workbook for creating successful direct mail letters, including sections on using computers and writing thank-you responses.

Warwick, Mal. *How to Write Successful Fundraising Letters.* Berkeley, CA: Strathmoor Press, 1994.

Warwick, Mal. *Raising Money by Mail: Strategies for Growth and Financial Stability.* Revised ed. Berkeley, CA: Strathmoor Press, 1994.
Covers all aspects of direct mail fundraising, with numerous examples and illustrations.

Warwick, Mal, et al. *999 Tips, Trends and Guidelines for Successful Direct Mail and Telephone Fundraising.* Berkeley, CA: Strathmoor Press, 1993.
Provides an overview of testing of direct mail and telephone fundraising methods. Discusses guidelines for a first mailing: exactly what should be tested; how much to ask for; tailoring methods to a particular organization; limits of testing; analyzing results.

PLANNED GIFTS

Barrett, Richard D., and Molly E. Ware. *Planned Giving Essentials: A Step-by-Step Guide to Success.* Frederick, MD: Aspen Publishers, 1997.
Introduces basic planned giving principles and practices and provides a guide to implementing a planned giving program.

Clough, Leonard G., et al. *Practical Guide to Planned Giving, 1998.* Detroit, MI: Taft Group, 1997.
> Provides marketing and technical information to help development officers establish permanent planned giving programs. Contains operational definitions of major forms of planned giving programs and a step-by-step guide to preparing and setting up a program.

Gregg, Keith E. *Do Well by Doing Good: The Complete Guide to Charitable Remainder Trusts.* Chicago, IL: Bonus Books, 1996.
> Covers different types and popular uses of charitable remainder trusts, and explains how to set them up and market them.

Jordan, Ronald R., Katelyn L. Quynn, and Carolyn M. Osteen. *Planned Giving: Management, Marketing, and Law.* New York, John Wiley & Sons, 1995.
> Divided into six parts: building a development program, marketing planned giving, planned giving assets, deferred gifts, related disciplines, and planned giving in context.

Moerschbaecher, Lynda S. *Start at Square One: Starting and Managing the Planned Gift Program.* Chicago, IL: Precept Press, 1998.
> Explains how to integrate a planned giving program with an overall development effort, and provides instructions for getting started.

Internet resource:

National Committee on Planned Giving (www.ncpg.org)
> Professional association for people whose work involves developing, marketing, and administering charitable planned gifts.

Prospect Research

Bergan, Helen. *Where the Money Is: A Fund Raiser's Guide to the Rich.* 2nd ed. Alexandria, VA: BioGuide Press, 1992.
> Techniques for locating biographical information on prospective donors.

Lane, Carole A., Helen Burwell, and Owen B. Davies, eds. *Naked in Cyberspace: How to Find Personal Information Online.* Somerville, MA: Pemberton Press Books, 1997.

Internet resources:

Association of Professional Researchers for Advancement (weber.u.washington.edu/~dlamb/apra/APRA.html)
   Professional association for prospect researchers whose Web site contains links to private and government resources.

Internet Prospector (w3.uwyo.edu/~prospect/)
   This nonprofit service to the prospect research community is located on the University of Wyoming's server and produced by volunteers nation-wide who "mine" the Net for prospect research nuggets for nonprofit fundraisers.

SPECIAL EVENTS

Freedman, Harry A., and Karen Feldman. *The Business of Special Events: Fundraising Strategies for Changing Times.* Sarasota, FL: Pineapple Press, 1998.
   Detailed step-by-step planning guide, with checklists, for all types of events.

Kaitcer, Cindy R. *Raising Big Bucks: The Complete Guide to Producing Pledge-Based Special Events.* Chicago, IL: Bonus Books, 1996.
   Covers planning, budgeting, publicity, staff and volunteers, logistics, and other issues related to this specialized fundraising option.

Levy, Barbara R., and Barbara H. Marion. *Successful Special Events: Planning, Hosting, and Evaluating.* Frederick, MD: Aspen Publishers, 1997.
   An overview of the management of successful special events, from the definition of a special event through goal setting, choice of theme and site, determinations of costs, time frame, and human resources needed, to decor, public relations, and legal considerations.

Schmader, Steven Wood, and Robert Jackson. *Special Events: Inside and Out.* 2nd ed. Champaign, IL: Sagamore Publishing, 1997.
   In a workbook format, covers most aspects of conducting special events.

Other Sources of Nonprofit Support

GOVERNMENT FUNDING

Catalog of Federal Domestic Assistance. Washington, D.C.: United States Office of Management and Budget, annual.
   Guide to financial assistance available to state and local governments, private for-profit and nonprofit agencies, and individuals.

Commerce Business Daily. Washington, D.C.: U.S. International Trade Administration, U.S. Department of Commerce, daily.
   Synopsis of United States government proposed procurement, sales, and contract awards. Contains a listing of products and services the government needs, with information on how and when to bid.

Dumouchel, J. Robert. *Government Assistance Almanac.* Detroit, MI: Omnigraphics, Inc., annual.
   Outlines the more than 1,300 federal domestic programs currently available, providing information about the type or types of assistance offered, with complete contact details.

Federal Register. Washington, D.C.: U.S. Office of the Federal Register, National Archives and Records Administration, daily.
   Provides proposed and final rules issued by more than 250 federal agencies, as well as all presidential proclamations and executive orders.

Internet resources:

Catalog of Federal Domestic Assistance (www.gsa.gov/fdac/default.htm)
   Information about financial and non-financial assistance programs administered by departments and agencies of the federal government.

Federal Information Exchange (web.fie.com/fedix/index.html)
  FEDIX, a database of federal funding opportunities, is searchable by
  agency, audience, and subject.

National Assembly of State Arts Agencies (www.nasaa-arts.org)
  Sponsored by the National Endowment for the Arts, this site is a clearinghouse of Internet information for arts organizations.

NonProfit Gateway (www.nonprofit.gov)
  Created by the White House Office of Public Liaison, this is the starting
  point for information about services from federal agencies.

In-kind Gifts

Gingold, Diane J. *Strategic Philanthropy in the 1990s: Handbook of Corporate
Development Strategies for Nonprofit Managers.* Washington, D.C.: Diane Gingold and
Associates, 1993.
  Guide to corporate strategic philanthropy, which includes corporate giv-
  ing, sponsorship, cause-related marketing, in-kind donations, public
  relations, marketing, government relations, and more.

Nelson, Donald T., and Paul H. Schneiter. *Gifts-in-Kind: The Fund Raiser's Guide to
Acquiring, Managing, and Selling Charitable Contributions Other Than Cash and
Securities.* Rockville, MD: Fund Raising Institute, 1991.
  Emphasizing the importance of a gifts-in-kind program to overall fundraising strategy, this book provides case histories, analyses, and recommendations on the acquisition, management, and selling of non-cash
  gifts. Includes sample policies and procedures manual.

Internet resource:

Gifts in Kind International (www.GiftsInKind.org)
  Gifts in Kind manages product donations from companies to support
  charities and schools addressing needs such as housing, health care, education, and youth development.

Memberships

Ellis, Susan J. *The Volunteer Recruitment and Membership Development Book.* 2nd ed. Philadelphia, PA: Energize, 1996.
  Provides one chapter about building memberships, based on principles of successful volunteer recruitment.

Ethier, Donald, and David Karlson. *Association Membership Basics: A Workbook for Membership Directors and Members.* Menlo Park, CA: Crisp Publications Inc., 1997.
  Provides how-to information about recruiting members, the membership cycle, establishing dues, special handling for new members, forecasting revenue, building value-added services and other challenges for membership directors.

Nonprofit Entrepreneurship

Boschee, Jerr. *Merging Mission and Money: A Board Member's Guide to Social Entrepreneurship.* Washington, D.C.: National Center for Nonprofit Boards, 1998.
  Potential pitfalls as well as specific steps for success as a social entrepreneur.

Brinckerhoff, Peter C. *Financial Empowerment: More Money for More Mission.* Dillon, CO: Alpine Guild, 1996.
  Covers characteristics and outcomes of empowerment, how to estimate cash needs, working with traditional funders, how to develop a new business, financial reporting, a review of different financing options, budgeting, pricing, corporate structures, roles of the CEO and the board.

Firstenberg, Paul B. *The Twenty-First Century Nonprofit: Remaking the Organization in the Post-Government Era.* New York: The Foundation Center, 1996.
  Encourages managers to: adopt the strategies developed by the for-profit sector in recent years; expand their revenue base by diversifying grant sources and exploiting the possibilities of for-profit enterprises; develop human resources by learning how to attract and retain talented people; and explore the nature of leadership.

Proposal Development

Belcher, Jane C., and Julia M. Jacobsen. *From Idea to Funded Projects: Grant Proposals That Work.* 4th revised ed. Phoenix, AZ: Oryx Press, 1992.
  Presents a method for nurturing an idea from inception through the development of a proposal; finding sources of support; administering grants; and evaluating your program.

Bowman, Joel P., and Bernardine P. Branchaw. *How to Write Proposals That Produce.* Phoenix, AZ: Oryx Press, 1992.
  A detailed and technical treatment of the process of writing proposals. Directed toward readers from both the corporate and nonprofit sectors.

Burns, Michael E. *Proposal Writer's Guide.* Revised ed. New Haven, CT: Development and Technical Assistance Center, 1993.
  Step-by-step approach to preparing written fund requests. Includes four sample proposals.

Carlson, Mim. *Winning Grants Step by Step.* San Francisco, CA: Support Centers of America, 1995.
  Contains exercises designed to help with proposal planning and writing skills and to meet the requirements of both government agencies and private funders.

Geever, Jane C., and Patricia McNeill. *The Foundation Center's Guide to Proposal Writing.* Revised ed. New York: The Foundation Center, 1997.
  This in-depth manual guides the grantseeker from pre-proposal planning to post-grant follow-up. Incorporates excerpts from actual grant proposals and interviews with foundation and corporate grantmakers revealing what they look for in a proposal.

Grant your Wish. [videotape] Ft. Lauderdale, FL: Successful Images, 1998.
  Concise 30-minute presentation on the elements of proposals, with numerous examples and tips.

Hale, Phale D., Jr. *Writing Grant Proposals That Win.* 2nd ed. Washington, D.C.:
Capitol Publications, 1997.
    Covers the major elements in any proposal and discusses the difference
    between applying to federal and private-sector funders.

Miner, Lynn E., Jeremy T. Miner, and Jerry Griffith. *Proposal Planning and Writing.*
2nd ed. Phoenix, AZ: Oryx Press, 1998.
    Covers the proposal development process for federal government, private
    foundation, and corporate funding sources.

Orlich, Donald C. *Designing Successful Grant Proposals.* Alexandria, VA: Association
for Supervision and Curriculum Development, 1996.
    Presents the standard elements of grant writing, with checklists.

Internet resources:

Elements of a Grant Proposal (www.silcom.com/~paladin/promaster.html)
    Information on proposal writing compiled by the Center for Nonprofit
    Management in Los Angeles, CA.

Foundation Center's Proposal Writing Short Course (www.fdncenter.org/onlib/
shortcourse/prop1.html)
    Basic information about proposal writing, excerpted from *The Foundation
    Center's Guide to Proposal Writing.*

Specialized Funding Directories

Directory of Research Grants. 24th ed. Phoenix, AZ: Oryx Press, 1999.

Eckstein, Richard M., ed. *Directory of Building and Equipment Grants.* 5th ed.
Loxahatchee, FL: Research Grant Guides, 1999.

Eckstein, Richard M., ed. *Directory of Computer and High Technology Grants.* 3rd ed.
Loxahatchee, FL: Research Grant Guides, 1996.

Eckstein, Richard M., ed. *Directory of Education Grants.* Loxahatchee, FL: Research Grant Guides, 1996.

Eckstein, Richard M., ed. *Directory of Grants for Organizations Serving People with Disabilities.* 10th ed. Loxahatchee, FL: Research Grant Guides, 1997.

Eckstein, Richard M., ed. *Directory of Health Grants.* 2nd ed. Loxahatchee, FL: Research Grant Guides, 1998.

Eckstein, Richard M., ed. *Directory of Operating Grants.* 4th ed. Loxahatchee, FL: Research Grant Guides, 1998.

Eckstein, Richard M., ed. *Directory of Social Service Grants.* 2nd ed. Loxahatchee, FL: Research Grant Guides, 1998.

Environmental Grantmaking Foundations. 6th ed. Rochester, NY: Resources for Global Sustainability, Inc. 1998.

Ferguson, Jacqueline. *Grants for Schools: How to Find and Win Funds for K-12 Programs.* 3rd ed. Alexandria, VA: Capitol Publications, 1997.

Ferguson, Jacqueline. *Grants for Special Education and Rehabilitation: How to Find and Win Funds for Research, Training and Services.* 3rd ed. Alexandria, VA: Capitol Publications, 1997.

Foundation Grants to Individuals. 11th ed. New York: The Foundation Center, 1999.

Funding Sources for Community and Economic Development 1998: A Guide to Current Sources for Local Programs and Projects. 4th ed. Phoenix, AZ: Oryx Press, 1998.

Funding Sources for K-12 Schools and Adult Basic Education. Phoenix, AZ: Oryx Press, 1998.

Guide to Funding for International and Foreign Programs. 4th ed. New York: The Foundation Center, 1998.

Hubbard, Monica M., and Laurie Fundukian. *Fund Raiser's Guide to Human Service Funding.* 10th ed. Detroit, MI: Taft Group, 1998.

Jankowski, Bernard. *Fund Raiser's Guide to Religious Philanthropy.* 12th ed. Detroit, MI: Taft Group, 1998.

Kerber, Beth-Ann. *The Health Funds Grants Resources Yearbook.* 8th ed. Manasquan, NJ: Health Resources Publishing, 1999.

Klein, Kim. *Fundraising for Social Change.* 3rd ed. Inverness, CA: Chardon Press, 1994.

Krebs, Arlene. *The Distance Learning Funding Sourcebook: A Guide to Foundation, Corporation and Government Support for Telecommunications and the New Media.* 4th ed. Dubuque, IA: Kendall/Hunt Publishing, 1998.

Meiners, Phyllis A., ed. *Corporate and Foundation Fundraising Manual for Native Americans.* Kansas City, MO: Corporate Resource Consultants, 1996.

Meiners, Phyllis A., ed. *National Directory of Foundation Grants for Native Americans.* Kansas City, MO: Corporate Resource Consultants, 1998.

Morris, James McGrath, and Laura Adler. *Grant Seekers Guide: Foundations that Support Social & Economic Justice.* 5th ed. Wakefield, RI: Moyer Bell, 1998.

National Guide to Funding for Children, Youth and Families. 5th ed. New York: The Foundation Center, 1999.

National Guide to Funding for Community Development. 2nd ed. New York: The Foundation Center, 1998.

National Guide to Funding for Elementary and Secondary Education. 5th ed. New York: The Foundation Center, 1999.

National Guide to Funding for Information Technology. 2nd ed. New York: The Foundation Center, 1999.

National Guide to Funding for Libraries and Information Services. 5th ed. New York: The Foundation Center, 1999.

National Guide to Funding for the Environment and Animal Welfare. 4th ed. New York: The Foundation Center, 1998.

National Guide to Funding for Women and Girls. 5th ed. New York: The Foundation Center, 1999.

National Guide to Funding in Aging. 5th ed. New York: The Foundation Center, 1998.

National Guide to Funding in AIDS, 1st ed. New York: The Foundation Center, 1999.

National Guide to Funding in Arts and Culture. 5th ed. New York: The Foundation Center, 1998.

National Guide to Funding in Health. 6th ed. New York: The Foundation Center, 1999.

National Guide to Funding in Higher Education. 5th ed. New York: The Foundation Center, 1998.

National Guide to Funding in Religion. 5th ed. New York: The Foundation Center, 1999.

National Guide to Funding in Substance Abuse. 2nd ed. New York: The Foundation Center, 1998.

Reyes, Rosana, ed. *Activist's Guide to Religious Funders.* 3rd ed. Oakland, CA: Center for Third World Organizing, 1993.

Robinson, Kerry, ed. *The Catholic Funding Guide: A Directory of Resources for Catholics.* Washington, D.C.: Foundations and Donors Interested in Catholic Activities, Inc., 1998.

Robinson, Kerry, ed. *Foundation Guide for Religious Grant Seekers.* 5th ed. Decatur, GA: Scholars Press, 1995.

Taft Group. *The Big Book of Library Grant Money.* 1998-99 ed. Detroit, MI: The Taft Group, 1998.

Weinhard, William, ed. *Grants for School Technology: A Guide to Federal and Private Funding.* Alexandria, VA: Capitol Publications, 1998.

Working Group on Funding Lesbian and Gay Issues. *Funders of Lesbian, Gay and Bisexual Programs: A Directory for Grantseekers.* 3rd ed. New York: Working Group on Funding Lesbian and Gay Issues, 1997.

Periodicals on Foundations and Fundraising—A Selected Listing

Advancing Philanthropy. National Society of Fund Raising Executives, 1101 King Street, Suite 700, Alexandria, VA 22314. Quarterly. (www.nsfre.org/index.html)
 Trends and issues impacting philanthropy and fundraising, new ideas and success stories, interviews with nonprofit leaders, and book reviews.

Chronicle of Philanthropy. 1255 23rd Street, N.W., Washington, D.C. 20037. Biweekly. (philanthropy.com)
 Reports on issues and trends in the nonprofit sector, covering corporate and individual giving, foundation profiles, updates on fundraising campaigns, taxation, regulation, and management.

Corporate Giving Watch. The Taft Group, 27500 Drake Rd., Farmington Hills, MI 48331-3535. Monthly. (www.thomson.com/taft)
 Articles analyzing corporate philanthropy, corporate sources of support, and fundraising ideas.

Corporate Philanthropy Report. Aspen Publishers, Inc., 1101 King Street, Suite 444, Alexandria, VA 22314. Monthly.
 Articles on issues and trends, reviews of current giving by companies and industry, and news items.

Currents. Council for the Advancement and Support of Education, 1307 New York Avenue, Suite 1000, Washington, D.C. 20005-1973. Monthly. (www.case.org/ CURRIndex/main.html)
  Articles on management, fundraising, and development for educational institutions. Book reviews and conference listings included.

Foundation Giving Watch. The Taft Group, 27500 Drake Rd., Farmington Hills, MI 48331-3535. Monthly. (www.thomson.com/taft)
  Brief reports on new foundation programs, giving trends, and recent grants. Updates the annual *Foundation Reporter.*

Foundation News & Commentary. Council on Foundations, 1828 L Street, N.W., Washington, D.C. 20036. Bimonthly. (www.cof.org/foundationnews)
  Articles on grantmaking activities, foundation leaders and people in the news, and trends in the field.

FRI Monthly Portfolio. Fund Raising Institute, The Taft Group, 27500 Drake Rd., Farmington Hills, MI 48331-3535. Monthly. (www.thomson.com/taft)
  Provides practical advice to fundraisers, with a focus on direct mail and capital campaigns.

Fund Raising Management. Hoke Communications, 224 Seventh Street, Garden City, NY 11530-5771. Monthly. (www.hokecomm.com/frmmagazine/index.html)
  Articles on all aspects of fundraising, book reviews, and a calendar of events.

Grantsmanship Center Magazine. The Grantsmanship Center, P.O. Box 17220, Los Angeles, CA 90017. Quarterly. (www.tgci.com/publications/magazine.htm)
  Articles, summaries of publications, and listings for Grantsmanship Center training programs and seminars.

Grassroots Fundraising Journal. P.O. Box 11607, Berkeley, CA 94712. Bimonthly.
  Articles about basic fundraising techniques, alternative sources of funding, book reviews, and bibliographies, especially for the smaller nonprofit.

New Directions for Philanthropic Fundraising. Jossey-Bass Inc. 350 Sansome Street, San Francisco, CA 94194. Quarterly. (www.jbp.com/JBJournals/ndpf.html)
  Quarterly journal addressing how the concepts of philanthropy pertain to fundraising practice.

NonProfit Times. 240 Cedar Knolls Rd., Suite 318, Cedar Knolls, NJ 07927. (www.nptimes.com)
  News articles focusing on trends, legislation, fundraising, and management of nonprofits.

ONLINE JOURNALS

American Philanthropy Review (www.philanthropy-review.com)
  Reviews of nonprofit periodicals, books, and software.

Internet Prospector (w3.uwyo.edu/~prospect)
  Monthly newsletter focusing on information for prospect researchers.

Nonprofit Online News (www.gilbert.org/news)
  A compilation of current news in the nonprofit area, with added opinions and observations.

Philanthropy Journal Online (www.pj.org/)
  Daily updates of news for the nonprofit sector, including jobs.

Philanthropy News Digest (www.fdncenter.org/pnd/current/index.html)
  Weekly summary of news about philanthropy, taken from the popular press.

Appendix B

State Charities Registration Offices

ALABAMA

Office of the Attorney General
11 South Union Street
Montgomery, AL 36130
(334) 242-7320

ALASKA

Attorney General's Office
1031 West 4th, Suite 200
Anchorage, AK 99501
(907) 269-5198

ARIZONA

Secretary of State
Attn: Charities
1700 West Washington, 7th Floor
Phoenix, AZ 85007
(602) 542-4285

ARKANSAS

Attorney General's Office
Consumer Protection
200 Tower Building
323 Center Street
Little Rock, AR 72201
(501) 682-2341

CALIFORNIA

Attorney General
Registry of Charitable Trusts
P.O. Box 903447
Sacramento, CA 94203-4470
(916) 445-2021

COLORADO

Secretary of State
Licensing Division
1560 Broadway, Suite 200
Denver, CO 80202
(303) 894-2680

CONNECTICUT

Office of the Attorney General
Public Charities
P.O. Box 120
Hartford, CT 06141-0120
(860) 808-5030

DELAWARE

Office of the Attorney General
Carvel State Building
820 North French Street, 6th Floor
Wilmington, DE 19801
(302) 577-8600

DISTRICT OF COLUMBIA

Department of Consumer and Regulatory
    Affairs
614 H Street N.W., Room 100
Washington, DC 20001
(202) 727-7287

FLORIDA

Department of Agriculture
Division of Consumer Services
Mayo Building
407 South Calhoun Street
Tallahassee, FL 32399
(850) 413-0840

GEORGIA

Secretary of State
Securities and Business Regulation
2 Martin Luther King Jr. Drive SE
Suite 808, West Tower
Atlanta, GA 30334
(404) 656-4910

HAWAII

Department of Commerce and Consumer
    Affairs
1010 Richards Street
P.O. Box 40
Honolulu, HI 96810
(808) 586-2737

IDAHO

Office of the Attorney General
Consumer Protection
P. O. Box 83720
Boise, ID 83720-0010
(208) 334-2424

ILLINOIS

Office of the Attorney General
Charitable Trusts
100 West Randolph, 11th Floor
Chicago, IL 60601
(312) 814-2595

INDIANA

Indiana Department of Revenue
Not for Profit Section
Room N203
100 North Senate Avenue
Indianapolis, IN 46204
(317) 232-2188

IOWA

Consumer Protection Division
1300 East Walnut
Des Moines, IA 50319
(515) 281-5926

KANSAS

Secretary of State
300 SW 10th Avenue
State Capitol, 2nd Floor
Topeka, KS 66612-1594
(785) 296-2236

KENTUCKY

Office of the Attorney General
Consumer Protection Division
1024 Capitol Center Drive
Frankfort, KY 40601
(502) 696-5389

LOUISIANA

Department of Justice
301 Main Street, Suite 1250
Baton Rouge, LA 70801
(504) 342-9638

MAINE

Department of Professional and Financial
    Regulation
62 State House Station
Augusta, ME 04333
(207) 624-8624

MARYLAND

Secretary of State
Charitable Organizations Division
State House
Annapolis, MD 21401
(410) 974-5534

MASSACHUSETTS

Office of the Attorney General
Charities Division, 14th Floor
1 Ashburton Place
Boston, MA 02108
(617) 727-2200

MICHIGAN

Office of the Attorney General
Charitable Trust Section
525 West Ottowa
670 Williams Building
Lansing, MI 48913
(517) 373-1152

MINNESOTA

Office of the Attorney General
Charities Division
1200 NCL Tower
445 Minnesota Street
St. Paul, MN 55101-2130
(612) 296-6172

MISSISSIPPI

Secretary of State
Customer Services Division
P.O. Box 136
Jackson, MS 39205
(601) 359-1350

MISSOURI

Office of the Attorney General
Consumer Protection Division
P.O. Box 899
Jefferson City, MO 65102
(573) 751-4471

MONTANA

Office of the Attorney General
P.O. Box 201401
Helena, MT 59620-1401
(406) 444-2026

NEBRASKA

Attorney General's Office
Consumer Protection Division
2115 State Capitol
Lincoln, NE 68509
(402) 471-2682

NEVADA

Nevada Department of Business &
   Industry
Consumer Affairs Division
1850 East Sahara Avenue, Suite 101
Las Vegas, NV 89104
(702) 486-7355

NEW HAMPSHIRE

Office of the Attorney General
Division of Charitable Trusts
33 Capitol Street
Concord, NH 03301-6397
(603) 271-3591

NEW JERSEY

Charitable Registration Section
P.O. Box 45021
Newark, NJ 07102
(973) 504-6262

NEW MEXICO

Office of the Attorney General
Consumer Protection Division/Charities
   Office
P.O. Drawer 1508
Santa Fe, NM 87504
(505) 827-6009

NEW YORK

Attorney General
Charities Bureau
120 Broadway, 3rd Floor
New York, NY 10271
(212) 416-8975

NORTH CAROLINA

Department of Health and Human Services
Division of Facilities Services
Solicitation Licensing Branch
P.O. Box 29530
Raleigh, NC 27626-0530
(919) 733-4510

NORTH DAKOTA

Secretary of State
600 East Boulevard Avenue
Bismarck, ND 58505-0500
(701) 328-3665

OHIO

Office of the Attorney General
Charitable Foundation Section
101 East Town Street, 4th Floor
Columbus, OH 43215-5148
(614) 466-3180

OKLAHOMA

Secretary of State
2300 North Lincoln, Room 101
Oklahoma City, OK 73105-4897
(405) 521-3049

OREGON

Department of Justice
Charities Division
1515 SW 5th Avenue, Suite 410
Portland, OR 97201
(503) 229-5725

PENNSYLVANIA

Department of State
Bureau of Charitable Organizations
P.O. Box 8723
Harrisburg, PA 17105
(717) 783-1720

RHODE ISLAND

Office of the Attorney General
Charitable Trusts
150 South Main Street
Providence, RI 02903
(401) 274-4400

SOUTH CAROLINA

Secretary of State
Public Charities Division
P.O. Box 11350
Columbia, SC 29211
(803) 734-9180

SOUTH DAKOTA

Office of the Attorney General
Division of Consumer Protection
500 East Capitol
Pierre, SD 57501
(605) 773-4400

TENNESSEE

Department of State
Division of Charitable Solicitations
Suite 1700, James K. Polk Building
Nashville, TN 37243
(615) 741-2555

TEXAS

Office of the Attorney General
Consumer Protection
Charitable Trusts Section
P.O. Box 12548
Austin, TX 78711-2548
(512) 463-2185

UTAH

Department of Commerce
Division of Consumer Protection
160 East 300 South
P.O. Box 146704
Salt Lake City, UT 84114-6704
(801) 530-6601

VERMONT

Secretary of State
109 State Street
Montpelier, VT 05609
(802) 828-2386

VIRGINIA

Department of Consumer Affairs
1100 Bank Street, Suite 103
Richmond, VA 23218
(804) 786-1343

WASHINGTON

Secretary of State
Charities Program
P.O. Box 40234
Olympia, WA 98504-0234
(360) 753-7118

WEST VIRGINIA

Secretary of State
Building 1, Suite 157K
1900 Kanawha Boulevard East
Charleston, WV 25305
(304) 558-6000

WISCONSIN

Department of Regulation Licensing
P.O. Box 8935
Madison, WI 53708
(608) 266-5511

WYOMING

Office of the Attorney General
123 State Capitol
Cheyenne, WY 82002
(307) 777-5838

Appendix C

The Foundation Center's Grants Classification System and The National Taxonomy of Exempt Entities (NTEE)

The Foundation Center began to record and categorize grants in 1961. It established a computerized grants reports system in 1972. From 1979 to 1988, the Center relied on a "facet" classification system, employing a fixed vocabulary of four-letter codes that permitted categorization of each grant by subject, type of recipient, population group, type of support, and scope of grant activity.

In 1989, following explosive growth in the number of grants indexed annually, the Center introduced a new classification system with links to the National Taxonomy of Exempt Entities (NTEE), a comprehensive coding scheme developed by the National Center for Charitable Statistics. This scheme established a unified national standard for classifying nonprofit organizations while permitting a multidimensional structure for analyzing grants. The new system also provided a more concise and consistent hierarchical method with which to classify and index grants.

The Center's Grants Classification System uses two- or three-character alphanumeric codes to track institutional fields and entities, governance or auspices, population groups, geographic focus, and types of support awarded. The universe of institutional fields is organized into twenty-six "major field" areas (A to Z), following the ten basic divisions established by the NTEE:

I.	Arts, Culture, Humanities	A
II.	Education	B
III.	Environment/Animals	C, D
IV.	Health	E, F, G, H
V.	Human Services	I, J, K, L, M, N, O, P
VI.	International/Foreign Affairs	Q
VII.	Public Affairs/Society Benefit	R, S, T, U, V, W
VIII.	Religion	X
IX.	Mutual/Membership Benefit	Y
X.	Nonclassifiable Entities	Z

The first letter of each code denotes the field, such as "A" for Arts and "B" for Education. Within each alpha subject area, numbers 20 to 99 identify services, disciplines, or types of institutions unique to that field, organized in a hierarchical structure. These sub-categories cover most activities in the nonprofit field. As a result, hundreds of specific terms can be researched with consistent results and grant dollars can be tallied to determine distribution patterns.

While based on NTEE, the Center's system added indexing elements not part of the original taxonomy, including the ability to track awards to government-sponsored organizations such as public schools, state universities, and municipal or federal agencies; a secondary set of codes to classify thirty-four specific types of grant support; and a third set of codes to track forty different grant beneficiary populations. More evolutionary than revolutionary, the new system does introduce two new fields not previously tracked by the Foundation Center: Auspices (NTEE'S governance codes are used) and Country of Activity (not part of NTEE). This last field is used to track the foreign locations of grant activities, for example, an award to the New York office of UNESCO for relief services in Ethiopia.

For a complete explanation of the Foundation Center's Grants Classification System, see *The Foundation Center's Grants Classification System Indexing Manual with Thesaurus*, available in all Center libraries, at the Center's Web site on the Internet (www.fdncenter.org), and in many Cooperating Collections. The *Manual* can also be purchased from the Center at its libraries, via telephone (1-800-424-9836), or on the Center's Web site.

Appendix D

Types of Support Definitions

Annual campaigns: Any organized effort by a nonprofit to secure gifts on an annual basis; also called annual appeals.

Building/renovation: Grants for constructing, renovating, remodeling, or rehabilitating property. Includes general or unspecified capital support awards.

Capital campaigns: Campaigns to raise funds for a variety of long-term purposes such as building construction or acquisition, endowments, land acquisition, etc.

Cause-related marketing: The practice of linking gifts to charity with marketing promotions. This may involve donating products that will then be auctioned or given away in a drawing with the proceeds benefiting a charity. The advertising campaign for the product will be combined with the promotion for the charity. In other cases it will be advertised that when a customer buys the product a certain amount of the proceeds will be donated to charity.

Conferences/seminars: Includes workshops.

Consulting services: Professional staff support provided by the foundation to a nonprofit to consult on a project of mutual interest or to evaluate services (not a cash grant).

Continuing support: Grants renewed on a regular basis.

Curriculum development: Awards to schools, colleges, universities, and educational support organizations to develop general or discipline-specific curricula.

Debt reduction: Grant to reduce the recipient organization's indebtedness; also referred to as deficit financing. Frequently refers to mortgage payments.

Donated equipment: Surplus furniture, office machines, paper, appliances, laboratory apparatus, or other items that may be given to charities, schools, or hospitals.

Donated land: Land or developed property. Institutions of higher education often receive gifts of real estate; land has also been given to community groups for housing development or for parks or recreational facilities.

Donated products: Companies giving away what they make or produce. Product donations can include periodic clothing donations to a shelter for the homeless or regular donations of pharmaceuticals to a health clinic resulting in a reliable supply.

Emergency funds: One-time grants to cover immediate short-term funding needs of a recipient organization on an emergency basis.

Employee matching gifts: Usually made by corporate foundations to match gifts made by corporate employees.

Employee volunteer services: Effort through which a company promotes involvement with nonprofits on the part of employees.

Employee-related scholarships: Scholarship programs funded by a company-sponsored foundation usually for children of employees; programs are frequently administered by the National Merit Scholarship Corporation which is responsible for selection of scholars.

Endowments: Bequests or gifts intended to be kept permanently and invested to provide income for continued support of an organization.

Equipment: Grants to purchase equipment, furnishings, or other materials.

Exchange programs: Usually refers to funds for educational exchange programs for foreign students.

Fellowship funds: Usually indicates funds awarded to educational institutions to support fellowship programs. A few foundations award fellowships directly to individuals.

General/operating support: Grants for the day-to-day operating costs of an existing program or organization or to further the general purpose or work of an organization. Also called unrestricted grants.

Grants to individuals: These awards are given directly to individuals, not through other nonprofit organizations. Many grantmakers have a specific limitation stating no grants to individuals. In order to make grants to individuals, a foundation must have a program that has received formal IRS approval.

In-kind gifts: Contributions of equipment, supplies, or other property as distinct from monetary grants.

Internship funds: Usually indicates funds awarded to an institution or organization to support an internship program.

Land acquisition: Grants to purchase real estate property.

Loaned talent: Usually involves loaned professionals and executive staff who are helping a nonprofit in an area involving their particular skills.

Matching/challenge support: Grants made to match funds provided by another donor and grants paid only if the donee is able to raise additional funds from another source.

Professorships: Grants to educational institutions to endow a professorship or chair.

Program development: Grants to support specific projects or programs as opposed to general purpose grants.

Program evaluation: Grants to evaluate a specific project or program; includes awards both to agencies to pay for evaluation costs and to research institutes and other program evaluators.

Program-related investments/loans: Loans or other investments (as distinguished from grants) to organizations to finance projects related to the foundation's stated charitable purpose and interests. Student loans are classified under Student aid funds.

Public relations services: May include printing and duplicating, audiovisual and graphic arts services, helping to plan special events such as festivals, piggyback advertising (advertisements that mention a company while also promoting a nonprofit), and public service advertising.

Publication: Grants to fund reports or other publications issued by a nonprofit resulting from research or projects of interest to the foundation.

Research: Funds to cover the costs of investigations and clinical trials, including demonstration and pilot projects. (Research grants for individuals are usually referred to as fellowships.)

Scholarship funds (institutional support): Grants to educational institutions or organizations to support a scholarship program, mainly for students at the undergraduate level; the donee institution then distributes the funds to individuals through their own programs.

Scholarships (to individuals): These are funds awarded to individuals through programs administered by the grantmaker.

Seed money: Grants to start, establish, or initiate new projects or organizations; may cover salaries and other operating expenses of a new project. Also called start-up funds.

Sponsorships: Endorsements of charities by corporations or corporate contributions to charitable events.

Student loans (to individuals): These are loans distributed directly to individuals through programs administered by the grantmaker.

Technical assistance: Operational or management assistance given to nonprofit organizations, including fundraising assistance, budgeting and financial planning, program planning, legal advice, marketing, and other aids to management.

Use of facilities: May include rent free office space for temporary periods, dining and meeting facilities, telecommunications services, mailing services, transportation services, or computer services.

Appendix E

Resources of the Foundation Center

The Foundation Center is a national service organization founded and supported by foundations to provide a single authoritative source of information on foundation and corporate giving. The Center's programs are designed to help grantseekers select those funders that may be most interested in their projects from the close to 50,000 active U.S. grantmakers. Among its primary activities toward this end are publishing reference books and CD-ROMs on foundation and corporate philanthropy and disseminating information on grantmaking, grantseeking, and related subjects through its site on the World Wide Web and a nationwide public service program.

Publications of the Foundation Center are the primary working tools of every serious grantseeker. They are also used by grantmakers, scholars, journalists, and legislators—in short, by anyone seeking any type of factual information on philanthropy. All private foundations and a significant number of corporate grantmakers actively engaged in grantmaking, regardless of size or geographic location, are included in one or more of the Center's publications. The publications are of three kinds: directories that describe specific funders, characterizing their program interests and providing fiscal and personnel data; grants indexes that list and classify by subject recent foundation and corporate awards; and guides, monographs, and bibliographies that introduce the reader to funding research, elements of proposal writing, and nonprofit management issues.

For those who wish to access information on grantmakers and their grants electronically, the Center issues *FC Search: The Foundation Center's Database on CD-ROM* containing the full universe of close to 50,000 grantmakers and more than 200,000 associated grants. In addition, the Center's award-winning Web site features a wide array of free information about the philanthropic community.

The Foundation Center's publications and electronic products may be ordered from the Foundation Center, 79 Fifth Avenue, New York, NY 10003-3076, or online at our Web site. For more information about any aspect of the Center's programs or for the name of the Center's library collection nearest you, call 1-800-424-9836, or visit us on the Web at www.fdncenter.org. At our Web site you will also find the most current information on new products and services of the Foundation Center.

GENERAL RESEARCH DIRECTORIES

THE FOUNDATION DIRECTORY, 1999 Edition

The Foundation Directory includes the latest information on all foundations whose assets exceed $2 million or whose annual grants total $200,000 or more. The 1999 Edition includes more than 10,000 of these foundations, over 2,000 of which are new to this edition. *Directory* foundations hold more than $304 billion in assets and award $14 billion in grants annually.

Each *Directory* entry contains precise information on application procedures, giving limitations, types of support awarded, the publications issued by the foundation, and staff. In addition, each entry features such data as the grantmaker's giving interests, financial data, grant amounts, address, and telephone number. This edition includes close to 35,000 selected grants. The Foundation Center works closely with foundations to ensure the accuracy and timeliness of the information provided.

The *Directory* includes indexes by foundation name; subject areas of interest; names of donors, officers, and trustees; geographic location; international interests; types of support awarded; and grantmakers new to the volume. Also included are analyses of the foundation community by geography, asset and grant size, and the different foundation types.

March 1999
Softbound: ISBN 0-87954-874-6 / $185
Hardbound: ISBN 0-87954-870-3 / $215
Published annually

THE FOUNDATION DIRECTORY PART 2, 1999 Edition

The Foundation Directory Part 2 has the same coverage for the next largest set of foundations, those with assets between $1 million and $2 million or grant programs from $50,000 to $200,000. Data on over 5,700 foundations is included along with more than 18,100 recently awarded foundation grants. Access to foundation entries is facilitated by seven indexes, including foundation name; subject areas of interest; names of donors, officers, and trustees; geographic location; international interests; types of support awarded; and grantmakers new to the volume.

March 1999 / ISBN 0-87954-871-1 / $185
Published annually

THE FOUNDATION DIRECTORY SUPPLEMENT

The Foundation Directory Supplement provides updated information on *Foundation Directory* and *Foundation Directory Part 2* grantmakers six months after those volumes are published. The *Supplement* ensures that users of the *Directory* and *Directory Part 2* have the latest addresses, contact names, policy statements, application guidelines, and financial data for *Directory*-size foundations.

September 1999 / ISBN 0-87954-886-X / $125
Published annually

GUIDE TO U.S. FOUNDATIONS, THEIR TRUSTEES, OFFICERS, AND DONORS, 1999 Edition

This reference tool provides fundraisers with current, accurate information on over 46,000 private grantmaking foundations in the U.S. The two-volume set also includes a master list of the names of the people who establish, oversee, and manage those institutions. Each entry includes asset and giving amounts as well as geographic limitations, and also tells you whether you can find more extensive information on the grantmaker in another Foundation Center reference work.

The *Guide to U.S. Foundations* is the only source of published data on thousands of local foundations. (It includes more than 25,000 grantmakers not covered in other print publications.)

April 1999 / 0-87954-872-X / $215
Published annually

THE FOUNDATION 1000

The Foundation 1000 provides access to extensive and accurate information on the nation's 1,000 largest foundations. *Foundation 1000* grantmakers hold over $208 billion in assets and each year award close to 250,000 grants worth $9 billion to nonprofit organizations nationwide.

The Foundation 1000 provides the most thorough analyses available of the 1,000 largest foundations and their extensive grant programs. Each multi-page foundation profile features a full foundation portrait, a detailed breakdown of the foundation's grant programs, and extensive lists of recently awarded foundation grants.

Five indexes help fundraisers target potential funders in a variety of ways: by subject field, type of support, geographic location, international giving, and the names of foundation donors, officers, trustees, and staff.

October 1999 / ISBN 0-87954-887-8 / $295
Published annually

NATIONAL DIRECTORY OF CORPORATE GIVING, 6th Edition

The *National Directory of Corporate Giving* offers authoritative information on approximately 3,000 corporate foundations and direct-giving programs.

This volume features detailed portraits of 1,900+ corporate foundations plus close to 1,000 direct-giving programs, including application information, key personnel, types of support generally awarded, giving limitations, financial data, and purpose and activities statements. Included in the 6th Edition are over 10,000 selected grants. The volume also provides data on the corporations that sponsor foundations and direct-giving programs. Each entry gives the company's name and address, a listing of its types of business, its financial data (complete with *Forbes* and *Fortune* ratings), a listing of its subsidiaries, divisions, plants, and offices, and a charitable-giving statement.

The *National Directory of Corporate Giving* also features an extensive bibliography. Seven essential indexes help target funding prospects by geographic region; international giving; types of support; subject area; officers, donors, and trustees; types of business; and the names of the corporation, its foundation, and its direct-giving program.

October 1999 / ISBN 0-87954-888-6 / $195
Published biennially

CORPORATE FOUNDATION PROFILES, 10th Edition

This biennially updated volume includes comprehensive information on 195 of the largest corporate foundations in the U.S., grantmakers who each give at least $1.2 million annually. Each profile includes foundation giving interests, application guidelines, recently awarded grants, and information on the sponsoring company. A section on financial data provides a summary of the size and grantmaking capacity of each foundation and contains a list of assets, gifts or contributions, grants paid, operating programs, expenditures, scholarships, and loans. A quick-scan appendix lists core financial data on some 1,000 additional corporate foundations, all of which give at least $50,000 in grants every year. Five indexes help grantseekers search for prospective funders by names of donors, officers, trustees, and staff; subject area; types of support; geographic region; and international giving.

February 1998 / ISBN 0-87954-761-8 / $155
Published biennially

NATIONAL DIRECTORY OF GRANTMAKING PUBLIC CHARITIES, 2nd Edition

The 2nd Edition of this volume features current information on more than 1,000 public charities, including over 450 community foundations. All offer some form of financial support to nonprofit organizations or individuals, whether it be grants, scholarships, fellowships, loans, or in-kind gifts. The *National Directory* includes descriptions of over 5,100 selected grants, which often provide the best indication of giving interests, and indexes by subject interest, types of support, geographic preferences, and names of officers and trustees.

July 1998 / ISBN 0-87954-802-9 / $115
Published biennially

SOUTHEASTERN FOUNDATIONS II: A Profile of the Region's Grantmaking Community, 2nd Edition

Southeastern Foundations II provides a detailed examination of foundation philanthropy in the 12-state Southeast region. The report includes an overview of the Southeast's share of all U.S. foundations, measures the growth of Southeastern foundations since 1992, profiles Southeastern funders by type, size, and geographic focus, compares broad giving trends of Southeastern and all U.S. foundations in 1992 and 1997, and details giving by non-Southeastern grantmakers to recipients in the region.

November 1999 / ISBN 0-87954-775-8 / $19.95

GUIDE TO GREATER WASHINGTON D.C. GRANTMAKERS, 3rd Edition

The *Guide to Greater Washington D.C. Grantmakers* provides current data on over 1,200 grantmakers—foundations, corporate giving programs, and public charities. Each grantmaker portrait includes an application address, financial data, giving limitations, and the names of key officials. For larger foundations—those that give at least $50,000 in grants annually—application procedures and giving interest statements are also provided. In addition, there are over 1,800 descriptions of recently awarded grants.

August 1998 / ISBN 0-87954-803-7/ $60
Published biennially

NEW YORK STATE FOUNDATIONS: A Comprehensive Directory, 6th Edition

New York State Foundations offers complete coverage of over 7,000 independent, corporate, and community foundations that fund New York nonprofits. Close to 5,900 of these foundations are located in New York state. An additional 1,200+ are out-of-state grantmakers with a documented interest in New York. Over 12,600 grant descriptions are included. Six indexes offer access to foundations according to their fields of interest; international interests; types of support awarded; city and county; names of donors, officers, and trustees; and foundation names.

June 1999 / ISBN 0-87954-891-6 / $180
Published biennially

DIRECTORY OF MISSOURI GRANTMAKERS, 3rd Edition

The *Directory of Missouri Grantmakers* provides a comprehensive guide to grantmakers in the state—approximately 1,000 foundations, corporate giving programs, and public charities—from the largest grantmakers to local family foundations. Entries list giving amounts, fields of interest, purpose statements, selected grants, and much more.

Indexes help you target the most appropriate funders by subject interest, types of support, and names of key personnel.

July 1999 / ISBN 0-87954-884-3 / $75
Published biennially

FOUNDATION GRANTS TO INDIVIDUALS, 11th Edition

The 11th Edition of this volume features more than 3,800 entries, all of which profile foundation grants to individuals. Entries include foundation addresses and telephone numbers, financial data, giving limitations, and application guidelines.

May 1999 / ISBN 0-87954-883-5 / $65
Published biennially

Subject Directories

The Foundation Center's *National Guide to Funding* series is designed to facilitate grantseeking within specific fields of nonprofit activity. Each of the directories described below identifies a set of grantmakers that have already stated or demonstrated an interest in a particular field. Entries provide access to foundation addresses, financial data, giving priorities, application procedures, contact names, and key officials. Many entries also feature recently awarded grants. A variety of indexes help target potential grant sources by subject area, geographic preferences, types of support, and the names of donors, officers, and trustees.

Subject guides are published biennially.

GUIDE TO FUNDING FOR INTERNATIONAL AND FOREIGN PROGRAMS, 4th Edition

The 4th Edition of the *Guide to Funding for International and Foreign Programs* covers over 800 grantmakers interested in funding projects with an international focus, both within the U.S. and abroad. Program areas covered include international relief, disaster assistance, human rights, civil liberties, community development, education, and more. The volume also includes descriptions of more than 6,000 recently awarded grants.

May 1998 / ISBN 0-87954-772-3 / $115

NATIONAL GUIDE TO FUNDING IN AGING, 5th Edition

The 5th Edition provides essential facts on close to 1,400 grantmakers with a specific interest in the field of aging. This funding tool includes up-to-date addresses, financial data, giving priorities statements, application procedures, contact names, and key officials. The volume also provides recent grants lists with descriptions of over 2,200 grants for nearly 500 foundation entries. Section II of this volume includes basic descriptions and contact information for approximately 85 voluntary organizations which offer valuable technical assistance or information to older Americans and the agencies that serve them.

December 1998 / ISBN 0-87954-804-5 / $95

NATIONAL GUIDE TO FUNDING IN AIDS, 1st Edition

This volume covers more than 600 foundations, corporate giving programs, and public charities that support AIDS- and HIV-related nonprofit organizations involved in direct relief, medical research, legal aid, preventative education, and other programs to empower persons with AIDS and AIDS-related diseases. Over 760 recently awarded grants show the types of projects funded by grantmakers.

July 1999 / ISBN 0-87954-882-7 / $75

NATIONAL GUIDE TO FUNDING IN ARTS AND CULTURE, 5th Edition

The 5th Edition of this volume covers more than 5,200 grantmakers with an interest in funding art colonies, dance companies, museums, theaters, and other types of arts and culture projects and institutions. The volume also includes more than 12,700 descriptions of recently awarded grants.

May 1998 / ISBN 0-87954-768-5 / $145

NATIONAL GUIDE TO FUNDING FOR CHILDREN, YOUTH AND FAMILIES, 5th Edition

The *National Guide to Funding for Children, Youth and Families* provides access to essential facts on over 5,100 grantmakers that together award millions of dollars each year to organizations committed to causes involving children, youth, and families. Each entry includes the grantmaker's address and contact person, purpose statement, and application guidelines. There are also useful descriptions of over 19,100 sample grants recently awarded by many of these foundations.

June 1999 / ISBN 0-87954-877-0 / $150

NATIONAL GUIDE TO FUNDING FOR COMMUNITY DEVELOPMENT, 2nd Edition

The *National Guide to Funding for Community Development* contains essential facts on over 2,600 grantmakers. Entries feature: address and contact names, giving interest statements, current financial data, key personnel, application guidelines, and 10,000 recently awarded grants. Indexes help identify appropriate funders by subject field, geographic area, and type of support.

June 1998 / ISBN 0-87954-769-3 / $135

NATIONAL GUIDE TO FUNDING FOR ELEMENTARY AND SECONDARY EDUCATION, 5th Edition

The 5th Edition of this volume provides information on more than 3,300 grantmakers that support nursery schools, bilingual education initiatives, remedial reading/math programs, drop-out prevention services, educational testing programs, and many other nonprofit organizations and initiatives. The volume also includes descriptions of over 8,800 recently awarded grants, the best indication of a grantmaker's funding interests.

July 1999 / ISBN 0-87954-880-0 / $140

NATIONAL GUIDE TO FUNDING FOR INFORMATION TECHNOLOGY, 2nd Edition

This volume provides facts on over 700 grantmakers that award grants to projects involving information technology. The guide also includes descriptions of more than 2,400 recently awarded grants for computer science, engineering and technology, tele-communications, and media and communications.

June 1999 / ISBN 0-87954-879-7 / $115

NATIONAL GUIDE TO FUNDING FOR THE ENVIRONMENT AND ANIMAL WELFARE, 4th Edition

The 4th Edition of this guide covers over 2,000 grantmakers that fund nonprofits involved in international conservation, ecological research, waste reduction, animal welfare, and much more. The volume includes descriptions of over 4,800 recently awarded grants.

June 1998 / ISBN 0-87954-770-7 / $95

NATIONAL GUIDE TO FUNDING IN HEALTH, 6th Edition

The 6th Edition of the *National Guide to Funding in Health* contains essential facts on over 7,700 grantmakers interested in funding hospitals, universities, research institutes, community-based agencies, national health associations, and a broad range of other health-related programs and services. The volume also includes descriptions of more than 16,900 recently awarded grants.

June 1999 / ISBN 0-87954-876-2 / $150

NATIONAL GUIDE TO FUNDING IN HIGHER EDUCATION, 5th Edition

The 5th Edition of the *National Guide to Funding in Higher Education* includes information on over 5,200 grantmakers with an interest in funding colleges, universities, graduate programs, and research institutes, as well as descriptions of more than 15,000 recently awarded grants.

June 1998 / ISBN 0-87954-771-5 / $145

NATIONAL GUIDE TO FUNDING FOR LIBRARIES AND INFORMATION SERVICES, 5th Edition

The 5th Edition of this volume provides essential data on 880 grantmakers that support a wide range of organizations and initiatives, from the smallest public libraries to major research institutions, academic/research libraries, art, law, and medical libraries, and other specialized information centers. The volume also includes descriptions of close to 1,600 recently awarded grants.

June 1999 / ISBN 0-87954-878-9 / $95

NATIONAL GUIDE TO FUNDING IN RELIGION, 5th Edition

With the 5th Edition of this volume, fundraisers who work for nonprofits affiliated with religious organizations have access to information on over 6,700 grantmakers that have demonstrated or stated an interest in funding churches, missionary societies, religious welfare and education programs, and many other types of projects and institutions. The volume also includes descriptions of more than 8,000 recently awarded grants.

May 1999 / ISBN 0-87954-875-4 / $140

NATIONAL GUIDE TO FUNDING IN SUBSTANCE ABUSE, 2nd Edition

The 2nd Edition of this volume contains essential facts on more than 580 grantmakers interested in funding counseling services, preventive education, treatment, medical research, residential care and halfway houses, and projects addressing alcohol and drug abuse, smoking addiction, and drunk driving. The volume also includes descriptions of over 680 recently awarded grants.

May 1998 / ISBN 0-87954-773-1 / $95

NATIONAL GUIDE TO FUNDING FOR WOMEN AND GIRLS, 5th Edition

The 5th Edition of this volume covers over 1,200 grantmakers with an interest in funding such projects as education scholarships, shelters for abused women, girls' clubs, health clinics, employment centers, and other diverse programs. The volume also provides descriptions of 5,400 recently awarded grants.

July 1999 / ISBN 0-87954-881-9 / $115

Grant Directories

GRANT GUIDES

This series of guides lists actual foundation grants of $10,000 or more in thirty-five key areas of grantmaking.

Each title in the series affords access to the names, addresses, and giving limitations of the foundations listed. The grant descriptions provide the grant recipient's name and location; the amount of the grant; the date the grant was authorized; and a description of the grant's intended use.

In addition, each *Grant Guide* includes three indexes: the type of organization generally funded by the grantmaker, the subject focus of the foundation's grants, and the geographic area in which the foundation has already funded projects.

Each *Grant Guide* also includes a concise overview of the foundation spending patterns within the specified field. The introduction uses a series of statistical tables to document such findings as (1) the twenty-five top funders in each area of interest (by total dollar amount of grants); (2) the fifteen largest grants reported; (3) the total dollar amount and number of grants awarded for specific types of support, recipient organization type, and population group; and (4) the total grant dollars received in each U.S. state and many foreign countries.

Series published annually in December, 1999 / 2000 Editions / $75 each

THE FOUNDATION GRANTS INDEX, 2000 Edition

A foundation's recently awarded grants offer the best indication of its future funding priorities. The 2000 (28th) Edition of *The Foundation Grants Index* covers the grantmaking programs of over 1,000 of the largest independent, corporate, and community foundations in the U.S. and includes more than 86,000 grant descriptions in all.

Grant descriptions are divided into twenty-eight broad subject areas, such as health, higher education, and arts and culture. Within each of these broad fields, the grant descriptions are listed geographically by state and alphabetically by the name of the foundation.

December 1999 / ISBN 0-87954-889-4 / $165

Guidebooks, Manuals, And Reports

AIDS FUNDRAISING

Published in conjunction with Funders Concerned About AIDS, *AIDS Fundraising* covers money-generating initiatives, from membership drives to special events, direct mail, and grant applications.

July 1991 / ISBN 0-87954-390-6 / $10

ARTS FUNDING: A Report on Foundation Trends, 3rd Edition

Arts Funding provides a framework for understanding recent trends in foundation support for arts and culture and spotlights new and leading arts funders. The report focuses on grantmaking in 1996 and analyzes over 11,000 arts grants awarded by 800+ foundations, providing a detailed picture of giving priorities in the field. This edition of *Arts Funding* includes several enhancements, such as an analysis of arts grantmakers and recipients by region, an examination of the impact of smaller grants on the field, and brief profiles of arts grantmakers that support individual artists.

November 1998 / ISBN 0-87954-813-4 / $19.95

ARTS FUNDING 2000: Funder Perspectives on Current and Future Trends
by Loren Renz and Caron Atlas

Arts Funding 2000 explores the current state of arts grantmaking and previews emerging themes and issues. Based on in-depth interviews conducted in 1999 with thirty-five leading foundations and corporations nationwide, the report offers an inside perspective on recent changes in arts funding priorities and strategies and on factors affecting decision making. Important issues and opportunities facing the arts community and arts funders at the turn of the century are identified. Conducted in cooperation with Grantmakers in the Arts, *Arts Funding 2000* also serves as a companion piece to the 1998

Arts Funding report, which documents changes in actual grantmaking patterns of foundations from 1992 to 1996.

September 1999 / ISBN 0-87954-776-6 / $14.95

HEALTH POLICY GRANTMAKING: A Report on Foundation Trends

Health Policy Grantmaking explores broad trends in grantmaker support for health policy-related activities during the 1990s, a period of dramatic growth in health policy funding. This report investigates health policy's share of all giving for health, presents areas of growth in health policy funding, spotlights emerging topics in the field, and identifies leading grantmakers by amount of funding and programmatic interests.

September 1998 / ISBN 0-87954-814 -2 / $14.95

INTERNATIONAL GRANTMAKING: A Report on U.S. Foundation Trends

This groundbreaking study maps the dimensions and patterns of international giving by U.S. foundations in the 1990s, revealing dynamic growth in overseas funding and a dramatic shift in priorities tied to the end of the Cold War. The study, prepared in cooperation with the Council on Foundations, examines more than 12,000 international grants made by 500 U.S. foundations.

The study investigates the practice and challenges of international grantmaking, drawn from in-depth interviews with experienced funders. Profiles of the international programs of sixty-three leading funders complete the portrait of U.S. giving trends. For a comparative view, the report features articles on the international activities of Japanese and European grantmakers. An extensive bibliography and summary of the regulatory framework for crossborder grants are included.

December 1997 / ISBN 0-87954-760-X / $50

THE FOUNDATION CENTER'S GRANTS CLASSIFICATION SYSTEM INDEXING MANUAL WITH THESAURUS, Revised Edition

The *Grants Classification Manual* includes a complete set of all classification codes to facilitate precise tracking of grants and recipients by subject, recipient type, and population categories. It also features a completely revised thesaurus to help identify the "official" terms and codes that represent thousands of subject areas and recipient types in the Center's system of grants classification.

May 1995 / ISBN 0-87954-644-1 / $95

THE FOUNDATION CENTER'S USER-FRIENDLY GUIDE: A Grantseeker's Guide to Resources, 4th Edition

This slim volume answers the most commonly asked questions about grantseeking. Specifically designed for novice grantseekers, the *User-Friendly Guide* leads the reader through the unfamiliar jargon and the wide range of print and electronic research tools used by professional fundraisers.

July 1996 / ISBN 0-87954-666-2 / $14.95

FOUNDATION GIVING: Yearbook of Facts and Figures on Private, Corporate and Community Foundations, 1999 Edition

Foundation Giving provides a comprehensive overview of the latest trends in foundation giving in the U.S. This volume uses a range of statistical tables to chart foundation giving by subject area and type of support, to categorize foundations by asset and giving amount, and to document other data such as the breakdown of grants awarded by the 100 largest foundations.

July 1999 / ISBN 0-87954-885-1 / $24.95
Published annually

THE FOUNDATION CENTER'S GUIDE TO GRANTSEEKING ON THE WEB

The *Guide to Grantseeking on the Web* provides both novice and experienced Web users with a gateway to the numerous online resources available to grantseekers. Foundation Center staff experts have team-authored this guide, contributing their extensive knowledge of Web content as well as their tips and strategies on how to evaluate and use Web-based funding materials.

The Foundation Center's Guide to Grantseeking on the Web also includes a guided tour of the Center's Web site, a glossary of common terms, and a bibliography of related resources in the field.

The 2nd edition, which is being developed at the time this book goes to press, will be available in the fall of 1999.

December 1998 / ISBN 0-87954-800-2 / $19.95
Published annually

THE FOUNDATION CENTER'S GUIDE TO PROPOSAL WRITING, 2nd Edition

The *Guide* is a comprehensive manual on the strategic thinking and mechanics of proposal writing. It covers each step of the process, from pre-proposal planning to the writing itself to the essential post-grant follow-up. The book features many extracts from actual grant proposals and also includes candid advice from grantmakers on the "dos and don'ts" of proposal writing.

February 1997 / ISBN 0-87954-703-0 / $34.95

PROGRAM-RELATED INVESTMENTS: A Guide to Funders and Trends

PRIs are alternative financing approaches for supplying capital to the nonprofit sector. This type of investment has been used to support community revitalization, low-income housing, microenterprise development, historic preservation, human services, and more.

Program-Related Investments: A Guide to Funders and Trends offers information on this little-understood field, including perspectives from providers and recipients; essays by experts in the field; strategies for success; and a directory of more than 100 leading PRI providers.

April 1995 / ISBN 0-87954-558-5 / $45

THE PRI INDEX: 500 Foundation Charitable Loans and Investments

This volume features crucial facts on loans and other charitable investments made by the growing community of foundations that make PRIs. Listings of some 500 recent PRIs by 125 foundations include funder name and state; recipient name, city, and state (or country); PRI amount; year of authorization or payment; and a description of the project funded. Four indexes guide PRI-seekers to records by foundation location, subject/type of support, recipient name, and recipient location.

June 1997 / ISBN 0-87954-758-8 / $75

Other Publications

AMERICA'S NONPROFIT SECTOR: A Primer, 2nd Edition
by Lester M. Salamon

In this revised edition, Lester M. Salamon clarifies the basic structure and role of the nonprofit sector in the U.S. and places the nonprofit sector into context in relation to the government and business sectors. He also shows how the position of the nonprofit sector has changed over time, both generally and in the major fields in which the sector is active. The book is illustrated with numerous charts and tables.

February 1999 / ISBN 0-87954-801-0 / $14.95

BEST PRACTICES OF EFFECTIVE NONPROFIT ORGANIZATIONS: A Practitioner's Guide
by Philip Bernstein

Philip Bernstein has drawn on his own extensive experience as a nonprofit executive, consultant, and volunteer to produce this review of "best practices" adopted by successful nonprofit organizations. The author identifies and explains the procedures which provide the foundation for social achievement in all nonprofit fields. Topics include defining purposes and goals, creating comprehensive financing plans, evaluating services, and effective communication.

February 1997 / ISBN 0-87954-755-3 / $29.95

THE BOARD MEMBER'S BOOK, 2nd Edition
by Brian O'Connell

Based on his extensive experience working with and on the boards of voluntary organizations, Brian O'Connell has developed this practical guide to the essential functions of voluntary boards. O'Connell offers practical advice on how to be a more effective board member as well as on how board members can help their organizations make a difference. He also provides an extensive reading list.

October 1993 / ISBN 0-87954-502-X / $24.95

CAREERS FOR DREAMERS AND DOERS: A Guide to Management Careers in the Nonprofit Sector
by Lilly Cohen and Dennis R.Young

A guide to management positions in the nonprofit world, *Careers for Dreamers and Doers* offers practical advice for starting a job search and suggests strategies used by successful managers throughout the voluntary sector.

November 1989 / ISBN 0-87954-294-2 / $24.95

ECONOMICS FOR NONPROFIT MANAGERS
by Dennis R. Young and Richard Steinberg

Young and Steinberg treat micro-economic analysis as an indispensable skill for nonprofit managers. They introduce and explain concepts such as opportunity cost, analysis at the margin, market equilibrium, market failure, and cost-benefit analysis. This volume also focuses on issues of particular concern to nonprofits, such as the economics of fundraising and volunteer recruiting, the regulatory environment, the impact of competition on nonprofit performance, interactions among sources of revenue, and more.

July 1995 / ISBN 0-87954-610-7 / $34.95

HANDBOOK ON PRIVATE FOUNDATIONS
by David F. Freeman and the Council on Foundations

Author David F. Freeman offers advice on establishing, staffing, and governing foundations and provides insights into legal and tax guidelines as well. Each chapter concludes with an annotated bibliography. Sponsored by the Council on Foundations.

September 1991
Softbound: ISBN 0-87954-404-X / $29.95
Hardbound: ISBN 0-87954-403-1 / $39.95

THE NONPROFIT ENTREPRENEUR: Creating Ventures to Earn Income
Edited by Edward Skloot

Nonprofit consultant and entrepreneur Edward Skloot demonstrates how nonprofits can launch successful earned-income enterprises without compromising their missions. Skloot has compiled a collection of writings by the nation's top practitioners and advisors in nonprofit enterprise. Topics covered include legal issues, marketing techniques, business planning, avoiding the pitfalls of venturing for smaller nonprofits, and a special section on museums and their retail operations.

September 1988 / ISBN 0-87954-239-X / $19.95

A NONPROFIT ORGANIZATION OPERATING MANUAL: Planning for Survival and Growth
by Arnold J. Olenick and Philip R. Olenick

This desk manual for nonprofit executives covers all aspects of starting and managing a nonprofit. The authors discuss legal problems, obtaining tax exemption, organizational planning and development, and board relations; operational, proposal, cash, and capital budgeting; marketing, grant proposals, fundraising, and for-profit ventures; computerization; and tax planning and compliance.

July 1991 / ISBN 0-87954-293-4 / $29.95

PEOPLE POWER: SERVICE, ADVOCACY, EMPOWERMENT
by Brian O'Connell

People Power, a selection of Brian O'Connell's writings, provides commentary on the nonprofit world. The essays included in this volume range from analyses of the role of voluntarism in American life, to advice for nonprofit managers, to suggestions for developing and strengthening the nonprofit sector of the future.

October 1994 / ISBN 0-87954-563-1 / $24.95

PROMOTING ISSUES AND IDEAS: A Guide to Public Relations for Nonprofit Organizations, Revised Edition
by M Booth & Associates

M Booth & Associates are specialists in promoting the issues and ideas of nonprofit groups. Included in their book are the "nuts-and-bolts" of advertising, publicity, speech-making, lobbying, and special events; how to write and produce informational literature; public relations on a shoe-string budget; how to plan and evaluate PR efforts; the use of rapidly evolving communication technologies; and a chapter on crisis management.

December 1995 / ISBN 0-87954-594-1 / $29.95

RAISE MORE MONEY FOR YOUR NONPROFIT ORGANIZATION: A Guide to Evaluating and Improving Your Fundraising
by Anne L. New

Anne New sets guidelines for a fundraising program that will benefit the incipient as well as the established nonprofit organization.

January 1991 / ISBN 0-87954-388-4 / $14.95

SECURING YOUR ORGANIZATION'S FUTURE: A Complete Guide to Fundraising Strategies
by Michael Seltzer

Beginners get bottom-line facts and easy-to-follow worksheets; veteran fundraisers receive a complete review of the basics plus new money-making ideas. Michael Seltzer supplements his text with an extensive bibliography of selected readings.

March 1987 / ISBN 0-87954-190-3 / $24.95

SUCCEEDING WITH CONSULTANTS: Self-Assessment for the Changing Nonprofit
by Barbara Kibbe and Fred Setterberg

Written by Barbara Kibbe and Fred Setterberg and supported by the David and Lucile Packard Foundation, this book guides nonprofits through the process of selecting and utilizing consultants to strengthen their organization's operations. The book emphasizes self-assessment tools and covers six different areas in which a nonprofit organization might benefit from a consultant's advice: governance, planning, fund development, financial management, public relations and marketing, and quality assurance.

April 1992 / ISBN 0-87954-450-3 / $19.95

THE 21ST CENTURY NONPROFIT
by Paul B. Firstenberg

The 21st Century Nonprofit encourages managers to adopt strategies developed by the for-profit sector in recent years. These strategies will help them to expand their revenue base by diversifying grant sources, exploit the possibilities of for-profit enterprises, develop human resources by learning how to attract and retain talented people, and explore the nature of leadership.

July 1996 / ISBN 0-87954-672-7 / $34.95

MEMBERSHIP PROGRAM

ASSOCIATES PROGRAM
Direct Line to Fundraising Information

Annual membership in the Associates Program provides vital information on a timely basis, including information from:

— IRS 990-PF information returns for close to 50,000 active grantmaking U.S. foundations

— Foundation and corporate annual reports, brochures, press releases, grants lists, and other announcements

— Books and periodicals on the grantmaking field, including regulation and nonprofit management

- The Associates Program provides access to information via a toll-free telephone number and e-mail. The annual fee of $495 for the Associates Program entitles you to ten toll-free telephone reference calls per month. Additional calls can be made at the rate of $30 per ten calls.

- Membership in the Associates Program allows you to request custom searches of the Foundation Center's computerized databases, which contain information on U.S. foundations and corporate givers. There is an additional cost for this service.

- Associates Program members may request photocopies of key documents. Important information from 990-PFs, annual reports, application guidelines, and other resources can be copied and either mailed or faxed to your office. The fee for this service, available only to Associate Members, is $2.00 for the first page of material and $1.00 for each additional page. Fax service is available at an additional charge.

- All Associates Program members receive the Associates Program quarterly newsletter, which provides news and information about new foundations, changes in boards of directors, new programs, and publications from both the Foundation Center and other publishers in the field.

For more information call 1-800-424-9836, or visit our World Wide Web site at www.fdncenter.org.

Electronic Resources

FC Search: The Foundation Center's Database on CD-ROM, Version 3.0

The Foundation Center's comprehensive database of grantmakers and their associated grants may be accessed in a fully searchable CD-ROM format. *FC Search* contains the Center's entire universe of close to 50,000 grantmaker records, including all known active foundations and corporate giving programs in the United States. It also includes over 200,000 newly reported grants from the largest foundations and the names of more than 200,000 trustees, officers, and donors which can be quickly linked to their foundation affiliations. Users can also link from *FC Search* to the Web sites of hundreds of grantmakers.**

Grantseekers and other researchers may select multiple criteria and create customized prospect lists, which can be printed or saved. Basic or Advanced search modes and special search options enable users to make searches as broad or as specific as required. Up to 21 different criteria may be selected.

FC Search is a sophisticated prospect research tool, but it is also user-friendly. It has been developed with both the novice and experienced fundraiser in mind. Assistance is available through Online Help, a *User Manual* that accompanies *FC Search,* as well as through a free User Hotline.

System Configurations
- Windows-based PC

241

- Microsoft Windows™ 98, Windows™ 95, or Windows™ NT

- Pentium microprocessor

- 16MB memory

For questions on system configurations, call the Hotline listed below.

FC Search, Version 3.0, April 1999 (prices include fall 1999 Update disk plus one User Manual).

Standalone (single user) version: $1,195
Local Area Network (2–8 users in one building) version: $1,895*
Additional copies of User Manual: $19.95
New editions of FC Search are released each spring.
*Larger local area network versions and wide area network versions are also available. For more information, call the FC Search Hotline (Mon–Fri., 9 am–5 pm EST)
1-800-478-4661.
**Internet access and Netscape's Navigator or Communicator or Microsoft's Internet Explorer browser required to access grantmaker Web sites and Foundation Center Web site.

Foundation and Grants Information Online

The Center's grantmaker and grants databases are also available online through The Dialog Corporation. Through this dial-up service, you can access the Center's database on your computer and design your own search for the foundations and corporate givers most likely to support your nonprofit organization.

For further information on accessing the Center's databases directly, contact The Dialog Corporation at 1-800-334-2564.

DIALOG User Manual and Thesaurus, Revised Edition

The *User Manual and Thesaurus* is a comprehensive guide that will facilitate your foundation and corporate giving research through our databases, offered online through Dialog.

November 1995 / ISBN 0-87954-595-X / $50

FC Scholar

The Center's new CD-ROM, *FC Scholar*, which is being developed at the time this book goes to press, is a searchable database containing information on the more than 3,000 foundations making grants to individuals for educational purposes. *FC Scholar* will be available in the fall of 1999.

Foundation Center's World Wide Web site (www.fdncenter.org)

Your gateway to philanthropy on the Web

Updated and expanded on an almost-daily basis, the Foundation Center's Web site provides grantseekers, grantmakers, researchers, journalists, and the general public with easy access to a range of online resources, among them:

- A Grantmaker Information directory with links to nearly 900 individual grantmaker sites.

- *Philanthropy News Digest,* a weekly compendium of philanthropy-related articles abstracted from major print and online media outlets. Also available as a listserv.

- *The Literature of the Nonprofit Sector Online,* a searchable bibliographical database with 17,100+ entries of works in the field of philanthropy, over 10,400 of which are abstracted.

- An Online Library, with comprehensive answers to FAQs, an online librarian to field questions about grantseeking and the Foundation Center, annotated links to useful nonprofit resources, and online orientations to the grantseeking process—one for individual grantseekers, the other for fundraisers at nonprofit organizations.

- Our popular Proposal Writing Short Course, an extensive glossary, valuable tips on the fundraising process, and downloadable common grant application forms.

- Information about Center-sponsored orientations, training programs, and seminars.

- The locations of our 200+ Cooperating Collections nationwide, and the activities and resources at our five main libraries.

- Foundation Finder, our free foundation look-up tool that provides a foundation's full name, address, telephone number, and contact person. Records also include brief background data, such as type of foundation, assets, total giving, and EIN.

All this and more is available at our Web site. The Center's publications and electronic resources can be ordered via the site's printable or interactive order forms.

FC FAX! Document Delivery Service
(212) 807-2577

FC FAX! is a free service, available 24 hours a day to provide the latest information on publications, electronic resources, programs, and services. Call to request a complete menu of Foundation Center documents that can be forwarded to your fax machine. FC FAX! includes *Profiles of the Top U.S Foundations*, in-depth individual profiles of the largest foundations included in *The Foundation 1000*. Profiles are available at a cost of $5.00 each, and can be ordered using Visa, MasterCard, or American Express (limit five profiles per phone call). Call for a free index of foundations.

Appendix F

Foundation Center
Cooperating Collections

Free Funding Information Centers

The Foundation Center is an independent national service organization established by
foundations to provide an authoritative source of information on foundation and corporate giving. The New York, Washington, D.C., Atlanta, Cleveland, and San Francisco
reference collections operated by the Foundation Center offer a wide variety of services
and comprehensive collections of information on foundations and grants. Cooperating
Collections are libraries, community foundations, and other nonprofit agencies that
provide a core collection of Foundation Center publications and a variety of supplementary materials and services in areas useful to grantseekers. The core collection consists of:

The Foundation Directory 1 and 2, and Supplement The Foundation Grants Index Quarterly
The Foundation 1000 Foundation Grants to Individuals
Foundation Fundamentals Guide to U.S. Foundations, their Trustees, Officers,
Foundation Giving   and Donors
The Foundation Grants Index

The Foundation Center's Guide to Grantseeking on
the Web
The Foundation Center's Guide to Proposal Writing
National Directory of Corporate Giving

National Directory of Grantmaking Public Charities
National Guide to Funding in. . . . (Series)
User-Friendly Guide

All five Center libraries and Cooperating Collections have *FC Search: The Foundation Center's Database on CD-ROM* available for public use. Also, many of the network members make available private foundation information returns (IRS Form 990-PF) for foundations in their state and/or neighboring states, as noted by the symbol (✳). Because the collections vary in their hours, materials, and services, it is recommended that you call the collection in advance of a visit. To check on new locations or current holdings, call toll-free 1-800-424-9836, or visit our Web site at www.fdncenter.org/collections/index.html.

Reference Collections Operated By The Foundation Center

THE FOUNDATION CENTER
2nd Floor
79 Fifth Ave.
New York, NY 10003
(212) 620-4230

THE FOUNDATION CENTER
312 Sutter St., Suite 606
San Francisco, CA 94108
(415) 397-0902

THE FOUNDATION CENTER
1001 Connecticut Ave., NW
Washington, DC 20036
(202) 331-1400

THE FOUNDATION CENTER
Kent H. Smith Library
1422 Euclid, Suite 1356
Cleveland, OH 44115
(216) 861-1933

THE FOUNDATION CENTER
Suite 150, Grand Lobby
Hurt Bldg., 50 Hurt Plaza
Atlanta, GA 30303
(404) 880-0094

Cooperating Collections

ALABAMA

BIRMINGHAM PUBLIC LIBRARY ✳
Government Documents
2100 Park Place
Birmingham   35203
(205) 226-3620

HUNTSVILLE PUBLIC LIBRARY
915 Monroe St.
Huntsville   35801
(256) 532-5940

UNIVERSITY OF SOUTH ALABAMA ✳
Library Building
Mobile   36688
(334) 460-7025

AUBURN UNIVERSITY AT MONTGOMERY
LIBRARY
7300 University Dr.
Montgomery   36124-4023
(334) 244-3200

ALASKA

UNIVERSITY OF ALASKA AT ANCHORAGE ✶
Library
3211 Providence Dr.
Anchorage   99508
(907) 786-1846

JUNEAU PUBLIC LIBRARY
Reference
292 Marine Way
Juneau   99801
(907) 586-5267

ARIZONA

FLAGSTAFF CITY–COCONINO COUNTY
PUBLIC LIBRARY
300 West Aspen Ave.
Flagstaff   86001
(520) 779-7670

PHOENIX PUBLIC LIBRARY ✶
Information Services Department
1221 N. Central
Phoenix   85004
(602) 262-4636

TUCSON PIMA LIBRARY ✶
101 N. Stone Ave.
Tucson   87501
(520) 791-4010

ARKANSAS

WESTARK COMMUNITY COLLEGE—
BORHAM LIBRARY
5210 Grand Ave.
Ft. Smith   72913
(501) 788-7200

CENTRAL ARKANSAS LIBRARY SYSTEM ✶
100 Rock St.
Little Rock   72201
(501) 918-3000

PINE BLUFF-JEFFERSON COUNTY LIBRARY
SYSTEM
200 E. Eighth
Pine Bluff   71601
(870) 534-2159

CALIFORNIA

HUMBOLDT AREA FOUNDATION
P.O. Box 99
Bayside   95524
(707) 442-2993

VENTURA COUNTY COMMUNITY
FOUNDATION ✶
Resource Center for Nonprofit Organizations
1317 Del Norte Rd., Suite 150
Camarillo   93010-8504
(805) 988-0196

FRESNO REGIONAL FOUNDATION
Nonprofit Advancement Center
1999 Tuolumne St., Suite 650
Fresno   93720
(559) 498-3929

CENTER FOR NONPROFIT MANAGEMENT
IN SOUTHERN CALIFORNIA
Nonprofit Resource Library
315 West 9th St., Suite 1100
Los Angeles   90015
(213) 623-7080

FLINTRIDGE FOUNDATION
Philanthropy Resource Library
1040 Lincoln Ave., Suite 100
Pasadena   91103
(626) 449-0839

GRANT & RESOURCE CENTER OF
NORTHERN CALIFORNIA ✶
Building C, Suite A
2280 Benton Dr.
Redding   96003
(530) 244-1219

LOS ANGELES PUBLIC LIBRARY
West Valley Regional Branch Library
19036 Van Owen St.
Reseda   91335
(818) 345-4393

RIVERSIDE PUBLIC LIBRARY
3581 Mission Inn Ave.
Riverside   92501
(909) 782-5202

NONPROFIT RESOURCE CENTER *
Sacramento Public Library
828 I St., 2nd Floor
Sacramento   95814
(916) 264-2772

SAN DIEGO FOUNDATION
Funding Information Center
1420 Kettner Blvd., Suite 500
San Diego   92101
(619) 239-8815

NONPROFIT DEVELOPMENT CENTER
Library
1922 The Alameda, Suite 212
San Jose   95126
(408) 248-9505

PENINSULA COMMUNITY FOUNDATION *
Peninsula Nonprofit Center
1700 S. El Camino Real, #300
San Mateo   94402-3049
(650) 358-9392

LOS ANGELES PUBLIC LIBRARY
San Pedro Regional Branch
9131 S. Gaffey St.
San Pedro   90731
(310) 548-7779

VOLUNTEER CENTER OF GREATER
   ORANGE COUNTY
Nonprofit Management Assistance Center
1901 E. 4th St., Suite 100
Santa Ana   92705
(714) 953-5757

SANTA BARBARA PUBLIC LIBRARY
40 E. Anapamu St.
Santa Barbara   93101-1019
(805) 564-5633

SANTA MONICA PUBLIC LIBRARY
1343 Sixth St.
Santa Monica   90401-1603
(310) 458-8600

SONOMA COUNTY LIBRARY
3rd & E Sts.
Santa Rosa   95404
(707) 545-0831

SEASIDE BRANCH LIBRARY
550 Harcourt St.
Seaside   93955
(831) 899-8131

SONORA AREA FOUNDATION
20100 Cedar Rd., N.
Sonora   95370
(209) 533-2596

COLORADO

EL POMAR NONPROFIT RESOURCE LIBRARY
1661 Mesa Ave.
Colorado Springs   80906
(719) 577-7000

DENVER PUBLIC LIBRARY *
General Reference
10 West 14th Ave. Pkwy.
Denver   80204
(303) 640-6200

CONNECTICUT

DANBURY PUBLIC LIBRARY
170 Main St.
Danbury   06810
(203) 797-4527

GREENWICH LIBRARY *
101 West Putnam Ave.
Greenwich   06830
(203) 622-7900

HARTFORD PUBLIC LIBRARY *
500 Main St.
Hartford   06103
(860) 543-8656

NEW HAVEN FREE PUBLIC LIBRARY *
Reference Dept.
133 Elm St.
New Haven   06510-2057
(203) 946-8130

DELAWARE

UNIVERSITY OF DELAWARE *
Hugh Morris Library
Newark   19717-5267
(302) 831-2432

FLORIDA

VOLUSIA COUNTY LIBRARY CENTER
City Island
105 E. Magnolia Ave.
Daytona Beach   32114-4484
(904) 257-6036

NOVA SOUTHEASTERN UNIVERSITY ✱
Einstein Library
3301 College Ave.
Fort Lauderdale   33314
(954) 262-4601

INDIAN RIVER COMMUNITY COLLEGE
Learning Resources Center
3209 Virginia Ave.
Fort Pierce   34981-5596
(561) 462-4757

JACKSONVILLE PUBLIC LIBRARIES ✱
Grants Resource Center
122 N. Ocean St.
Jacksonville   32202
(904) 630-2665

MIAMI-DADE PUBLIC LIBRARY ✱
Humanities/Social Science
101 W. Flagler St.
Miami   33130
(305) 375-5575

ORANGE COUNTY LIBRARY SYSTEM
Social Sciences Department
101 E. Central Blvd.
Orlando   32801
(407) 425-4694

SELBY PUBLIC LIBRARY
Reference
1331 First St.
Sarasota   34236
(941) 316-1181

TAMPA-HILLSBOROUGH COUNTY PUBLIC
   LIBRARY ✱
900 N. Ashley Dr.
Tampa   33602
(813) 273-3652

COMMUNITY FOUNDATION OF PALM
   BEACH & MARTIN COUNTIES ✱
324 Datura St., Suite 340
West Palm Beach   33401
(561) 659-6800

GEORGIA

ATLANTA-FULTON PUBLIC LIBRARY
Foundation Collection—Ivan Allen Department
1 Margaret Mitchell Square
Atlanta   30303-1089
(404) 730-1900

UNITED WAY OF GEORGIA ✱
Community Resource Center
277 Martin Luther King Jr. Blvd.,
Suite 301
Macon   31201
(912) 745-4732

SAVANNAH STATE UNIVERSITY
Asa Gordon Library
P.O. Box 20394
Savannah   31404
(912) 356-2185

THOMAS COUNTY PUBLIC LIBRARY
201 N. Madison St.
Thomasville   31792
(912) 225-5252

HAWAII

UNIVERSITY OF HAWAII ✱
Hamilton Library
2550 The Mall
Honolulu   96822
(808) 956-7214

HAWAII COMMUNITY FOUNDATION
   FUNDING RESOURCE LIBRARY
900 Fort St., Suite 1300
Honolulu   96813
(808) 537-6333

IDAHO

BOISE PUBLIC LIBRARY
715 S. Capitol Blvd.
Boise   83702
(208) 384-4024

CALDWELL PUBLIC LIBRARY ✱
1010 Dearborn St.
Caldwell   83605
(208) 459-3242

ILLINOIS

DONORS FORUM OF CHICAGO *
208 South LaSalle, Suite 735
Chicago   60604
(312) 578-0175

EVANSTON PUBLIC LIBRARY *
1703 Orrington Ave.
Evanston   60201
(847) 866-0305

ROCK ISLAND PUBLIC LIBRARY
401 - 19th St.
Rock Island   61201
(309) 788-7627

UNIVERSITY OF ILLINOIS AT SPRINGFIELD
Brookens Library
P.O. Box 19243
Springfield   62794-9243
(217) 206-6633

INDIANA

EVANSVILLE–VANDERBURGH COUNTY
   PUBLIC LIBRARY *
22 Southeast Fifth St.
Evansville   47708
(812) 428-8200

ALLEN COUNTY PUBLIC LIBRARY *
900 Webster St.
Ft. Wayne   46802
(219) 421-1200

INDIANAPOLIS–MARION COUNTY PUBLIC
   LIBRARY *
Social Sciences
P.O. Box 211
40 E. St. Clair
Indianapolis   46206
(317) 269-1733

VIGO COUNTY PUBLIC LIBRARY *
1 Library Sq.
Terre Haute   47807
(812) 232-1113

IOWA

CEDAR RAPIDS PUBLIC LIBRARY
Foundation Center Collection
500 First St., SE
Cedar Rapids   52401
(319) 398-5123

SOUTHWESTERN COMMUNITY COLLEGE
Learning Resource Center
1501 W. Townline Rd.
Creston   50801
(515) 782-7081

PUBLIC LIBRARY OF DES MOINES
100 Locust
Des Moines   50309-1791
(515) 283-4295

SIOUX CITY PUBLIC LIBRARY
529 Pierce St.
Sioux City   51101-1202
(712) 252-5669

KANSAS

DODGE CITY PUBLIC LIBRARY *
1001 2nd Ave.
Dodge City   67801
(316) 225-0248

TOPEKA AND SHAWNEE COUNTY PUBLIC
   LIBRARY *
1515 SW 10th Ave.
Topeka   66604-1374
(785) 233-2040

WICHITA PUBLIC LIBRARY *
223 S. Main St.
Wichita   67202
(316) 261-8500

KENTUCKY

WESTERN KENTUCKY UNIVERSITY
Helm-Cravens Library
Bowling Green   42101-3576
(502) 745-6125

LEXINGTON PUBLIC LIBRARY *
140 E. Main St.
Lexington   40507-1376
(606) 231-5520

LOUISVILLE FREE PUBLIC LIBRARY ✱
301 York St.
Louisville   40203
(502) 574-1611

LOUISIANA

EAST BATON ROUGE PARISH LIBRARY ✱
Centroplex Branch Grants Collection
120 St. Louis
Baton Rouge   70802
(225) 389-4967

BEAUREGARD PARISH LIBRARY
205 S. Washington Ave.
De Ridder   70634
(318) 463-6217

OUACHITA PARISH PUBLIC LIBRARY
1800 Stubbs Ave.
Monroe   71201
(318) 327-1490

NEW ORLEANS PUBLIC LIBRARY ✱
Business & Science Division
219 Loyola Ave.
New Orleans   70140
(504) 596-2580

SHREVE MEMORIAL LIBRARY ✱
424 Texas St.
Shreveport   71120-1523
(318) 226-5894

MAINE

MAINE GRANTS INFORMATION CENTER
University of Southern Maine Library
314 Forrest Ave.
Portland   04104-9301
(207) 780-5029

MARYLAND

ENOCH PRATT FREE LIBRARY ✱
Social Science & History
400 Cathedral St.
Baltimore   21201
(410) 396-5430

MASSACHUSETTES

ASSOCIATED GRANTMAKERS OF
  MASSACHUSETTS ✱
294 Washington St., Suite 840
Boston   02108
(617) 426-2606

BOSTON PUBLIC LIBRARY ✱
Soc. Sci. Reference
700 Boylston St.
Boston   02117
(617) 536-5400

WESTERN MASSACHUSETTS FUNDING
  RESOURCE CENTER
65 Elliot St.
Springfield   01101-1730
(413) 452-0615

WORCESTER PUBLIC LIBRARY ✱
Grants Resource Center
60 Fremont St.
Worcester   01603
(508) 799-1655

MICHIGAN

ALPENA COUNTY LIBRARY
211 N. First St.
Alpena   49707
(517) 356-6188

UNIVERSITY OF MICHIGAN–ANN ARBOR ✱
Graduate Library
Reference & Research Services Department
Ann Arbor   48109-1205
(313) 764-9373

WILLARD PUBLIC LIBRARY ✱
Nonprofit & Funding Resource Collections
7 W. Van Buren St.
Battle Creek   49017
(616) 968-8166

HENRY FORD CENTENNIAL LIBRARY ✱
Adult Services
16301 Michigan Ave.
Dearborn   48124
(313) 943-2330

WAYNE STATE UNIVERSITY *
Purdy/Kresge Library
5265 Cass Ave.
Detroit   48202
(313) 577-6424

MICHIGAN STATE UNIVERSITY LIBRARIES *
Reference
Main Library
100 Library
East Lansing   48824-1048
(517) 355-2344

FARMINGTON COMMUNITY LIBRARY *
32737 West 12 Mile Rd.
Farmington Hills   48334
(248) 553-0300

UNIVERSITY OF MICHIGAN—FLINT *
Library
Flint   48502-2186
(810) 762-3408

GRAND RAPIDS PUBLIC LIBRARY *
Business Dept.—3rd Floor
60 Library Plaza NE
Grand Rapids   49503-3093
(616) 456-3600

MICHIGAN TECHNOLOGICAL UNIVERSITY
Van Pelt Library
1400 Townsend Dr.
Houghton 49931
(906) 487-2507

MAUD PRESTON PALENSKE MEMORIAL
   LIBRARY
500 Market St.
Saint Joseph   49085
(616) 983-7167

NORTHWESTERN MICHIGAN COLLEGE *
Mark & Helen Osterin Library
1701 E. Front St.
Traverse City   49684
(616) 922-1060

MINNESOTA

DULUTH PUBLIC LIBRARY *
520 W. Superior St.
Duluth   55802
(218) 723-3802

SOUTHWEST STATE UNIVERSITY
University Library
North Hwy. 23
Marshall   56253
(507) 537-6176

MINNEAPOLIS PUBLIC LIBRARY *
Sociology Department
300 Nicollet Mall
Minneapolis   55401
(612) 630-6300

ROCHESTER PUBLIC LIBRARY
101 2nd St. SE
Rochester   55904-3777
(507) 285-8002

ST. PAUL PUBLIC LIBRARY
90 W. Fourth St.
St. Paul   55102
(651) 266-7000

MISSISSIPPI

JACKSON/HINDS LIBRARY SYSTEM *
300 N. State St.
Jackson   39201
(601) 968-5803

MISSOURI

CLEARINGHOUSE FOR MIDCONTINENT
   FOUNDATIONS *
University of Missouri
5110 Cherry, Suite 310
Kansas City   64110-0680
(816) 235-1176

KANSAS CITY PUBLIC LIBRARY *
311 E. 12th St.
Kansas City   64106
(816) 701-3541

METROPOLITAN ASSOCIATION FOR
   PHILANTHROPY, INC. *
211 North Broadway, Suite 1200
St. Louis   63102
(314) 621-6220

SPRINGFIELD-GREENE COUNTY LIBRARY *
397 E. Central
Springfield   65802
(417) 837-5000

MONTANA

MONTANA STATE UNIVERSITY—
BILLINGS *
Library—Special Collections
1500 North 30th St.
Billings   59101-0298
(406) 657-1662

BOZEMAN PUBLIC LIBRARY *
220 E. Lamme
Bozeman   59715
(406) 582-2402

MONTANA STATE LIBRARY *
Library Services
1515 E. 6th Ave.
Helena   59620
(406) 444-3004

UNIVERSITY OF MONTANA *
Maureen & Mike Mansfield Library
Missoula   59812-1195
(406) 243-6800

NEBRASKA

UNIVERSITY OF NEBRASKA—
LINCOLN
Love Library
14th & R Sts.
Lincoln   68588-0410
(402) 472-2848

W. DALE CLARK LIBRARY *
Social Sciences Department
215 S. 15th St.
Omaha   68102
(402) 444-4826

NEVADA

CLARK COUNTY LIBRARY
1401 E. Flamingo
Las Vegas   89119
(702) 733-3642

WASHOE COUNTY LIBRARY *
301 S. Center St.
Reno   89505
(775) 785-4190

NEW HAMPSHIRE

CONCORD PUBLIC LIBRARY *
45 Green St.
Concord   03301
(603) 225-8670

PLYMOUTH STATE COLLEGE *
Herbert H. Lamson Library
Plymouth   03264
(603) 535-2258

NEW JERSEY

CUMBERLAND COUNTY LIBRARY
800 E. Commerce St.
Bridgeton   08302
(609) 453-2210

FREE PUBLIC LIBRARY OF ELIZABETH
11 S. Broad St.
Elizabeth   07202
(908) 354-6060

COUNTY COLLEGE OF MORRIS *
Learning Resource Center
214 Center Grove Rd.
Randolph   07869
(973) 328-5296

NEW JERSEY STATE LIBRARY *
Governmental Reference Services
185 W. State St.
Trenton   08625-0520
(609) 292-6220

NEW MEXICO

ALBUQUERQUE COMMUNITY
FOUNDATION *
3301 Menaul NE, Suite 30
Albuquerque   87176-6960
(505) 883-6240

NEW MEXICO STATE LIBRARY *
Information Services
1209 Camino Carlos Rey
Santa Fe   87505-9860
(505) 476-9714

NEW YORK

NEW YORK STATE LIBRARY
Humanities Reference
Cultural Education Center, 6th Fl.
Empire State Plaza
Albany   12230
(518) 474-5355

SUFFOLK COOPERATIVE LIBRARY SYSTEM
627 N. Sunrise Service Rd.
Bellport   11713
(516) 286-1600

NEW YORK PUBLIC LIBRARY
Bronx Reference Center
2556 Bainbridge Ave.
Bronx   10458-4698
(718) 579-4257

THE NONPROFIT CONNECTION, INC.
One Hanson Place—Room 2504
Brooklyn   11243
(718) 230-3200

BROOKLYN PUBLIC LIBRARY
Social Sciences/Philosophy Division
Grand Army Plaza
Brooklyn   11238
(718) 230-2100

BUFFALO & ERIE COUNTY PUBLIC
   LIBRARY *
Business, Science & Technology Dept.
1 Lafayette Square
Buffalo   14203
(716) 858-7097

HUNTINGTON PUBLIC LIBRARY
338 Main St.
Huntington   11743
(516) 427-5165

QUEENS BOROUGH PUBLIC LIBRARY
Social Sciences Division
89-11 Merrick Blvd.
Jamaica   11432
(718) 990-0700

LEVITTOWN PUBLIC LIBRARY *
1 Bluegrass Lane
Levittown   11756
(516) 731-5728

NEW YORK PUBLIC LIBRARY
Countee Cullen Branch Library
104 W. 136th St.
New York   10030
(212) 491-2070

ADRIANCE MEMORIAL LIBRARY
Special Services Department
93 Market St.
Poughkeepsie   12601
(914) 485-3445

ROCHESTER PUBLIC LIBRARY
Social Sciences
115 South Ave.
Rochester   14604
(716) 428-8120

ONONDAGA COUNTY PUBLIC LIBRARY
447 S. Salina St.
Syracuse   13202-2494
(315) 435-1818

UTICA PUBLIC LIBRARY
303 Genesee St.
Utica   13501
(315) 735-2279

WHITE PLAINS PUBLIC LIBRARY
100 Martine Ave.
White Plains   10601
(914) 422-1480

YONKERS PUBLIC LIBRARY
Reference Department, Getty Square Branch
7 Main St.
Yonkers   10701
(914) 476-1255

NORTH CAROLINA

COMMUNITY FOUNDATION OF WESTERN
   NORTH CAROLINA
Nonprofit Resources Center
16 Biltmore Ave., Suite 201
P.O. Box 1888
Asheville   28802
(828) 254-4960

THE DUKE ENDOWMENT *
100 N. Tryon St., Suite 3500
Charlotte   28202
(704) 376-0291

DURHAM COUNTY PUBLIC LIBRARY ✷
301 North Roxboro
Durham   27702
(919) 560-0110

STATE LIBRARY OF NORTH CAROLINA ✷
Government and Business Services
Archives Bldg., 109 E. Jones St.
Raleigh   27601-2807
(919) 733-4488

FORSYTH COUNTY PUBLIC LIBRARY ✷
660 W. 5th St.
Winston-Salem   27101
(336) 727-2680

NORTH DAKOTA

BISMARCK PUBLIC LIBRARY ✷
515 N. Fifth St.
Bismarck   58501
(701) 222-6410

FARGO PUBLIC LIBRARY ✷
102 N. 3rd St.
Fargo   58102
(701) 241-1491

OHIO

STARK COUNTY DISTRICT LIBRARY
715 Market Ave. N.
Canton   44702
(330) 452-0665

PUBLIC LIBRARY OF CINCINNATI &
   HAMILTON COUNTY ✷
Grants Resource Center
800 Vine St.—Library Square
Cincinnati   45202-2071
(513) 369-6000

COLUMBUS METROPOLITAN LIBRARY
Business and Technology
96 S. Grant Ave.
Columbus   43215
(614) 645-2590

DAYTON & MONTGOMERY COUNTY
   PUBLIC LIBRARY ✷
Grants Resource Center
215 E. Third St.
Dayton   45402
(937) 227-9500 x211

MANSFIELD/RICHLAND COUNTY PUBLIC
   LIBRARY
42 W. 3rd St.
Mansfield   44902
(419) 521-3110

TOLEDO–LUCAS COUNTY
   PUBLIC LIBRARY ✷
Social Sciences Department
325 Michigan St.
Toledo   43624-1614
(419) 259-5245

PUBLIC LIBRARY OF YOUNGSTOWN &
   MAHONING COUNTY ✷
305 Wick Ave.
Youngstown   44503
(330) 744-8636

MUSKINGUM COUNTY LIBRARY
220 N. 5th St.
Zanesville   43701
(614) 453-0391

OKLAHOMA

OKLAHOMA CITY UNIVERSITY ✷
Dulaney Browne Library
2501 N. Blackwelder
Oklahoma City   73106
(405) 521-5822

TULSA CITY–COUNTY LIBRARY ✷
400 Civic Center
Tulsa   74103
(918) 596-7940

OREGON

OREGON INSTITUTE OF TECHNOLOGY
Library
3201 Campus Dr.
Klamath Falls   97601-8801
(541) 885-1780

PACIFIC NON-PROFIT NETWORK
Grantsmanship Resource Library
33 N. Central, Suite 211
Medford   97501
(541) 779-6044

MULTNOMAH COUNTY LIBRARY
Government Documents
801 SW Tenth Ave.
Portland   97205
(503) 248-5123

OREGON STATE LIBRARY
State Library Building
Salem   97310
(541) 378-4277

PENNSYLVANIA

NORTHAMPTON COMMUNITY COLLEGE
Learning Resources Center
3835 Green Pond Rd.
Bethlehem   18017
(610) 861-5360

ERIE COUNTY LIBRARY SYSTEM
160 East Front St.
Erie   16507
(814) 451-6927

DAUPHIN COUNTY LIBRARY SYSTEM
Central Library
101 Walnut St.
Harrisburg   17101
(717) 234-4976

LANCASTER COUNTY PUBLIC LIBRARY
125 N. Duke St.
Lancaster   17602
(717) 394-2651

FREE LIBRARY OF PHILADELPHIA ✱
Regional Foundation Center
Logan Square
Philadelphia   19103
(215) 686-5423

CARNEGIE LIBRARY OF PITTSBURGH ✱
Foundation Collection
4400 Forbes Ave.
Pittsburgh   15213-4080
(412) 622-1917

POCONO NORTHEAST
   DEVELOPMENT FUND
James Pettinger Memorial Library
1151 Oak St.
Pittston   18640-3795
(570) 655-5581

READING PUBLIC LIBRARY
100 South Fifth St.
Reading   19475
(610) 655-6355

MARTIN LIBRARY
159 Market St.
York   17401
(717) 846-5300

RHODE ISLAND

PROVIDENCE PUBLIC
   LIBRARY
225 Washington St.
Providence   02903
(401) 455-8000

SOUTH CAROLINA

ANDERSON COUNTY LIBRARY
202 East Greenville St.
Anderson   29621
(864) 260-4500

CHARLESTON COUNTY LIBRARY ✱
68 Calhoun St.
Charleston   29401
(843) 805-6950

SOUTH CAROLINA STATE LIBRARY ✱
1500 Senate St.
Columbia   29211-1469
(803) 734-8666

COMMUNITY FOUNDATION OF GREATER
   GREENVILLE
27 Cleveland St., Suite 101
P.O. Box 6909
Greenville   29606
(864) 233-5925

SOUTH DAKOTA

SOUTH DAKOTA STATE LIBRARY ✱
800 Governors Dr.
Pierre   57501-2294
(605) 773-5070
(800) 592-1841 (SD residents)

DAKOTA STATE UNIVERSITY
Nonprofit Grants Assistance
132 S. Dakota Ave.
Sioux Falls   57104
(605) 367-5380

SIOUXLAND LIBRARIES
201 N. Main Ave.
Sioux Falls   57104
(605) 367-7081

TENNESSEE

KNOX COUNTY PUBLIC LIBRARY *
500 W. Church Ave.
Knoxville   37902
(423) 544-5750

MEMPHIS & SHELBY COUNTY PUBLIC
   LIBRARY *
1850 Peabody Ave.
Memphis   38104
(901) 725-8877

NASHVILLE PUBLIC LIBRARY *
Business Information Division
225 Polk Ave.
Nashville   37203
(615) 862-5842

TEXAS

NONPROFIT RESOURCE CENTER
Funding Information Library
500 N. Chestnut, Suite 1511
P.O. Box 3322
Abilene   79604
(915) 677-8166

AMARILLO AREA FOUNDATION *
Funding Research and Nonprofit Management
Libary
Nonprofit Services Center
801 S. Fillmore, Suite 700
Amarillo   79101
(806) 376-4521

HOGG FOUNDATION FOR
   MENTAL HEALTH *
3001 Lake Austin Blvd.
Austin   78703
(512) 471-5041

BEAUMONT PUBLIC LIBRARY
801 Pearl St.
Beaumont   77704-3827
(409) 838-6606

CORPUS CHRISTI PUBLIC LIBRARY *
Funding Information Center
805 Comanche St.
Reference Dept.
Corpus Christi   78401
(361) 880-7000

DALLAS PUBLIC LIBRARY *
Urban Information
1515 Young St.
Dallas   75201
(214) 670-1487

CENTER FOR VOLUNTEERISM &
   NONPROFIT MANAGEMENT
1918 Texas Ave.
El Paso   79901
(915) 532-5377

SOUTHWEST BORDER NONPROFIT
   RESOURCE CENTER
Nonprofit Resource Center
1201 W. University Dr.
Edinburgh   78539
(956) 384-5900

FUNDING INFORMATION CENTER OF FORT
   WORTH *
329 S. Henderson
Ft. Worth   76104
(817) 334-0228

HOUSTON PUBLIC LIBRARY
Bibliographic Information Center
500 McKinney
Houston   77002
(713) 236-1313

NONPROFIT MANAGEMENT AND
   VOLUNTEER CENTER
Laredo Public Library
1120 East Calton Rd.
Laredo   78041
(956) 795-2400

LONGVIEW PUBLIC LIBRARY
222 W. Cotton St.
Longview   75601
(903) 237-1352

LUBBOCK AREA FOUNDATION, INC.
1655 Main St., Suite 209

Lubbock   79401
(806) 762-8061

NONPROFIT RESOURCE CENTER
    OF TEXAS ✱
111 Soledad, Suite 200
San Antonio   78205
(210) 227-4333

WACO-MCLENNAN COUNTY LIBRARY ✱
1717 Austin Ave.
Waco   76701
(254) 750-5975

NORTH TEXAS CENTER FOR NONPROFIT
    MANAGEMENT
624 Indiana, Suite 307
Wichita Falls   76301
(940) 322-4961

UTAH

SALT LAKE CITY PUBLIC LIBRARY ✱
209 East 500 South
Salt Lake City   84111
(801) 524-8200

VERMONT

VERMONT DEPT. OF LIBRARIES ✱
Reference & Law Info. Services
109 State St.
Montpelier   05609
(802) 828-3261

VIRGINIA

HAMPTON PUBLIC LIBRARY
4207 Victoria Blvd.
Hampton   23669
(757) 727-1312

RICHMOND PUBLIC LIBRARY ✱
Business, Science & Technology
101 East Franklin St.
Richmond   23219
(804) 780-8223

ROANOKE CITY PUBLIC LIBRARY SYSTEM ✱
Main Library
706 S. Jefferson
Roanoke   24016
(540) 853-2477

WASHINGTON

MID-COLUMBIA LIBRARY
405 South Dayton
Kennewick   99336
(509)586-3156

SEATTLE PUBLIC LIBRARY ✱
Fundraising Resource Center
1000 Fourth Ave.
Seattle   98104-1193
(206) 386-4620

SPOKANE PUBLIC LIBRARY ✱
Funding Information Center
West 811 Main Ave.
Spokane   99201
(509) 626-5347

UNITED WAY OF PIERCE COUNTY
Center for Nonprofit Development
1501 Pacific Ave., Suite 400
P.O. Box 2215
Tacoma   98401
(253) 597-7496

GREATER WENATCHEE COMMUNITY
    FOUNDATION AT THE WENATCHEE
    PUBLIC LIBRARY
310 Douglas St.
Wenatchee   98807
(509) 662-5021

WEST VIRGINIA

KANAWHA COUNTY
    PUBLIC LIBRARY ✱
123 Capitol St.
Charleston   25301
(304) 343-4646

WISCONSIN

UNIVERSITY OF WISCONSIN–
    MADISON ✱
Memorial Library, Grants Information Center
728 State St., Room 276
Madison   53706
(608) 262-3242

MARQUETTE UNIVERSITY MEMORIAL
LIBRARY ✱
Funding Information Center
1415 W. Wisconsin Ave.
Milwaukee   53201-3141
(414) 288-1515

UNIVERSITY OF WISCONSIN—
STEVENS POINT
Library—Foundation Collection
900 Reserve St.
Stevens Point   54481-3897
(715) 346-4204

WYOMING

NATRONA COUNTY PUBLIC LIBRARY ✱
307 E. 2nd St.
Casper   82601-2598
(307) 237-4935

LARAMIE COUNTY COMMUNITY
COLLEGE ✱
Instructional Resource Center
1400 E. College Dr.
Cheyenne   82007-3299
(307) 778-1206

CAMPBELL COUNTY PUBLIC LIBRARY ✱
2101 4-J Rd.
Gillette   82718
(307) 687-0115

TETON COUNTY LIBRARY
125 Virginian Lane
Jackson   83001
(307) 733-2164

ROCK SPRINGS LIBRARY
400 C St.
Rock Springs   82901
(307) 352-6669

PUERTO RICO

UNIVERSIDAD DEL SAGRADO CORAZON
M.M.T. Guevara Library
Santurce   00914
(809) 728-1515 x 4357

Participants in the Foundation Center's Cooperating Collections network are libraries or nonprofit information centers that provide fundraising information and other funding-related technical assistance in their communities. Cooperating Collections agree to provide free public access to a basic collection of Foundation Center publications during a regular schedule of hours, offering free funding research guidance to all visitors. Many also provide a variety of services for local nonprofit organizations, using staff or volunteers to prepare special materials, organize workshops, or conduct orientations.

The Foundation Center welcomes inquiries from libraries or information centers in the U.S. interested in providing this type of public information service. If you are interested in establishing a funding information library for the use of nonprofit organizations in your area or in learning more about the program, please contact a coordinator of Cooperating Collections: Erika Wittlieb, The Foundation Center, 79 Fifth Avenue, New York, NY 10003 (e-mail: eaw@fdncenter.org) or Janet Camarena, The Foundation Center, 312 Sutter Street, Suite 606, San Francisco, CA 94108 (e-mail: jfc@fdncenter.org).